Remedies

Authors

Colin Bobb-Semple, Solicitor, Senior Lecturer, The City Law School
Julie Browne, Barrister, Senior Lecturer, The City Law School
Nigel Duncan, Principal Lecturer, The City Law School
David Emmet, Barrister, Senior Lecturer, The City Law School
Ann Halpern, Barrister, former Reader, ICSL
Peter Hungerford-Welch, Barrister, Associate Dean, The City Law School
Robert McPeake, Barrister, Principal Lecturer, The City Law School
The late His Honour Judge William Rose
Margot Taylor, Solicitor, Principal Lecturer, The City Law School

Editor

David Emmet, Barrister, Senior Lecturer, The City Law School

Series Editor

Julie Browne, Barrister, Senior Lecturer, The City Law School

Remedies

The City Law School, City University, London

OXFORD
UNIVERSITY PRESS

OXFORD

UNIVERSITY PRESS

Great Clarendon Street, Oxford ox2 6dp

Oxford University Press is a department of the University of Oxford.
It furthers the University's objective of excellence in research, scholarship,
and education by publishing worldwide in

Oxford New York

Auckland Cape Town Dar es Salaam Hong Kong Karachi
Kuala Lumpur Madrid Melbourne Mexico City Nairobi
New Delhi Shanghai Taipei Toronto

With offices in

Argentina Austria Brazil Chile Czech Republic France Greece
Guatemala Hungary Italy Japan Poland Portugal Singapore
South Korea Switzerland Thailand Turkey Ukraine Vietnam

Oxford is a registered trade mark of Oxford University Press
in the UK and in certain other countries

Published in the United States
by Oxford University Press Inc., New York

A Blackstone Press Book
© City University, 2008

British Library Cataloguing in Publication Data
Data available

Typeset by Laserwords Private Limited, Chennai, India
Printed in Great Britain on acid-free paper by
Ashford Colour Press Ltd, Gosport, Hampshire

ISBN 978–0–19–955358–7

10 9 8 7 6 5 4 3 2 1

FOREWORD

I am delighted to write this Foreword to the manuals which are written by practitioners and staff of the Inns of Court School of Law (ICSL [now The City Law School]).

The manuals are designed primarily to support training on the Bar Vocational Course (BVC). They now cover a wide range, embracing both the compulsory and the optional subjects of the BVC. They provide an outstanding resource for all those concerned to teach and acquire legal skills wherever the BVC is taught.

The manuals for the compulsory subjects are updated and revised annually. The manuals for the optional subjects are revised every two years. To complement the Series, the publishers will maintain a website for the manuals which will be used to keep them up-to-date throughout the academic year.

The manuals, continually updated, exemplify the practical and professional approach that is central to the BVC. I congratulate the staff of The City Law School who have produced them to an excellent standard, and Oxford University Press for its commitment in securing their publication. As my predecessor the Hon. Mr Justice Gross so aptly said in a previous Foreword, the manuals are an important ingredient in the constant drive to raise standards in the public interest.

The Hon. Mr Justice Etherton
Chairman of the Advisory Board of the Institute of Law
City University, London
May 2008

OUTLINE CONTENTS

DETAILED CONTENTS

TABLE OF CASES

TABLES OF STATUTES

EC Primary Legislation

International Legislation

TABLE OF RULES AND REGULATIONS

EC Secondary Legislation

Introduction

1.1 Role and context of remedies

It is usually in the first months of practice that barristers come face to face with the realities of dealing with the problems and objectives of clients. Armed with a considerable amount of textbook law, practitioners soon discover that the task of finding a resolution or remedy to a specific problem demands additional skills: a knowledge of the range of major remedies, the ability to recognise which remedy can be sought in any situation and the likelihood of success of a particular remedy, how to choose between alternative remedies, and an understanding of how to calculate damages.

For most students, academic training has focused on substantive law: researching, classifying and analysing legal arguments. Such analysis has a central role in the barrister's work. However, to the client, it is of secondary importance. The client's crucial and primary question for you, as legal adviser, will be what solution the law offers to the client's problem, ie, what is the remedy? It is not uncommon to hear former students say that they simply had not appreciated the importance of knowing how to go about *solving* a problem, ie, what damages to claim, whether or not to seek an injunction, and how to find appropriate remedies in an unfamiliar area of law.

The term 'remedy' is wide-ranging and can include any positive solution to a client's problem. The Civil Procedure Rules 1998 use the term 'remedy' rather than 'relief', for example permitting a party to apply for remedy from sanctions previously ordered by the court. As an adviser you will wish to take an overview of all possible remedies, including routes which do not involve court intervention, such as self-help remedies, exhausting internal complaints procedures or filing complaints with agencies such as the Commission for Racial Equality. This manual will focus on remedies which a court can give, the most common being (a) the judgment of a money award of damages, and (b) orders that defendants refrain from certain acts or restore the position the claimant was in before the cause of the claim arose. Though the study of remedies involves both substantive law principles and rules of procedure and enforcement, it does not lie squarely in either of these areas. Substantive law is decided by the court and answers the question, 'Is the defendant liable?' Procedural rules govern the issue, 'How can that liability be enforced?' The law of remedies falls between them, overlapping but distinct. Having determined that the defendant is liable, it answers the question, 'What remedy will the law permit?'

1.2 Classifying remedies

While not all of the wide range of available remedies fit into set categories, most will fall into general areas and it is helpful to start with an understanding of these.

(a) *Compensatory remedies.* These compensate the claimant for losses suffered. The most common compensatory remedy is damages, ie, a sum of money to put the claimant in as good a position as before the harm and recognition of loss. If a defendant fails to satisfy a judgment ordering payment of damages, there are various methods of enforcement available against the defendant's assets and wages (see *Civil Litigation* manual). A winning claimant will normally be awarded costs and, although these compensate for costs expended, they are not deemed to be part of the damages award.

(b) *Coercive remedies.* These aim to prevent harm from occurring or re-occurring. The most common preventative remedy is an injunction, which is an order by the court that the defendant do or refrain from doing a certain act to prevent harm occurring. An injunction, by itself, normally does not involve compensation to the claimant. In addition to injunctions, courts have a variety of specialised orders, eg, an order for specific performance of a contract, which requires the defendant to perform contractual obligations. Failure to obey a court order is contempt of court for which the court may order payment of a fine and/or a period of imprisonment and/or sequestration of assets.

(c) *Declaratory remedies.* These interpret documents such as wills and contracts, and resolve disputes about the parties' rights. The most common is the declaration. In one sense a declaration can be a preventative remedy in that it will resolve uncertainty about the parties' rights or legal ownership before either side has taken steps based on an (erroneous) view of the matter. In another sense these types of remedies can be seen as indirectly 'coercive' in that a declaration puts the parties on notice of the legal interpretation of the matter. If either side subsequently acts contrary to that interpretation, the courts are likely to award compensation to the injured party and possibly an injunction preventing further acts.

(d) *Exemplary or punitive remedies.* These aim to punish the offending party for deliberate or particularly grave wrongful acts. The most common is an order requiring a defendant to pay a sum of money as exemplary or punitive damages. This remedy is distinct as it does not 'compensate' in the sense of restoring the claimant's position. Nor is it coercive in the sense of requiring the defendant to do or refrain from doing an act. Rather it is to penalise the defendant through civil rather than criminal litigation, and is often done to send a clear message of the court's view of particular conduct.

Remedies can also be categorised as either legal or equitable. Damages are the most common legal remedy. The most frequently used equitable remedies are injunctions and specific performance, although the list is extensive and includes *quantum meruit,* rescission, rectification, constructive trust, subrogation, contribution and receivership. Traditionally there were separate courts of law and equity, each providing their own specific type of remedies. Although the merger of modern courts diffused the distinction, it remains important in at least one respect: a claimant will often be denied an equitable remedy if the legal remedy (eg, an award of monetary damages) would be adequate (see *Civil Litigation* manual).

1.3 Further sources of information

In addition to the information contained in this manual, the course manuals on specialist areas of law will assist with an in-depth study of remedies relevant to those areas. A list of practitioners' works on speciflc subjects can also be found in the legal research section of the **Case Preparation** manual. Increasingly texts are appearing in electronic form which may also be helpful. The following practitioner texts are of particular interest:

Burrows, A., *Remedies for Torts and Breach of Contract,* 3rd edn, Oxford University Press, 2004.

Goff and Jones, *The Law of Restitution,* 7th edn, Sweet & Maxwell, 2007.

Kemp and Kemp, *Quantum of Damages,* Sweet & Maxwell, looseleaf.

McGregor, H., *Damages,* 17th edn, Sweet & Maxwell, 2003.

2

Who to sue?

2.1 Introduction

When considering the remedies available to your client, it is important to consider the client's legal status and that of the person from whom the remedy is sought. This involves an awareness of the different types of legal persons and the limits on some persons' legal capability and liability.

2.2 Legal personality

2.2.1 General

Where the claimant and defendant are individuals acting on their own behalf, you will need to consider whether they are treated differently before the law. For example, there are limits placed on the legal capacity of minors or persons suffering from mental disorder.

The claimant or defendant may be a group of people acting together, eg, a business which wishes to sue a supplier for breach of contract or a sports club seeking damages for the negligence of builders. You will need to determine precisely who the legal persons are for whom you are acting and against whom you are seeking a remedy. The three principal legal forms which the group may take are: a trust, a corporation and an unincorporated association. These different forms may be used for a variety of purposes from running a business to a local social club.

Once you have determined the legal status of the claimant and defendant, you need to consider what, if any, limits are placed on the capacity of such legal persons and who can bind the group (ie, how do the rules of agency apply to this type of legal status?).

2.2.2 Trusts

When dealing with a problem which involves a trust, you need to ensure that you are clear on the distinct roles of the settlor, trustees and beneficiaries. The legal ownership of any property is vested in the trustees, who are under a duty to hold it for the benefit of the beneficiaries. Thus, for example, when acting for the trust, you will need to ensure that whatever action is being proposed is within the trustees' power both in equity and under the specific terms of the trust.

2.2.3 Corporations

A corporation is a legal person separate from its members. A corporation may be formed (a) by Royal Charter, eg, the BBC, (b) by statute, eg, local authorities, or (c) under the Companies Acts as a private or public company. You will need to ensure that you are clear which individual(s) have the legal authority to act on behalf of the corporation.

2.2.4 Unincorporated associations

Unincorporated associations have no legal personality separate from their members. The principal legal effect is that one member may be liable for the acts of another member. The three main types of such associations are (a) trade unions and employers' associations, (b) clubs (where the difference between a proprietary and a members' club is important), and (c) partnerships. You will need to ensure that you know what type of unincorporated association you are dealing with and who has the authority to act for it.

2.3 Business associations

Although the different forms of legal person may be used for a variety of reasons, eg, a club may incorporate as a limited company, the main use of incorporation is to trade. It is important to understand the different legal forms used to trade: (a) sole trader (an individual who sets up in business and trades in his own name), (b) partnership (persons carrying on a business in common with a view of profit), and (c) a company (a corporation created by registration under Companies Act 1985 (CA 1985)).

The Companies Act 2006 received the Royal Assent in November 2006. It incorporates provisions in the Companies Act 1985, restating some of them, and codifies some of the current case law. However, the basic principles remain the same. The provisions of the Companies Act 2006 (CA 2006) are being brought into force over time. Some are already in force but many of the provisions will not come into force until October 2009. Where the provisions are in force this manual includes the new provisions. Where they are not yet in force, the manual indicates the date which is presently given as the likely commencement date.

2.3.1 Formation

2.3.1.1 Sole traders

No formalities are required to set up as a sole trader and the personality of the 'trader' is indistinguishable in law from that of the individual. The debts of the business are the liability of the sole trader personally and without limit. For accounting purposes, however, the sole trader will distinguish between assets 'owned' by the business and personal assets.

2.3.1.2 Partnerships

No formalities are required to form a partnership. It will exist if it satisfies the definition in s 1(1) of the Partnership Act 1890 (PA 1890) 'the relation which subsists between persons carrying on a business in common with a view of profit' (companies are expressly excluded by s 1 (2)). There are few restrictions on the formation of partnerships although the business must be lawful.

The Limited Liability Partnerships Act 2000 (in force from 6 April 2001) creates a new form of legal entity known as a limited liability partnership. Forming such a partnership requires similar formalities to those needed to form a company (see **2.3.1.3**), ie, registration with the Registrar of Companies and filing of certain documents with the Registrar. As with a company, the liability of the partnership itself will be unlimited and the liability of the individual partners will be limited to contribute to the assets on the winding up of the partnership to such extent as set out in the Act. The 2000 Act specifically provides that the law relating to partnerships does not apply to a limited liability partnership and that the law relating to companies on relevant matters such as registration, insolvency and winding up shall be applied to such partnerships. These entities will be more like companies than partnerships. It is not known how many will choose to use this new form of entity to trade. Although the limitation on partners liability is attractive, the price paid is disclosure of information about the partnership including financial matters.

2.3.1.3   Companies

A company can only be formed by complying with the formalities set out in the CA 1985, which requires certain documents including the memorandum (the company's constitution) and the articles (the rules for the conduct of internal affairs) to be filed with the Registrar of Companies who will issue a certificate of incorporation, enter it in the register of companies and open a file for the new company at Companies House.

A company exists as a legal person distinct from its members from the date in the certificate of incorporation. The principal effect of this is that the company alone is liable for its debts. While the company has unlimited liability for its debts (ie, can be liquidated to obtain assets to pay creditors), the members are not liable for the debts of the company, and their liability to contribute to the company's assets, to enable it to pay its creditors, may be limited by share or guarantee.

Companies can be categorised on the following basis:

(a) The liability of members to contribute to assist the company to pay its debts:
  (i) company limited by shares—members' liability to contribute (at any time) limited to nominal value and any premium on shares (mostly used for trading purposes);
  (ii) company limited by guarantee—members' liability to contribute (on liquidation only) limited to amount of guarantee given (mostly used for non-trading organisations, eg, educational institutions);
  (iii) unlimited company—members' liability to contribute (on liquidation only) is unlimited (rare).
(b) The ability to offer its securities (shares and debentures) to the public:
  (i) public company—the memorandum states that it is a public company and the name must end with the words 'Public Limited Company' (or 'plc').
  (ii) private company—any other company. Unless it is an unlimited company, the name of a private company must end with the word 'Limited' (or 'Ltd'). All unlimited companies and companies limited by guarantee must be private. Some guarantee companies are exempt from the requirement that the name must end with the word 'Limited'.

A group of companies exists where one company controls one or more other companies, either through voting rights of members or determining the composition of the board of directors. The holding (controlling) company is (usually) the principal shareholder of the subsidiary (controlled) company. The law, for most purposes, treats the various companies in the group as distinct legal persons with liability only for their own debts.

The CA 2006 provisions, in respect of formation of a company and its constitutional documents, are likely to come into force in October 2009. The major change is that the main constitutional document will be the Articles of Association; the Memorandum will contain limited information and will no longer be a constitutional document.

2.3.2 Internal management and control of the association

2.3.2.1 Sole traders

A sole trader is free to employ others and whatever 'say' is given to others in the running of the organisation is a matter between them; the law has no impact here, save to provide contractual remedies if appropriate.

2.3.2.2 Partnerships

The term 'partner' is usually used to describe an 'equity' partner (ie, one with full rights). Other types of partners usually have very limited if any 'partnership' rights, eg, 'sleeping' partners (who take no active part in management) or 'salaried' partners (usually in fact employees).

The equity partners own the firm (ie, have invested their capital) and manage the business (ie, have the right to attend meetings and participate in the decision-making process running the business). The rights of the partners should be set out in a partnership agreement. However, PA 1890 implies terms into any partnership in so far as they are not inconsistent with what has been agreed. Section 24 contains most of these provisions, which include the right to take part in the management and have access to the books and that differences may be decided by simple majority of the partners (except a change in the nature of the business, introduction and expulsion of a partner, all of which require unanimity). Section 24 is subject to agreement to the contrary, express or implied (except expulsion of a partner which must be express), and s 19 provides that the rights and duties of partners may be varied by consent of all the partners, express or inferred by conduct.

PA 1890, ss 28 to 30, require partners to act in good faith towards one another, eg, give full information and account for benefits derived from the firm. Although not expressly stated in PA 1890, partners have a duty to act within their actual authority.

2.3.2.3 Companies

A company as a legal person must make decisions but this must be done by the individuals controlling it. It is necessary to determine what decisions are decisions of the company and not just of the individuals. The members, as owners, make decisions collectively by voting in general meeting (on most matters a simple majority is sufficient but some decisions, mostly those which relate to the company's constitution, require a 75 per cent majority). Such decisions will be decisions of the company. CA 2006 requires certain formalities for such meetings which are much more stringent for public than private companies. Decisions made without following the proper procedures can be challenged as irregular and invalid.

It is impractical for members to have general meetings to make all the decisions necessary to run the business. Much of the decision-making power is therefore delegated to the directors who must also act collectively through decisions at board meetings unless the power to sub-delegate has been given. There are thus two decision-making organs of the company, the general meeting and the board. As a general rule, once members have delegated their decision-making powers to the board, they cannot simultaneously exercise the delegated powers. In most public companies, the members and directors will not be the same people, and ownership (which is with the members) is therefore separated from the management powers (which are with the directors). This can cause problems where there is disagreement about the manner in which the business should be conducted. Small private companies are more likely to have a few members who are also directors of the company (ie, the same people own and control the business).

Directors' powers are limited by the general law applicable to fiduciaries, which requires them to act in the best interests of the company as a whole (ie, the shareholders collectively), to exercise their powers for proper purpose (ie, in accordance with the memorandum of association and articles) and not to put themselves in a position where their duty to the company conflicts with their own personal interests (eg, restrictions are placed on their contracting with the company, particularly substantial property transactions, without consent of the members, and there are outright prohibitions on certain loans). Directors also owe a duty of care and can be sued in negligence if they fall below the requisite standard.

Members' rights are contained in the articles of association, which are deemed to be a contract by CA 1985, s 14 (to become CA 2006, s 33 when brought into force in October 2009). The articles usually have detailed provisions on calling of meetings, appointment, removal and powers of directors, paying of dividends etc. A company limited by shares can adopt a model form of articles (Table A) set out in a statutory instrument.

Where directors act wrongfully or some other person commits a wrong against the company, it is the company which must sue (*Foss v Harbottle* [1935] 2 KB 113). The power to institute proceedings is usually delegated to the directors. If the directors refuse, the members may be permitted to take collective action on behalf of the company but will have to do this collectively (ie, a majority of the members will have to agree to initiate action and follow the proper rules, usually by calling a meeting of members and putting the matter to a vote, to make the decision valid). While this option appears attractive, it has not been favoured in more recent cases; see *Breckland Group Holdings Ltd v London and Suffolk Properties Ltd* [1989] BCLC 100. A simple majority of members can always dismiss directors with whom they disagree. Only in very rare circumstances can an individual member bring an action on behalf of the company.

CA 2006, s 994, which reenacts CA 1985, s 459, affords some protection to members by enabling them to petition the court for an order where the company's affairs are conducted in a manner which is unfairly prejudicial to them. In addition, the DTI has the power to investigate a company in a variety of circumstances.

2.3.3 Contractual capacity and agency rules

2.3.3.1 General agency rules

Where one person (the agent) negotiates a contract on behalf of another (the principal), there are two matters you should check to determine who is bound by the contract.

The authority of the agent

An agent's *actual* authority is that which is agreed between the agent and the principal. This can be *express actual authority,* ie expressly agreed, or *implied actual authority,* ie impliedly given by the principal. Implied authority can include authority to do everything necessarily and ordinarily incidental to the carrying out of the activity expressly authorised (called *implied* or sometimes *incidental authority),* to do whatever an agent in that trade, profession or business would usually have the authority to do (called *usual authority*) or to act in accordance with reasonable customs and usages of the places they act (called *customary authority*).

An agent's *apparent* (sometimes also called *ostensible*) authority is the authority as it appears to others based on the principle that third parties are entitled to assume that an agent has the authority he appears to, or would normally, have because of his position. Generally an agent's actual and apparent authority are the same. However, an agent's apparent authority may be greater than his actual authority, for example where restrictions have been placed on his authority (perhaps a car salesman whose authority is limited to contracts of a certain relatively low value), but the principal has not notified third parties of these restrictions. His actual authority may exceed his apparent authority, for example where the principal specifically gives the agent more authority than an agent in his position would usually have, but third parties are unaware of this.

Whatever the agent's actual authority, the principal will generally be bound by contracts which come within the agent's apparent authority. However, even where the principal is bound on the contract, if an agent has acted outside his actual authority, the principal will have an action against the agent for breach of the agency agreement.

Disclosed/undisclosed principal

Usually an agent discloses to the third party that he is acting as an agent for a principal. The contract is between the principal and the third party. The general rule is that the agent is not liable on the contract, nor can he enforce it. There are exceptions to this, eg where by custom or trade the agent is liable or where the agent in signing accepts personal liability.

Where an agent does not disclose that he is acting on behalf of someone else, the agent can sue and be sued on the contract as the agent appeared to be the contracting party. The undisclosed principal can usually intervene and claim against the third party provided the terms of the contract are not inconsistent with such intervention.

2.3.3.2 Sole traders

The contractual capacity of a sole trader is determined by the general rules for contractual capacity of the individual in the law of contract.

General agency rules will apply to acts of employees and the sole trader will be personally liable for torts and breaches of contract committed in the course of business. The assets available to satisfy judgment debts will be the personal and business assets of the trader.

2.3.3.3 Partnerships

As with sole traders, there is no limit on the contractual capacity of partners except the general rules of contract law.

Normal agency rules have been applied to partnerships and codified in PA 1890, ss 5 to 18. Each partner is both agent and part of the principal. Acts of individual partners carrying on the business of the partnership in the usual way will bind all the partners unless the partner is acting outside his authority and the third party is aware of this or is not aware of dealing with a partner (s 5). Case law has established that all partners will have usual authority to buy and sell goods and pay debts, give receipts and draw cheques but that the 'usual' authority of partners in trading partnerships is wider than non-trading (eg, professional) partnerships and includes borrowing money. Where limits are placed on a partner's authority, the firm will still be bound unless the third party has notice of the limitation (ss 5 and 8). Section 6 deals specifically with acts done and instruments executed in the firm's name and s 7 with pledging the firm's credit.

Tortious liability is covered by ss 10 and 11. Section 10 makes the firm liable for loss or damage caused in the ordinary course of business or with the authority of copartners. Under s 11 the firm is liable to make good loss suffered from misapplication of money or property received by a partner within his apparent authority or by the firm in the course of business.

The combined effect of ss 14, 17 and 36 on the liability of incoming and outgoing partners is that partners are not liable for acts done before or after the time they were partners unless they have been held out to be partners outside this period (s 14), eg, by having their names on the letterhead as partners or by failing to give proper notice of retirement from the partnership under s 36. They remain liable for debts and obligations incurred while a partner even after their retirement (unless discharged by agreement of all the parties).

Although it enjoys no separate legal status, a firm (ie, the partners), may sue or be sued in the firm name (RSC, Ord 81, preserved in CPR, Sch 1), in which case all the partners who were partners at the date of the action will be parties (see *Civil Litigation* manual).

2.3.3.4   Companies

A company's contractual capacity is limited to activities authorised by the objects clause of its memorandum, which sets out the purpose for which the company was formed, eg, to make and sell bicycles. Any contract not within the scope of this clause is theoretically ultra vires and void. The theory behind the rule was to protect the investors (at the expense of the outsider dealing with the company) in that their money could only be used for the stated purposes. However, the effect of this rule has been almost eradicated (a) by companies having very broad objects clauses (under CA 1985, s 3A, companies can incorporate with the object 'to carry on any trade or business whatsoever'), (b) because companies can easily change their objects (CA 1985, s 4), and (c) because statute gives considerable protection to outsiders. CA 1985, s 35, allows both the company and the outsider to enforce an ultra vires act but retains the right of members to restrain proposed ultra vires acts and makes directors liable for them.

Companies formed under CA 2006 will not have an objects clause so the companies objects will be unrestricted unless they are specifically restricted by the Articles of Association. These provisions are likely to be brought into force in October 2009.

2.3.3.5   Business Names Act 1985

Whether acting for or against a business association, it is important to get the legal name correct. This will not be difficult where the business name is the legal name of the person running it; in the case of sole traders and partners, their surnames and, in the case of a company, its corporate name (in the memorandum). However, the business may use a 'trade' name (ie, not the legal name of the person running it). In these circumstances, the Business Names Act 1985 requires disclosure of the legal name on correspondence, at business premises etc.

The Business Names Act 1985 will be repealed and replaced by similar provisions in the Companies Act 2006. These provisions are likely to be brought into force in October 2009.

2.3.4   Cessation of business: termination of association

2.3.4.1   Sole traders

A sole trader may cease trading at any time for any reason. If there are business debts on cessation, she or he will remain personally liable for them.

2.3.4.2 Partnerships

PA 1890, s 32, provides that a partnership formed for a fixed term will end at the end of the term and a partnership at will (ie, without a fixed term) may be ended by any partner giving notice to the others of intention to dissolve, the partnership being dissolved from the date in the notice. Section 32 is subject to agreement to the contrary, eg, that dissolution may occur only by mutual agreement of all the partners, in which case a single partner cannot terminate by notice. The court does have power to order dissolution on one of the grounds in PA 1890, s 35, which include a partner being in wilful or persistent breach of the agreement. Resort will be made to this provision only where the partners have no power to dissolve or cannot reach agreement to dissolve.

2.3.4.3 Companies

A company ceases to exist when the name is removed from the register of companies. It may be liquidated voluntarily by the members passing a resolution. The court may order the company to be liquidated if one of the grounds set out in the Insolvency Act 1986, s 122, is proved. These grounds include that it would be 'just and equitable'.

2.3.4.4 Insolvency

Where an individual becomes insolvent (ie, unable to pay debts), creditors may institute bankruptcy proceedings. All the individual's assets, subject to a few exceptions such as essential living items, vest in the trustee in bankruptcy. These assets include all causes of action held by the individual except personal claims such as a right to sue for defamation. Where a company becomes insolvent, any creditor may apply to have the company put into liquidation. All the company's assets then vest in the liquidator, including any causes of action held by the company. Both the trustee in bankruptcy and the liquidator have a duty to use the assets to pay the creditors according to the rules under the Insolvency Act 1986. Proceedings against the estate of a bankrupt or the assets of a company must not be taken without the court's permission.

3

Liability for breach of contract

3.1 Introduction

A claim for damages arises in circumstances where there has been a failure to perform, without lawful excuse, one or more of the obligations (whether conditions, warranties, or innominate or intermediate terms) contained in a contract. The innocent party may also have the right to rescind (terminate) the contract or choose to affirm. A failure to perform in this sense includes a refusal to perform, defective performance, delayed performance, and action taken which prevents performance.

3.1.1 Performance

Generally, failure to perform amounts to breach of contract. However, where obligations are concurrent, each party's right to the other's performance depends on being able to show readiness, willingness and ability to perform. One party may be contractually bound to perform fully before the other party is under any obligation to perform at all (sometimes known as an entire contract). However, the doctrine of part performance provides that where one party has substantially performed but not completed performance of the contractual obligations, the other party cannot assume a discharge of obligations and a counterclaim can be made to compensate for minor discrepancies in performance. Alternatively, a claim for *quantum meruit* can be made where it is possible to infer a fresh agreement between the parties that payment will be made for the performance completed because a benefit has been conferred by it, provided that it is possible for the benefit of the performance to be accepted or rejected and one party is preventing the other from completing performance.

In cases where the parties agree otherwise, or where the contract is frustrated or the contract provides for the situation which has occurred or the limitation period has run out, there will be no actionable breach of contract for non-performance.

The right of the innocent party to *terminate* for breach of contract arises where the other has repudiated the contractual duty to perform, either before the time for performance falls due (known as an 'anticipatory breach' of contract) or whilst the contract remains only partly performed, or where the breach of contract complained of goes to the root of the contract. Repudiation can be express or implied reasonably from the circumstances, which must show either an intention to renounce the obligations under the contract or an absolute refusal to perform. It entitles the other party to an immediate cause of action, although if preferred, that party can choose to wait until the time for performance falls due.

3.1.2   What is the effect of a repudiatory breach or a breach which goes to the root of the contract?

The innocent party can *affirm* the contract or choose to rescind (terminate or discharge) it.

If affirmation is chosen, the contract remains alive, and the 'guilty' party can repent the breach and complete the performance as originally agreed, whilst the 'innocent' party can claim damages to compensate for any loss remaining. If the contract remains unperformed, the 'innocent' party can claim damages for that failure at the date when performance falls due. Where damages are calculated by reference to market price, the damages payable may be more or less than would have been payable at the date when the breach could have been anticipated.

If rescission is chosen, then, once communicated to the 'guilty' party, that election is final and terminates all the contractual obligations as to the future, such that the guilty party is, as a rule of construction, not entitled to take advantage of the wrong by relying on any of the terms in the contract (see *Briggs v Oates* [1991] 1 WLR 407).

Parties can agree to avoid the normal consequences of the common law, so the contract can provide for termination for a minor breach or without cause.

The consequences of a breach as to time for performance will depend upon whether time is of the essence. Time will be of the essence when the parties have expressly agreed that it will be so, when reasonable notice is given to make time of the essence or where the circumstances or subject matter of the contract make it imperative.

Where one party offers to perform all obligations under the contract and the other refuses to accept performance, the first party will be discharged from all further performance.

3.1.3   What are the terms of a contract?

Express terms are those which the court finds as a fact were agreed orally between the parties, and those which were stated in writing. The parol evidence rule states that agreed terms not included in a written contract between the parties must be ignored. There are several exceptions to this rule and, in limited circumstances, a written contract can be rectified if it was executed by both parties under a common mistake. Some contracts may be made partly in writing and partly by word of mouth and whether or not a court will accept this will depend on the intention of the parties. Distinguish a *mere* representation from an express term.

Implied terms are those which will be included in a contract:

(a) because there is a custom of the trade to that effect and nothing in the contract contradicts their implication, or

(b) because they are implied by statute, such as the terms implied under the Sale of Goods Act 1979 (as amended by the Sale and Supply of Goods Act 1994) and the Supply of Goods and Services Act 1982, or

(c) because the parties must have intended to include them. Such terms must have been obvious—the officious bystander test—or necessary so as to give the transaction the business efficacy which the parties intended it to have or be those which the 'nature of the contract itself implicitly requires' *(Liverpool City Council v Irwin* [1977] AC 239).

3.1.4 What is the relative importance of contractual terms?

Although a claim for damages will be available for any breach of any term of a contract, the importance of the term broken will determine the availability of the remedy of rescission. A breach of a *condition* will entitle the innocent party to claim *rescission and damages,* whereas the breach of a *warranty* will entitle the innocent party to claim only damages. The parties can agree on which terms are to be conditions of the contract, or the court can decide, by looking at the consequences of breach, whether the term concerned did, in the events which have happened, go to the root of the contract.

3.2 Preliminary issues

3.2.1 The breach of contract must have caused the loss

The breach must be the effective or dominant cause of loss rather than providing merely an opportunity to sustain loss. It is for the court to exercise common sense in assessing whether a breach was the cause or merely the occasion for the loss. The breach must be the dominant or effective cause of the loss. The 'but for' test is insufficient (see *Galoo Ltd v Bright Grahame Murray* [1994] 1 WLR 1360). The claimant must be able to prove that but for the defendant's breach of contract there would have been no loss (see *Banque Bruxelles Lambert SA v Eagle Star Insurance Co Ltd* [1995] QB 375). Where the breach is one of a number of causes of the loss, and all have had an equal impact in causing that loss, the breach will be taken to have caused the loss (see *Monarch SS v Karishamns* [1949] AC 196).

Where the breach partly causes the loss and the loss is otherwise due to the actions of a third party, liability for breach will arise if the acts of that party were contemplated by the defendant (see *De La Bere v Pearson Ltd* [1908] 1 KB 48; *Beoco Ltd v Alfa Laval Co Ltd* [1994] 3 WLR 1179).

3.2.2 What is the standard of proof?

The general rule is that the claimant must prove both the fact of damage and its amount, although where it is clear that a loss has been caused, difficulty in actually assessing that loss will not bar relief (see *Chaplin v Hicks* [1911] 2 KB 786).

It is said that the standard of proof is therefore one of *reasonable* certainty. What is required is evidence from which the existence of damage can be reasonably inferred and which provides adequate data for calculating the amount (see *McGregor on Damages).* Where absolute certainty is possible, detailed and precise evidence will be required.

Difficult cases are those where the claim is necessarily somewhat speculative, for example, a claim for loss of profit. In *E. Bailey and Co Ltd v Balholm Securities Ltd* [1973] 2 Lloyd's Rep 404, it was suggested that a claim for loss of profit will be reasonably certain where the claimant has lost the opportunity of making profit in circumstances where there was no equal exposure to the risk of loss—for example, in commodity trading the chance of profit is entirely speculative and hence there is insufficient certainty of loss for a claim to be successful. There must be a substantial chance or probability, a mere possibility must be ignored (see *Obagi v Stanborough* The Times, 15 December 1993).

Case law suggests that there is a sufficient degree of certainty in claims for loss of reputation arising from a loss of publicity. For example, cases where an actor or author is denied, in breach of contract, the chance of enhancing his reputation, and cases where the whole purpose of the contract is for publicity, ie, advertising contracts, where the breach causes a loss of business.

Where the loss depends upon a large number of contingencies a claim can be made for the value of the chance which the claimant has lost. The greater the number of contingencies, the lower the value of that chance (see *Chaplin v Hicks* [1911] 2 KB 786).

3.2.3 Can the parties to contract plan for its breach?

Sophisticated contracts often plan for a breach of contract through clauses aimed at, for example, limiting, restricting or excluding liability.

3.2.4 Can liability for breach be excluded or restricted?

The first issue in relation to exclusion and exemption clauses is whether the clause has been *incorporated* into the contract (see *Chitty on Contracts,* vol 1, Pt 3).

If the clause is found to be a part of the contract the court will then have to *construe* the clause to see whether it covers the damage which has been suffered and operates in the circumstances which have occurred. The *contra proferentem* rule applies, ie, where there is any ambiguity, the clause will be strictly construed against the party for whose benefit it was inserted. Such clauses, if intended to cover negligence, must do so expressly or be capable of no other interpretation.

In some cases the power to exclude liability is prevented or is made subject to court review by statute, for example, the Unfair Contract Terms Act 1977 (UCTA 1977). The main protections which are afforded by the Act as they apply here are to be found in ss 2–7 and 11. The Act only applies to business liability and prevents, in any circumstances, an attempt to exclude, etc, liability for death or personal injury arising from negligence. Negligence is defined as a failure to exercise reasonable care and skill. Otherwise, if a party to a contract attempts to rely on an exclusion clause to excuse a negligent performance of the contract or, in cases involving consumers or contracts in a standard form, a failure to perform substantially or at all or to exclude or restrict liability, the clause will be subjected to the *test of reasonableness,* as defined in s 11. The burden of proving reasonableness rests with the party seeking to rely on the clause.

The Unfair Terms in Consumer Contracts Regulations 1999 (SI 1999/2083) supplement UCTA 1977. They apply in a broad range of areas, eg, retail, banking, mortgage agreements and real property transactions including tenancies. Under the 1999 Regulations an unfair term in a contract between a seller or supplier and a consumer is not binding on the consumer. It is unfair if it has not been individually negotiated (ie, it is a standard term of the seller or supplier) and, contrary to the requirement of good faith, it causes a significant imbalance in the parties' rights and obligations arising under the contract to the detriment of the consumer. A seller or supplier is obliged to ensure that any written term is expressed in plain intelligible language, and if there is doubt as to the meaning of a term, the interpretation most favourable to the consumer prevails. The parties can agree that different or additional remedies to those provided by the common law should be applicable, for example, liquidated damages clauses, forfeiture clauses, repossession clauses and arbitration clauses. Such clauses may need to be construed by the court to establish their precise ambit.

A liquidated damages clause specifies the amount of damages to be paid in the event of a particular breach. Apart from consideration under UCTA 1977, in these cases the issue is whether such a term will be enforced by the court, or whether it will fail because it is found to be a penalty clause. In *Dunlop Pneumatic Tyre Co Ltd v New Garage and Motor Co Ltd* [1915] AC 79 it was held that the resolution of this issue depends upon the intention of the parties at the time when the contract was made. In construing that intention the court will have regard to the following matters:

- Was the clause intended to terrorise the other party into performing or was it a genuine pre-estimate of the damage likely to be suffered?
- Was it extravagant or unconscionable?
- Did it provide for the payment of a sum which is greater than the loss suffered?
- Did it provide for the payment of a single sum upon the occurrence of any of many different events?

See *Philips Hong Kong v Attorney-General of Hong Kong* (1990) 61 BLR 41.

Liability in tort

4.1 Introduction

There are three torts whose practical significance is so great that we need to reintroduce them to you from a practitioner's point of view.

The commonest by far of all tortious claims is the action for damages for personal injury. Such claims will almost always be founded on negligence, occupiers' liability or breach of statutory duty. Although you will have studied these at the academic stage, you are likely to have done so in a rather academic way, and some practical notes on these three important causes of action now follow.

4.2 Negligence

4.2.1 Ingredients of the tort of negligence

These are:

- the existence of a duty of care;
- the duty owed to the claimant;
- negligence, ie, breach of the duty of care;
- causation of damage;
- damage not too remote.

As well as these ingredients, in many cases the court is concerned with the question of quantum, ie, the extent of the damage recoverable in financial terms.

4.2.2 The practitioner's view of negligence

At the academic stage you will largely have been concerned with the duty situation, the principles of reasonable foreseeability etc. The practitioner is largely concerned with breach of duty, ie, negligence. The situations in which a duty of care is owed by one person to another are on the whole so well established that in practice it is rare for an issue to arise as to duty. It is only in the comparatively rare cases where there is no clear authority on whether a duty is owed, or a claimant seeks to establish a new situation, that a court will be concerned with this aspect of the tort. A general practitioner is, however, concerned almost every day with the question of whether someone has been negligent or not.

4.2.3   Duty situations

Particularly common and important duty of care situations in practice are:

(a) The duty owed by users of the highway to other users and to those beside the highway.

(b) The duty owed by manufacturers of products to users or consumers of these products. This has now largely been superseded by product liability under Part I of the Consumer Protection Act 1987.

(c) The duty owed by professional persons to their clients: such duties are usually contractual as well as tortious, but may arise in tort alone, particularly in cases of medical negligence.

(d) The duty owed by builders (and others responsible for safety in buildings) to owners and occupiers of buildings. Specific cases have severely restricted the scope of these duties (see *D & F Estates Ltd v Church Commissioners* [1989] AC 177, and *Murphy v Brentwood District Council* [1991] 1 AC 398, in which the House of Lords held that *Anns v Merton London Borough Council* [1978] AC 728 was wrongly decided).

(e) The duty owed by employers to their employees. Frequently known as the three-fold duty laid down by *Wilson's and Clyde Coal Co Ltd v English* [1938] AC 57, it is strictly a single duty, but for practical purposes it is a duty with five identifiable limbs:

   (i)   to provide a safe place of work,

   (ii) to provide a safe system of work,

   (iii) to provide effective supervision,

   (iv) to provide proper plant and materials,

   (v)   to provide a competent staff of men.

The duty arises both in tort and contract, but for practical purposes treat it as a tortious duty. It is a duty of reasonable care, not an absolute duty, but the standard of care expected can be surprisingly high on occasions. The duty is non-delegable: that is to say no one can discharge it but the employer, who cannot avoid liability by appointing someone else to discharge it.

4.2.4   Other important or current topics under the general heading of negligence

(a) Limits on the scope of the duty with regard to the recoverability of economic loss (see **6.1.3**).

(b) The development of the doctrine of 'assumption of responsibility' in determining whether a duty of care is owed and the scope of such a duty. The leading case is *Henderson v Merrett Syndicates Ltd* [1994] AC 145. Other recent cases showing the application of the doctrine are: *Williams v Natural Life Health Foods Ltd* [1998] 2 All ER 577; *Costello v Chief Constable of the Northumbria Police* [1999] 1 All ER 550; *Leach v Chief Constable of Gloucestershire Constabulary* [1999] 1 All ER 215; *Watson v British Board of Boxing Control* [2001] 2 WLR 1256; and *Lennon v Metropolitan Police Commissioner* [2004] 2 All ER 266.

(c) The issue of whether a duty of care can be owed by a statutory body which acts negligently in the discharge of its statutory functions. The leading cases are *X v Bedfordshire County Council* [1995] 3 All ER 353 and *Stovin v Wise* [1996] 3 All

ER 801. Other recent cases involving public authorities are: *Barrett v Enfield LBC* [1997] 3 All ER 171; *O'Rourke v Camden LBC* [1997] 3 All ER 23; *Clunis v Camden & Islington Health Authority* [1998] 3 All ER 180; *W v Essex County Council* [1998] 3 All ER 111 and [2000] 2 All ER 237; *Harris v Evans* [1998] 3 All ER 522; *Barrett v Enfield LBC* [1999] 3 All ER 193; *Phelps v Hillingdon LBC* [2000] 4 All ER 504; *S v Gloucestershire CC* [2000] 3 All ER 346; *A v Essex County Council* [2003] NLJ 22; *B v A-G of New Zealand* [2003] 4 All ER 833; *Gorringe v Calderdale Metropolitan Borough Council* [2004] 2 All ER 326; *Carty v Croydon LBC* [2005] 2 All ER 517; and *Neil Martin Ltd v Revenue and Customs Commissioners* [2006] All ER (D) 137 (Revenue and Customs owe no duty of care to a taxpayer). Other cases involving emergency services are: *Capital and Counties plc v Hampshire CC* [1997] 2 All ER 865; *OLL Ltd v Secretary of State for Transport* [1997] 3 All ER 897; *Kent v Griffiths* [2000] 2 All ER 474; and *Bailey v HSS Alarms Ltd* The Times, 20 June 2000.

(d) The scope of the duty with regard to causing nervous shock in someone other than the primary victim. The leading case is *Alcock v Chief Constable of South Yorkshire Police* [1992] 1 AC 310. Other recent cases are: *Vernon v Bosley* [1997] 1 All ER 577; *Frost v Chief Constable of South Yorkshire Police* [1997] 1 All ER 540; *Hunter v British Coal* [1998] 2 All ER 97; *White v Chief Constable of South Yorkshire Police* [1999] 1 All ER 1; and *Greatorex v Greatorex* [2000] 4 All ER 769. The scope of the duty was extended in *Walters v North Glamorgan NHS Trust* [2002] All ER (D) 65 (Mar).

(e) The duty owed by solicitors drafting a will to potential beneficiaries. The leading case is *White v Jones* [1995] 2 AC 207. Other recent cases are: *Carr-Glynn v Frearsons* [1998] 4 All ER 225; and *Gibbons v Nelsons* The Times, 21 April 2000. An analogous situation arises in respect of pensions: *Gorham v British Telecom* [2000] All ER 867. However, no duty of care is owed to an executor claiming on behalf of a beneficiary: *Chappell v Somers & Blake* [2003] 3 All ER 1076.

(f) Other important recent cases concerned with the circumstances in which a duty of care will be owed, its nature and its scope are: *Arthur JS Hall v Simons* [2000] 3 All ER 673 (abolition of the immunity from civil liability of advocates (including barristers); *Barber v Somerset County Council* [2004] 2 All ER 385 (the duty of care owed by an employer to an employee suffering from work-related stress or depression); *Blake v Galloway* [2004] 3 All ER 315 (the duty and standard of care expected of someone taking part in rough horseplay to which the claimant has tacitly consented); *Customs and Excise Commissioners v Barclays Bank plc* [2006] 4 All ER 256 (a bank does not owe a duty of care to a claimant in whose favour a freezing order has been granted); *Brooks v Metropolitan Police Commissioner* [2005] 2 All ER 489 (no duty of care is owed by the police to a victim of crime or a witness to a crime); *D v East Berkshire Community Health NHS Trust* [2005] 2 All ER 443 (no duty of care is owed by health professionals to parents they mistakenly suspect or accuse of abusing their children).

(g) In a recent case, *Rothwell v Chemical & Insulating Co Ltd ('the Pleural Plaques Litigation')* [2007] 4 All ER 1047, the House of Lords held that the existence of a condition, which does not cause injury in itself, but merely evidences the possibility of injury in the future, is not damage capable of giving rise to liability in tort, even when combined with anxiety about the risk of injury.

(h) The principle of *res ipsa loquitur*. This is frequently pleaded, but rarely successful. It raises a presumption of negligence on the defendant's part in certain circumstances, in the absence of any evidence of negligence. It is always preferable to prove negligence by evidence rather than rely on *res ipsa loquitur.* It is therefore very much a last resort for a claimant in difficulties.

(i) Causation: see **6.1.2.**

(j) Remoteness: see **6.1.4.**

(k) The defence of *volenti non fit injuria.* This is not frequently raised and not easy to establish. For a fairly recent example of a successful defence of *volenti,* see *Morris v Murray* [1991] 2 QB 6. The defence cannot be relied upon where the defendant has a duty to protect the claimant against himself (*Reeves v Metropolitan Police Commissioner* [1999] 3 All ER 897).

(l) Contributory negligence. Frequently raised, frequently established, and very important in practice. See **6.3.1.** It has recently been held that failure by a claimant to give up smoking may amount to contributory negligence: *Badger v Ministry of Defence* [2005] EWHC 2941 (QB).

(m) Vicarious liability. Nowadays it is very rare for an employee or agent to be outside the scope of his employment. The test in *Harrison v Michelin Tyre Co Ltd* [1985] 1 All ER 918 is very difficult to satisfy. Particular difficulties arise where the employee has committed a crime or some other wholly unauthorised act while employed by the defendant. The test to be applied in such cases was considered by the House of Lords in *Lister v Helsey Hall Ltd* [2001] 2 All ER 769 and applied in *Mattis v Pollock* [2003] All ER (D) 10 (Jul). It has recently been held in *Viasystems (Tyneside) Ltd v Thermal Transfer (Northern) Ltd* [2005] 4 All ER 1181 that it is possible for more than one employer to be vicariously liable for the acts of the same individual workman. In *Majrowski v Guy's and St Thomas's NHS Trust* [2006] 4 All ER 395 the House of Lords held an employer vicariously liable for harassment by one employee against another. In practice the majority of tortious actions are probably founded on vicarious rather than direct liability.

(n) Limitation periods. These are particularly important in cases of latent injury and damage. See the ***Civil Litigation*** manual, **Chapter 23.**

(o) Compensation Act 2006. Two significant new principles have been enacted.

By s 1 of the Act:

> *A court considering a claim in negligence or breach of statutory duty may, in determining whether the defendant should have taken particular steps to meet a standard of care (whether by taking precautions against a risk or otherwise), have regard to whether a requirement to take those steps might—*
> *(a) prevent a desirable activity from being undertaken at all, to a particular extent or in a particular way, or*
> *(b) discourage persons from undertaking functions in connection with a desirable activity.*

The section is entitled 'Deterrent effect of potential liability' and explains the purpose of the provision. There has been concern that fear of litigation, and the demands of insurers, have tended to produce a defensive attitude to the conduct of public affairs, particularly by local authorities and schools, and s 1 seeks to reverse this trend.

By s 2 of the Act:

> *An apology, an offer of treatment or other redress, shall not of itself amount to an admission of negligence or breach of statutory duty.*

This is intended to put paid to the possibility that saying 'Sorry' after an accident, or behaving in a considerate manner to the victim of an accident (for example offering a lift to someone whose vehicle has been damaged) could be taken as an admission of liability.

4.3 Occupiers' liability

The liability of occupiers to visitors and non-visitors is statutory. The liability to lawful visitors is laid down by the Occupiers' Liability Act (OLA) 1957, which imposes a duty of care similar in standard and scope to the common law duty of care. Liability to non-visitors or trespassers is governed by the Occupiers' Liability Act 1984, which imposes no general duty but lays down the circumstances in which a duty will arise, and then defines a duty of a lower standard and narrower scope than that owed to lawful visitors.

Liability under the 1957 Act is based on negligence, ie, breach of a duty of reasonable care. The statutory guidelines and defences included within the Act equate occupiers' liability with common law negligence to a considerable extent. Although the Act covers the relationship of employer and employee, it is not usually appropriate in such circumstances. Where the occupier is the employer of the visitor, a claim will usually be brought in negligence or for breach of statutory duty rather than under the OLA 1957.

Liability under the 1984 Act is very difficult to establish. The danger must be due to the state of the premises, not the claimant's activity on the premises: *Keown v Coventry Healthcare NHS Trust* [2006] EWCA Civ 39. In essence, a claim is only likely to succeed where the danger is not one which the claimant can appreciate, but which the defendant is aware of. As a result, while child trespassers may occasionally succeed in claims under the 1984 Act, adults will almost always fail, unless there is some hidden trap—see for example *Donoghue v Folkestone Properties Ltd* [2003] 3 All ER 1101. The decision of the Court of Appeal in *Tomlinson v Congleton BC,* which somewhat surprisingly allowed a claim by an adult trespasser in respect of a perfectly obvious risk, has now been overruled by the House of Lords (both decisions are reported at [2003] 3 All ER 1122).

Tomlinson was applied and extended in *Evans v Kosmar Villa Holidays plc* [2008] 1 All ER 530. The rule that there is no duty to protect people against obvious risks (unless they do not have an informed choice or lack capacity) applies equally where a duty would otherwise arise under a contract or under the Occupiers' Liability Act 1957.

4.4 Breach of statutory duty

4.4.1 Introduction

Breach of statutory duty has considerably more importance in practice than it does to an academic studying the law of tort. There are thousands and thousands of specific duties imposed upon various people, usually employers, with regard to safety and health in various places of work, industrial processes and commercial premises. A great many injuries are suffered by people in the course of their work. In most cases of industrial injury, a claim is likely to be brought not only in negligence, but also under a statute or statutory regulation.

Statutory duties are to be found covering more or less any workplace, work situation or industrial process you can think of. They are laid down by statute (eg, the Factories Act 1961) or by statutory instrument (eg, the Construction (General Provisions) Regulations 1961). Most statutes and regulations are currently in the process of being replaced by new regulations based on European Directives.

The relevant directives and statutory provisions are gathered together in the major reference work *Redgrave's Health and Safety,* 4th edn by M. Ford and E. Brown (London: Butterworths, 2002) where you will find such delights as the Manufacture of Cinematograph Film Regulations 1928, the Magnesium (Grinding of Castings and Other Articles) Special Regulations 1946, the Genetically Modified Organisms (Contained Use) Regulations 2000 and the Equipment and Protective Systems Intended for Use in Potentially Explosive Atmospheres Regulations 1996.

The duties laid down by statute are unlike common law duties. They are not general, but highly specific. They do not, for the most part, involve any principles of negligence or reasonable foreseeability. Three broad types of duty can be identified.

4.4.2 Absolute duties

Many duties are absolute. They require that something 'shall be done' without further qualification. They are very strictly construed, and breach of an absolute duty will give rise to liability even where there is no fault on the part of the defendant. So, for example, it is no defence that compliance with a duty would mean the defendant could not operate machinery at all (*John Summers & Sons Ltd v Frost* [1955] AC 740), or that all the evidence showed that the accident which in fact happened was an impossibility (*Galashiels Gas Co Ltd v O'Donnell* [1949] AC 275). However, the courts may construe duties as less than absolute in order to avoid unintended liabilities—see *Fytche v Wincanton Logistics plc* [2004] 4 All ER 221 (HL).

4.4.3 Duties of reasonable care

Such duties require persons to act with reasonable care; the standard of care is similar to the common law standard, and a reasonable foreseeability test will be applied. In such cases the word 'reasonably' usually appears in the statute: eg, a duty to prevent something happening 'so far as is reasonably practicable'; a duty to 'take such steps as are reasonable in all the circumstances to ensure that' something does or does not happen.

4.4.4 Hybrid duties

These are duties which are less than absolute, but which require more than reasonable care: for example, a duty to 'take such steps as may be necessary to prevent . . .'; or to 'take all appropriate precautions'. There is no single test for breach of such duties. The standard of care required is a question of the interpretation of each individual statutory section or regulation. Words which tend to indicate a hybrid duty are words such as: adequate, secure, appropriate, sufficient, necessary, practicable.

4.4.5 To establish liability

There are as many as eight conditions to be satisfied before a claimant can succeed in a claim for damages for breach of statutory duty.

(a) That the legislation applies. The statutes are not of general application. For example, the Workplace (Health, Safety and Welfare) Regulations 1992 (SI 1992/3004) only apply to workplaces as defined in reg 2. It may well be that the defendant has done something prohibited by the Regulations, but if it was not done in a workplace there will be no liability. Always check the application of the statute or regulations. This will usually be found in the legislation itself.

(b) That the duty is imposed upon the defendant or upon someone for whom the defendant is vicariously liable. Somewhere in the regulations or statute will be a section or regulation stating upon whom the duties are imposed. Different duties are imposed on different people: eg, under the Railway Safety (Miscellaneous Provisions) Regulations 1997, some duties are imposed upon Railtrack, others upon train operators, and yet others on employers contracted to work on the railway. Always make sure you are suing the right person.

(c) That the duty is owed to the claimant. The statute or regulations may state to whom a duty is owed, or it may be a matter of construction. The duty will usually be owed to the person(s) whose safety the statute is intended to protect. Others may be injured by a breach of statutory duty, but will be unable to claim (eg, *Hartley v Mayoh & Co* [1954] 1 QB 383).

(d) That breach of the legislation gives rise to civil liability. Not every statute or regulation aimed at safety will give rise to civil liability. Either it must expressly state that it does so, or it must be construed by the court as doing so. There will usually be no difficulty where the claimant has suffered the harm the statute was intended to prevent; but there may well be doubt where the statute imposes a criminal sanction, though this is not necessarily fatal. Modern statutes usually make this point clear (see, eg, Health and Safety at Work etc Act 1974, s 47). For older statutes, check in *Redgrave*.

(e) That the defendant is in breach of duty. This sounds obvious, but it may need careful examination of the facts and the legislation. Regulations are specific, not general. The defendant is only in breach if he has done exactly what he is forbidden to do; conversely he will be in breach unless he has done *exactly* what is required. Note that where a regulation requires a defendant to do something so far as 'practicable' or 'reasonably practicable' the claimant need not show that it was practicable or reasonably practicable, only that it was not done. It is for the defendant to show that it was not practicable or reasonably practicable. See, for example, *Larner v British Steel plc* [1993] 4 All ER 102.

(f) That the claimant has suffered damage. This must usually amount to personal injury or death. There are few, if any, statutory duties giving rise to liability for damage to property.

(g) That the damage is of the kind the statute was intended to prevent. There is no liability if the damage is of a different kind from that which was contemplated (*Gorris v Scott* (1874) LR 9 Ex 125). But the damage need not have been caused in the precise manner anticipated.

(h) That the breach of statutory duty caused the damage. Causation is obviously an essential requirement, as in negligence. But there are some particularly important aspects of causation, explained in the next paragraph.

4.4.6 Causation

Causation is established by applying the 'but for' test. This results in the important principle that the defendant will have a good defence if he can establish that the claimant would still have been injured even if the defendant had fulfilled his statutory duty (*McWilliams v Sir William Arrol & Co Ltd* [1962] 1 WLR 295). Where the duty is to provide a safety device, and the defendant has failed to provide it, there will still be no liability if the defendant shows that even if he had provided the safety device, the claimant would probably not have used it.

A further particular difficulty of causation arises where the duty is imposed not only on the defendant but also on the claimant. Some duties are imposed not only upon employers, but also upon employees: both may therefore be in breach of the same duty. If the only reason that the defendant is in breach of an absolute duty is that the claimant put the defendant in breach by his own breach, should the defendant be liable? The answer is a qualified no.

If the defendant's breach is coextensive with and consists of the claimant's own wrongful act and nothing more, then the defendant will not be liable for his own breach (*Ginty v Belmont Building Supplies Ltd* [1959] 1 All ER 414). But this is a strict rule and it involves the defendant establishing that there is absolutely no fault on his part beyond the technical breach of an absolute duty brought about by the claimant's own, unpreventable act.

More usually, however, a claimant will be able to establish some fault on the part of the defendant which makes the defendant's breach wider and so not coextensive with the claimant's breach. This can usually be done by showing that the defendant has not done all that he reasonably could to prevent the breach occurring, and so has caused or permitted it to happen, as well as having implicitly committed it himself (eg, *Boyle v Kodak Ltd* [1969] 1 WLR 661). In practice you can frequently get round the *Ginty* principle on this basis.

The coextensive breach principle does not even arise where the duty is imposed not upon the defendant directly, but upon someone for whom he is vicariously liable. In such a case, the defendant's liability will depend on whether the tortfeasor for whom he is vicariously liable could have raised a defence of *volenti non fit injuria* against the claimant. If so, the defendant may also raise that defence; if not, he will be liable (*Imperial Chemical Industries Ltd v Shatwell* [1965] AC 656). This is an exception to the general rule that *volenti* is not a defence to breach of statutory duty where the duty is imposed on the defendant himself (*Wheeler v New Merton Board Mills Ltd* [1933] 2 KB 669).

Contributory negligence is a good partial defence to breach of statutory duty, however.

Damages in contract

5.1 The legal remedy: damages

Where a contract has been breached, damages are available as a matter of right. Even where loss cannot be proved, nominal damages may be claimed, although cases of this type are relatively rare. The underlying principle of the damage award is to compensate the claimant for his losses, rather than measure the award by the amount of gain derived by the defendant. In a few situations the defendant's gain may also be taken into account, for example, where a defendant in the position of a fiduciary is required to account for the profit made by his acts. Compensation for the claimant can also be measured by lost opportunity, for example, where the defendant in breach of contract uses the claimant's car, the defendant may be required to pay a reasonable rental value for the use of the car for the relevant period, notwithstanding that the claimant would not have used it or otherwise leased it to someone else during the period.

A claimant's 'loss' includes any harm to the person or property of the claimant including any diminution of the claimant's assets caused by the breach. However, in calculating the total 'loss', any benefits which the claimant has enjoyed (or savings made) as a result of the breach must be set off against (reduce) the loss. The court will not generally award damages which will put the claimant in a better position than he would have been in if the breach had not occurred, although the practical effect of some damage awards may do just that.

There are three basic methods of calculating 'loss':

- expectation (or loss of bargain) basis;
- reliance (or wasted expenditure) basis; and
- restitution.

The choice of which basis to use in calculating the claim for damages will depend on the kind of loss which has occurred as a result of the breach, and which method achieves the most advantageous result for the client.

5.1.1 Expectation (loss of bargain) basis

Damages for loss of bargain are forward looking (*Robinson v Harman* (1848) 1 Ex 850) and are intended to put the claimant into the position in which he would have been if the contract had actually been performed. This includes both the loss of the promised performance and the loss of profit resulting from not being able to put the performance to use. For example, if C purchases a car for business from D and D cancels at the last minute, C has lost the benefit of the car itself, but has also lost the chance to use it in his or her business until he or she can secure another car, ie, a loss of profit.

All losses which are not too remote from the breach may be recovered, provided that the claimant has acted reasonably to mitigate his or her loss.

5.1.1.1   How is expectation loss quantified?

There are two alternative ways of calculating the amount of damages necessary to compensate for the loss of bargain: the cost of cure measure (reinstatement cost); or the difference in value measure (diminution in value). Which of these two measures is the appropriate one seems to depend largely on common sense. Consideration should be given to why the performance was wanted, what impact the claimant's duty to mitigate has had, and whether the court believes that the claimant, awarded damages on the cost of cure basis, either has carried out or will carry out the cure.

In *Radford v De Froberville* [1977] 1 WLR 1262 a contract for the sale of land required a wall to be built separating the land sold from that belonging to the claimant. In a claim for damages for breach of contract the claimant was held entitled to receive the cost of building the wall as compensation from the defendant because the claimant genuinely wanted the work done and convinced the court that the money would be used for that purpose, even though the land had not been diminished in value by the failure to carry out the contractual obligation.

In *Tito v Waddell (No 2)* [1977] Ch 106 a mining company had agreed to replant land after it had been mined and had then failed to do so. It was held, in an action for damages seeking the cost of replanting, that the claimants could not succeed since there was no evidence that they intended to use the money to carry out the contractual obligation. Instead, damages were assessed on the basis of the diminution in the value of the land—a much smaller sum of money.

Where a claim for negligent performance of a contract is made against a surveyor, the rule is that the correct measure of damages is normally diminution of value. However, this is not an absolute and invariable rule and will not be followed if its application would manifestly not do justice in the case (see *Hipkins v Jack Cotton Partnership* [1989] 2 EGLR 157).

Where a finance company lends money on the basis of a negligent valuation of the property, it is entitled to recover, as part of the measure of damages, interest at a proper rate of interest but not necessarily the rate provided by the loan. (See *Swing-castle Ltd v Alastair Gibson* [1991] 2 AC 223.)

Subject to the principles of remoteness and mitigation, damages arising from some common breaches of contract are quantified in the ways illustrated by **Table 5.1**. See further **6.2.5**.

5.1.2   Reliance (or wasted expenditure) basis

Reliance loss arises where the claimant has expended money which is then wasted in preparation for, or in partial performance of, the contract. It covers out-of-pocket expenses. Like the expectation loss basis, the reliance loss method aims to put the claimant in as good a position as he was in before the contract was made (see Fuller and Perdue, 'Reliance Interest in Contract Damages' (1936) 46 *Yale Law Journal* 52).

Reliance loss will be claimed in cases where expectation loss is too speculative to recover (see, eg, *McRae v Commonwealth Disposals Commission* (1950) 84 CLR 377; *Anglia Television Ltd v Reed* [1972] 1 QB 60).

Common examples of reliance expenses are for collection of goods (where the buyer is required by the contract to collect the goods and after incurring charges the seller repudiates the contract), storage and transport charges. According to *Anglia Television*

Table 5.1 Damages arising from some common breaches of contract

Type of contract	Where a claim is made against the person who confers the benefit			Where the claim is against the person who receives the benefit
	Non-performance	*Delayed performance*	*Defective performance*	*Non-performance*
Transfer of property or goods	(a) The difference between the cost of buying the same goods in the market and the contract price if it has not been paid. (b) Or, if there is no market, then the loss of user profit. (The rule in *Bain v Fothergill*, relating to sale of land, that only expenses can be recovered has been abolished so now normal expectation damages will be available.)	(a) The difference between the market value at the due date for delivery and the market value at the date of actual delivery. (b) or, if intended to be used, then the loss of profit which could have been expected from that use. (The rule in *Bain v Fothergill*, relating to sale of land, that only the expenses which have been incurred can be recovered, has been abolished so now normal expectation damages will be available.)	Where the goods are defective, or are not of contract quality, then the value of the goods in their expected or intended condition less their market value in the defective condition (diminution of value), and, if wanted for use, the loss of user profit. However, if the defect can be cured, then the measure is the cost or cure. Betterment will be ignored.	(a) Where there is a failure to pay or accept the goods, then the difference between the contract price and the selling price on the market. (b) Or, if there is no market, then the loss of user profit suffered.
Contract for a loan	The difference between the contract cost of the loan and the market cost of the loan.	Same as for non-performance.		
Contract for services	The difference between the market cost of the same service and the contract cost, less the contract price if it has not already been paid.	The value of the service if rendered on the due date, less its value on the date when rendered.	Where the value of the property is reduced, then the diminution in the value of that property. However, if reasonable, the cost of cure measure will be awarded instead if the work has been or will be done. If there is no reduction in value, then such consequential losses as arise.	Where there is a failure to accept a service: (a) A failure to supply cargo in a contract of carriage, then the difference between the contract rate and the market rate for carriage. (b) In a wrongful dismissal, the difference between the contract wage and any substitute wage. (c) Where there is a failure to allow work to proceed, then the contract price less the costs saved by not having to carry out the work.

Source: Table compiled from *McGregor on Damages* and Burrows, *Remedies for Tort and Breach of Contract*.

Ltd v Reed, pre-contractual expenses are recoverable as part of the reliance loss, provided 'it was such as would reasonably be in the contemplation of the parties as likely to be wasted if the contract was broken' (per Lord Denning MR at p 64).

5.1.3   Restitution (unjust enrichment)

The third basis of calculating loss is where the claimant, in performing his obligations under the contract, has conferred a benefit on the defendant and wishes to claim back the benefit (or the value) given. For example, where the claimant has paid in advance for a product which is not delivered, he is entitled to the return of the money paid. The 'loss' to the claimant is measured by reference to the amount of benefit (including the reasonable value of services) given to the defendant, rather than focusing on the amount of the claimant's loss, although in some cases this may be the same amount. In breach of contract cases, actions based on a claim for restitution may be for *quantum meruit,* and where there has been a total failure of consideration (failure to perform), the action will be for the recovery of money had and received.

The effect of a restitutionary claim is to restore both parties to the position they would have been in if the contract had never been made. This differs from the expectation basis, which is meant to put the claimant in the position he would have been in if the contract had been performed. It also differs from the reliance basis in that a restitution claim assumes that no contract had been made but the party in breach may be left in a worse position. Damages for breach of contract which are awarded purely for restitutionary loss have been rare (see *Wrotham Park Estate Co. Ltd v Parkside Homes Ltd* [1974] 1 WLR 798). It is important to bear in mind that claims for restitution are not limited to cases of breach of contract and are frequently part of claims for other equitable remedies (see later in this chapter and **Chapter 13**).

5.1.4   Choosing between expectation, reliance and restitution

Generally the claimant will be permitted to choose the method on which to base his or her claim, and the defendant is not entitled to insist that the claimant must pursue one basis over another. There are, however, several guiding principles which will apply. First a claimant will not be permitted to claim damages for a reliance loss where this would compensate him, in effect, for a bad bargain, thereby putting him in a better position than he would have been in had the contract been performed. Where the loss flows from having entered into the contract rather than from its breach, only the lower expectation loss will be recoverable. (See *CCC Films (London) Ltd v Impact Quadrant Films Ltd* [1985] QB 16 and *C & P Haulage v Middleton* [1983] 1 WLR 1461.)

A claimant will not be permitted to claim for expectation losses that are too speculative to be capable of satisfactory proof. In such a case, the claim will be limited to reliance losses and the value of any restitutionary claim.

A claim in restitution will only be permitted if the breach is a serious one which amounts to a total failure of consideration. If this is proved, restitution may be claimed even if the result is to leave the claimant in a better position than he would have been in if the contract had been performed. This is a complex area and practitioners are advised to consult specialist texts on contract law.

The various bases may also be combined within one claim provided the losses are not duplicated, allowing the claimant to recover twice for the same loss. It is possible to have a situation where the claimant paid in advance for a product, and incurred installation expenses. After installation the product was found to be defective. The claimant may recover the money paid for the product (in restitution) and the costs of installation (incurred in reliance). If expected profits were also lost as a result of the breach, the net (not the gross) profits could be recovered as well.

5.2 When can loss of profit be claimed?

A claim for loss of profit will arise in cases where the business use of the goods or service contracted for is lost or delayed as a result of the breach of contract.

Where there is no difference between the market price and the contract price, a claim for loss of profit will succeed only if it can be established that there was a market— that is, that the supply of the goods or services in question outstripped the demand for them—otherwise only nominal damages will be available (see *W.L. Thompson Ltd v Robinson (Gunmakers) Ltd* [1955] Ch 177; *Lazenby Garages Ltd v Wright* [1976] 1 WLR 459). Whether or not there is an available market depends upon whether there is an available buyer who is prepared to pay a fair price on that day. Where there is only a hypothetical sale, there is an available market only where, on the relevant day, there were sufficient possible traders in touch with each other to evidence a market in which the goods could have been sold (see *Shearson Lehman Hutton Inc v Maclaine Watson & Co Ltd (No 2)* [1990] 3 All ER 723).

Where there has been an inadequate repair causing an explosion, and thereby loss of profit, that loss of profit cannot be claimed because the further damage arises from another cause. Damages will then be limited to the replacement of the defective equipment and to the loss of profit while the repair is being effected.

5.3 Can incidental losses be included in the assessment of damages?

Such items as the cost of stopping delivery, holding goods in store, defending a sub-buyer's claim, etc are included in the assessment of damages and can be recovered.

5.4 When can damages be obtained for loss of reputation?

The general rule is that damages cannot be awarded for loss of reputation caused by wrongful dismissal or because a wrongful dismissal may make it more difficult to find alternative employment (see *Addis v Gramophone Co Ltd* [1909] AC 488). However, in cases where the obtaining of publicity is the main purpose of the contract, damages for the lost chance of enhancing reputation will be recoverable (breaches of actors' contracts, and breach of advertising contracts). Equally, dishonouring a trader's cheque in breach of contract will entitle the trader to damages for lost reputation and, where goods or services are provided directly to the claimant's customers but are not of contract quality, again, damages for lost reputation can be recovered.

5.5 When can damages be obtained for distress and disappointment?

The general rule is that damages for distress are not available in an action for breach of contract. However, recent cases suggest some slackening in the strictness of this rule, so that in contracts entered into for purposes of enjoyment (see *Jarvis v Swans Tours Ltd* [1973] QB 233) damages will be available for disappointment, and in contracts entered into to avoid distress or to gain peace of mind damages will be available for the failure to prevent that distress (see *Heywood v Wellers* [1976] QB 446). The scope of this exception has now been extended by the House of Lords in *Farley v Skinner* [2001] 4 All ER 801. It is not necessary that the very purpose of the contract should have been to provide pleasure, relaxation or peace of mind; it is sufficient that this was a major or important part of the contract. However, damages under this head should be restrained and modest. The House of Lords regarded £10,000 as right on the upper limit. Where the damages are for injury to feelings, the appropriate range is £500 to £25,000 (*Chief Constable of West Yorkshire v Vento* The Times, 20 December 2002).

Applying this principle, it was held in *Hamilton Jones v David & Snape* [2004] 1 All ER 657 that a claimant could recover damages for the distress caused by the loss of the company of her children, where this loss was caused by the negligence of her solicitors, who had been specifically instructed in order to avoid such a loss.

Damages for distress can also be claimed as consequential to physical inconvenience because this is taken to be obviously within the contemplation of the parties at the time of contracting (see *Perry v Sydney Phillips and Son* [1982] 1 WLR 1297). Damages for distress arising out of wrongful dismissal from a contract of employment cannot be recovered (*Addis v Gramophone Co Ltd* [1909] AC 488, recently reaffirmed in *Johnson v Unisys Ltd* [2001] UKHL 13, [2001] 2 All ER 801). No claim for inconvenience or distress can be made by a company (see *Firststeel Cold Rolled Products v Anaco Precision Pressings* The Times, 21 November 1994).

5.6 Exemplary or punitive damages

Exemplary damages are not available for breach of contract claims (see *Addis v Gramophone Co Ltd* [1909] AC 488).

5.7 When are damages assessed?

The general rule is that damages are assessed at the time of breach (the date of the accrual of the cause of action), that is, at the date when the damage occurs, because the innocent party is required to act reasonably (to mitigate) by going to the market to replace the goods or services as soon as is possible after the breach (see *C. Sharpe & Co Ltd v Nosawa* [1917] 2KB 814). However, where it appears probable that the defendant may make good his default, then damages will be assessed at the time when that probability ceases.

This general rule fails to take account of the problems caused by inflation and the consequent variability of the cost of goods and services, or of the changing world value of money. The rule is now often ignored where it would 'give rise to injustice, [and] the court has power to fix such other date as may be appropriate in the circumstances' (see *Johnson v Agnew* [1980] AC 367). However, *The Folias* [1979] AC 685 and *Attorney-General of the Republic of Ghana v Texaco Overseas Tankships Ltd* [1994] 1 Lloyd's Rep 473 held that if the contract discloses no intention as to the currency in which damages for breach are to be payable, they should be calculated in the currency in which the claimants incurred the loss.

So, where the price of the contract has already been paid, and it may not be reasonable to expect the innocent party to replace the goods or services by going to the market, since he or she may not have the money to do so (that party has not got the opportunity to act), damages will be assessed by reference to the market value at the time of judgment. Equally, a buyer of land is entitled to seek specific performance of the contract of sale and, if damages are awarded instead of specific performance, those damages will be assessed at the date of judgment rather than at the date of breach (see *Wroth v Tyler* [1974] Ch 30).

In cases where foreign currency liability arises, the sum in sterling to be paid is the applicable rate for exchange on the date of payment (see *Miliangos v George Frank (Textiles) Ltd* [1976] AC 443).

Where an anticipatory breach of contract occurs, the innocent party has the option of accepting the breach or continuing to press for performance. In the former situation there is an immediate obligation to mitigate and damages will be assessed at that time. However, in the latter case, damages will be assessed as at the date when performance should have taken place.

Where, after breach, an event occurs which has a material effect on the amount of loss that the claimant has suffered, that supervening event cannot be ignored. This is particularly so where the event was a contingency that was, or could have been, anticipated by the parties to the contract, since, if the event had not occurred, the damages would have had to be assessed with reference to the chance of its occurring: see *Golden Strait Corp v Nippon Yusen Kubishika Kaisha* [2007] 3 All ER 1.

See further **6.2.2**.

5.8 Taxation of damages

In assessing damages for a breach of contract, to what extent will a deduction be made for taxation?

The general rule is that where the loss which is compensated for by the payment of damages is loss of income, the tax which would have been paid on that income if earned in the normal way will be deducted from the damages awarded (see *British Transport Commission v Gourley* [1956] AC 185). This rule applies only if the damages are not themselves subject to taxation. Now, since sums in excess of £30,000 awarded for wrongful dismissal are taxable, the *Gourley* principle no longer applies to sums in excess of that amount (see *Shove v Downs Surgical plc* [1984] 1 All ER 7). The easiest way to calculate the correct sum to be paid by way of damages is to use the net effect approach.

The appropriate principles are set out in **Chapter 20**.

5.9 Limitations on compensatory damages

5.9.1 Loss in the contemplation of the parties

Compensatory damages are subject to the limitation imposed by the rules preventing claims for losses which are deemed to be too remote from the breach.

The test in contract is whether the loss was in the reasonable contemplation of the parties. In *Hadley v Baxendale* (1854) 9 Ex 341 two limbs to the test for judging whether the damage is too remote were identified: first, damage which arises naturally, that is, according to the usual course of things from such breach of contract (see further *Banque Keyser Ullmann SA v Skandia (UK) Insurance Co Ltd* [1991] 2 AC 249); or second, such as may reasonably be supposed to have been in the contemplation of both parties, at the time they made the contract, as a probable result of the breach of it. (See further *Victoria Laundry (Windsor) Ltd v Newman Industries Ltd* [1949] 2 KB 528, *The Heron II* [1969] 1 AC 350, and *H. Parsons (Livestock) Ltd v Uttley Ingham & Co Ltd* [1978] QB 791, which suggests that in contract there must be a serious possibility of the loss arising, whereas in the law of tort a slight risk of the loss is enough.) The test has been recently discussed yet again by the House of Lords in *Jackson v Royal Bank of Scotland* [2005] 2 All ER 71.

5.9.2   The claimant is under a duty to mitigate the loss

The general rule is that the claimant is required to take reasonable steps to reduce the loss and to avoid taking action which may increase the loss suffered (see *Payzu Ltd v Saunders* [1919] 2 KB 581 and *Banco de Portugal v Waterlow and Sons Ltd* [1932] AC 452). Where the effect of the mitigating act is to wipe out the loss from the breach, according to *British Westinghouse Co v Underground Electric Railways Co of London* [1912] AC 673 the claimant will be entitled to nominal damages only. (Note that no such duty arises in relation to claims for misrepresentation, see *Hussey v Eels* [1990] 2 QB 227.)

5.9.3   Other restrictions on the right to claim damages

If the claimant saves the cost of performance as a result of the breach, these savings will be deducted from the overall award of damages, as will any sums of money earned from new employment in a claim for wrongful dismissal.

It has been held that loss which results purely from the claimant's own impecuniosity is irrecoverable (see *Owners of Dredger Liesbosch v Owners of Steamship Edison* [1933] AC 449). However, it would seem that if the claimant's impecuniosity prevents him from mitigating the loss, this will not affect the claim for damages (see *Perry v Sidney Phillips and Son* [1982] 1 WLR 1297 and *Alcoa Minerals of Jamaica v Broderick* [2000] 3 WLR 23). It has also been held by the House of Lords in *Lagden v O'Connor* [2004] 1 All ER 277 that if a claimant incurs a greater loss as a result of his poverty than he would have done if he had been able to afford to mitigate, that greater loss is recoverable. It is now highly arguable that the principle of *The Liesbosch* is no longer good law.

Where a contract entitles the defendant to perform in a number of alternative ways, then it will be assumed that the defendant will choose to perform in the way most advantageous to him and damages will be assessed on that basis.

5.9.4   What is the effect of contributory negligence on a claim for damages for breach of contract?

There are three classes of case:

(a) Those where liability arises both in contract and tort coextensively, in which case the Law Reform (Contributory Negligence) Act 1945 applies and damages will be reduced to take account of any contributory negligence on the part of the claimant (see *Forsikringsaktieselskapet Vesta v Butcher* [1989] AC 852).

(b) Those where the breach does not amount to a tort as well, in which case the 1945 Act does not apply and any contributory negligence on the part of the claimant can be disregarded (see *Lambert v Lewis* [1982] AC 225).

(c) Those where there is both strict liability in contract and coextensive liability in contract and tort. In such a case there can be no defence of contributory negligence (*Barclays Bank plc v Fairclough Building Ltd* [1995] 1 All ER 289).

5.9.5 When is interest on damages recoverable?

The Supreme Court Act (SCA) 1981, s 35A and the County Courts Act (CCA) 1984, s 69, give the court discretion to award interest on all or any part of damages for all or any part of the period from the date of the cause of action until the date of payment or judgment. If the contract itself fixes interest, the court has no power to fix any different rate. Any claim for interest must be mentioned specifically in the appropriate statement of case.

5.10 Other remedies

5.10.1 Action for an agreed sum

This remedy is available where there is a duty to pay the sum of money agreed and the action providing the right to claim exists. For example, the Sale of Goods Act 1979, s 49, provides that an action for the price only arises once the property in the goods has passed to the buyer, even though the duty to pay arises as soon as the seller is willing and able to deliver.

If the injured party elects to affirm the contract, he can claim the agreed sum if all that is necessary has been done to make the action available or, arguably, if he can complete doing that which is necessary to make the action available (see *White & Carter (Councils) Ltd v McGregor* [1962] AC 413).

5.10.2 Quasi-contract—the law of restitution

Quasi-contract is sometimes described as an action for money had and received or unjust enrichment or benefit. This occurs: first 'where the claimant has been compelled to pay money for which the defendant is liable, he may sue the defendant for the money so paid' (*Cheshire, Fifoot and Furmston*, p 631). Second, where money has been paid under a mistake which, had it been true, would have required the payment of the money. It is no longer necessary to distinguish a mistake of fact from a mistake of law (*Kleinwort Benson Ltd v Lincoln City Council* [1998] 4 All ER 513). Accordingly, tax wrongly paid under a mistake of law is recoverable (*Deutsche Morgan Grenfell Group plc v IRC* [2007] 1 All ER 449. Third, where money is paid where there has been a total failure of consideration or where money is paid in pursuance of a void contract. Money paid in pursuance of an illegal contract is rarely recoverable in quasi-contract. Fourth, where one party is bound to pay a sum of money to another and agrees to pay that money to a third party and has informed that third party of the intention to pay, that party is liable in quasi-contract to make the payment. Fifth, where a wrongful (tortious) act has been committed against the claimant who, as a consequence, has suffered loss, the claimant may be entitled to recover for the loss in quasi-contract—where action can be brought in tort, the claims are alternatives to each other. Sixth, a claim to *quantum meruit* for reasonable remuneration for work done or services rendered where no price was fixed or where a new contract has been substituted for the old.

For an interesting analysis see *Rover International Ltd v Cannon Film Sales Ltd (No 3)* [1989] 3 All ER 423. See also *Lipkin Gorman v Karpnale* [1991] AC 548 for an example of unjust enrichment.

This area is developing rapidly as a method by which redress can be sought. See *D.O. Ferguson and Associates v Sohl* (1992) 62 BLR 95.

Damages in tort

6.1 Liability

To establish liability on the part of the defendant, in order to recover damages, a claimant must show:

- The elements of the tort.
- Causation.
- Loss and damage.
- Loss and damage not too remote.

6.1.1 Elements of the tort

To go into the elements of all the various torts is beyond the scope of this chapter. Many, but not all, torts involve the breach of some duty owed by the defendant to the claimant, eg, negligence, breach of statutory duty. Others involve the performance of some deliberate act calculated or likely to cause harm to the claimant, eg, assault and battery, conversion, defamation. Yet others are torts of strict liability, eg, *Rylands v Fletcher* liability, product liability. Whatever the elements of the tort may be, each of them must be made out.

6.1.2 Causation

The claimant must show causation—that the tortious act caused his or her injury, loss or damage. It need not have been the sole cause. It is usual to apply the 'but for' test: the claimant must show that *but for* the defendant's tortious act he or she would not, on the balance of probabilities, have suffered the injury or loss. It may be sufficient in some circumstances to show that the tortious act increased the likelihood of damage occurring (*McGhee v National Coal Board* [1973] 1 WLR 1), but it must still have caused the injury on the balance of probabilities (*Kay v Ayrshire andArran Health Board* [1987] 2 All ER 417). There is no claim in respect of a tortious act which has increased the likelihood of damage if it still would have occurred in any event on the balance of probabilities (*Hotson v Fitzgerald* [1987] AC 750; *Gregg v Scott* [2005] 4 All ER 812).

However, the 'but for' test will not be rigidly applied where the claimant can show that one or both of two defendants caused him damage, but is unable to show that either of them did so on the balance of probabilities. In such circumstances it is enough to show that either of them made a material contribution to the claimant's damage by materially increasing the risk of such damage (*Fairchild v Glenhaven Funeral Services Ltd* [2002] 3 All ER 305, followed in *Barker v Saint-Gobain Pipelines plc* [2005] 3 All ER 661). In cases of personal injury where the claimant has suffered mesothelioma as a result of exposure to asbestos, and there are several defendants potentially liable under the principle of *Fairchild,* but no evidence as to the extent to which each has exposed the claimant to risk, a special rule has been laid down by s 3 of the Compensation Act 2006. In such cases the potential defendants are jointly and severally liable, and each may therefore be liable for the whole of the claimant's loss, irrespective that some of the loss may have been caused by the claimant himself during a period of self-employment or by employers who are not liable in negligence. This section was enacted to reverse the decision of the House of Lords in *Barker v Corus (UK) Ltd* [2006] 3 All ER 785.

Another exception to the strict rule on causation was allowed by the House of Lords in *Chester v Afshar* [2004] 4 All ER 587. It was held that where a surgeon negligently failed to warn a patient of the risk of damage inherent in an operation, and the patient underwent the operation, and the risk materialised, the patient did not have to show that if properly advised she would not have had the operation, only that she would not have had it on the day she did. The court recognised that it was departing from the principles of the law on causation, but held that this departure was justified in the interests of justice. In the circumstances, this must therefore be seen as only a very narrow and specific exception to the rule.

Causation may be broken by a supervening act or event, in which case the claimant's claim will fail. The supervening act may come between the defendant's tortious act and damage, in which case the chain of causation may be broken altogether, but whether it is broken is a question of fact and degree. If the supervening act was reasonably foreseeable and/or made little difference to the chain of events, the chain is probably not broken. For example, in *Corr v IBC Vehicles Ltd* [2006] 2 All ER 929, having been injured as a result of the defendant's negligence, the deceased developed a psychiatric illness which made him suicidal, and he did eventually commit suicide. The Court of Appeal held that the chain of causation was not broken, because the suicide could not be regarded as an intentional act, and it was irrelevant whether the suicide was foreseeable: it was enough that psychiatric injury was reasonably foreseeable. If, on the other hand, it was not reasonably foreseeable and was a wholly new event, the chain of causation may be broken even if the 'but for' test is still satisfied. If the supervening act was one which the defendant had a duty to prevent, then the chain of causation is not broken (*Reeves v Metropolitan Police Commissioner* [1999] 3 All ER 897). Alternatively, the supervening event may occur after the claimant has suffered damage, and its effect is to add to the claimant's damage. In such circumstances the question is whether the second event was natural, in which case causation is broken (*Jobling v Associated Dairies Ltd* [1982] AC 794), or whether it was a tortious act, in which case causation is not broken (*Baker v Willoughby* [1970] AC 467). The principle of *Baker v Willoughby,* that the second tortfeasor should be liable only for the additional harm caused to a claimant who had already been injured by the first tortfeasor, was upheld in *Murrell v Healy* [2001] 4 All ER 345, where the court had to consider what loss of earnings would have flowed from the first accident even though it had been superseded by the second accident which caused a complete loss of earnings.

Where the supervening event was brought on by a second tortious act, but was such that it might well have resulted in due course from the first tortious act, the second tortfeasor will not be fully liable for the consequences of the event; rather, a discount should be made (*Heil v Rankin* The Times, 20 June 2000).

6.1.3 Loss and damage

The claimant must establish loss and damage in order to recover damages (with the exception of trespass to land, which is actionable without proof of loss). He or she does not, however, have to establish the extent of his or her loss, so long as he or she can prove it does exist: the court will then assess the damage as best it can. Difficulty of assessment is no bar to recovery. On this principle damages can be recovered for loss of a chance or opportunity.

There may, however, be some limitation in law as to the type of loss in respect of which damages can be recovered. The primary example is pure economic loss in negligence. Although the House of Lords ruled in *Junior Books Ltd v Veitchi & Co Ltd* [1983] 1 AC 520 that there is no fundamental rule that pure economic loss is not recoverable, consistent lines of case law show that such loss is in most cases not recoverable in negligence (eg, *Leigh & Sillavan Ltd v Aliakmon Shipping Co Ltd* [1986] AC 785; *Peabody Donation Fund v Sir Lindsay Parkinson & Co Ltd* [1985] AC 210). Even damage that at first sight appears to be damage to property may in fact be deemed pure economic loss (*D & F Estates Ltd v Church Commissioners* [1989] AC 177; *Murphy v Brentwood District Council* [1991] 1 AC 398). The major exception is economic loss resulting from negligent misstatement or negligent professional advice (*Hedley Byrne & Co Ltd v Heller and Partners Ltd* [1964] AC 465; *Caparo Industries plc v Dickman* [1990] 2 AC 605; *Henderson v Merrett Syndicates Ltd* [1994] AC 145).

Nevertheless, it should not be thought that economic loss is not generally recoverable in tort as a whole. Many torts result solely or primarily in pure economic loss to the claimant: misrepresentation, deceit, procuring breach of contract, conspiracy, slander of title, slander of goods, conversion, breach of copyright, infringement of patent. In all these cases damages for pure economic loss may be recovered.

6.1.4   Remoteness

Broadly speaking, the test for remoteness in tort is reasonable foreseeability: it must have been reasonably foreseeable that the damage suffered by the claimant might result from the defendant's act. With what degree of likelihood is not entirely clear, but the cases tend to suggest only a slight degree of likelihood is required in tort, with rather more likelihood in contract (eg, *H. Parsons (Livestock) Ltd v Uttley Ingham & Co Ltd* [1978] QB 791).

It is not necessary that the precise damage suffered should have been foreseeable; the broad type of damage will suffice. Personal injury is generally regarded as a broad type of damage in itself. It is not necessary that the damage should have come about in precisely the foreseeable manner. It is not necessary that the actual seriousness or quantum of damage should have been foreseeable. Reasonable foreseeability appears to be the correct test for all torts, except torts of strict liability and deceit (see **7.4.3**).

6.1.5   Recovery of sums paid to another by way of settlement

It is not a rule of law that a person (A) who has settled a claim against him by B and seeks to recover the sum paid as damages from a third party (C) must prove that he was or would have been liable to B. The question is whether the payment, and the amount of the payment were reasonable. If the settlement is reasonable, then it is likely to have been reasonably foreseeable that A would make the payment by way of settlement to B, and there is no reason why he cannot recover it from C. If it is unreasonable, then not only is payment unforeseeable, but the chain of causation is broken, and so A cannot recover the sum from C for both those reasons. If it is reasonable for A to make settlement with B, but the amount paid is not reasonable, then the amount paid is not foreseeable, and is not the correct measure of loss in A's claim against C. For all the above, see *John F Hunt Demolition Ltd v ASME Engineering Ltd* [2008] 1 All ER 180.

6.2 Quantum of damages

6.2.1 Compensatory nature of damages

Damages in tort are compensatory in nature and are designed to put the claimant into the position he or she would have been in had the tort not been committed. This means that a claimant may prima facie receive damages both in respect of any loss directly caused by the tortious act and in respect of any consequential loss, provided the rules of causation and remoteness are satisfied.

6.2.2 Time of assessment

Strictly speaking, damages are to be assessed at the date when damage occurs. This will frequently, but not necessarily, be the same as the date when the cause of action arose. However, courts are also bound to take account of all events which occur prior to trial, which would tend to suggest that damages should be valued as at the date of trial. This latter approach is adopted in cases of personal injury and death. In cases of damage to property and economic loss the courts seem to adopt a more discretionary and flexible approach. In *Dodd Properties (Kent) Ltd v Canterbury City Council* [1980] 1 All ER 928, it was held that damages for the cost of repair to property should be assessed at the date when it was reasonable for the claimant to undertake the repairs: this may be as late as the date of trial. The same result was achieved in *Alcoa Minerals of Jamaica v Broderick* [2000] 3 WLR 23.

6.2.3 Mode of assessment: general

The mode of assessing damages varies greatly according to the tort, the nature of the loss, etc. Without considering each tort separately, one can nevertheless identify certain types of damage and consider how they are quantified in general terms:

- Personal injury.
- Economic loss consequent on injury or death.
- Other kinds of personal non-financial damage.
- Damage to property.
- Interference with property.
- Pure economic loss.

Most torts are capable of giving rise to several of these different types of damage all at once. There may be some special rules as to how each type of damage is to be quantified in respect of the particular tort that has caused it: reference should be made to specialist textbooks, eg, *Clerk and Lindsell on Torts; McGregor on Damages*.

Personal injury and economic loss consequent on injury and death are dealt with in **Chapters 11** and **12**. This chapter will concentrate on the remaining four types of damage.

6.2.4 Other kinds of personal non-financial damage

This includes, for example, loss of liberty, mental distress, damage to reputation, and inconvenience and discomfort. It is not difficult to see how such damage may arise.

Loss of liberty may result from false imprisonment, malicious prosecution, or negligence (see *Meah v McCreamer* [1985] 1 All ER 367). Mental distress, or injury to feelings, which amounts to suffering is a personal injury and is dealt with under that head. Mental distress that falls short of suffering (eg, fear, grief and anguish) is prima facie not recoverable in tort but may be 'tacked on' to damages for defamation, malicious prosecution, assault, deceit and nuisance. Damage to reputation obviously results from defamation, but it can also result from defamation of goods, malicious prosecution, negligence, deceit, misrepresentation or breach of copyright. Inconvenience and discomfort can result from virtually any tort, and may be recoverable as a separate head where it does not overlap with loss of amenity.

Such losses are assessed with very little to go on but the judge's or jury's own intuitive judgment and comparison with awards in previous cases (so far as they can be ascertained), much as pain, suffering and loss of amenity are assessed in personal injury cases. Some observations can be made:

(a) Damages for loss of liberty, mental distress and inconvenience obviously overlap and may well be assessed together.

(b) Damages for injury to feelings involving mental distress are very similar to damages for pain and suffering and can be assessed in the same way.

(c) Damages for loss of reputation may be substantial in cases of defamation. In most other cases the loss of reputation may well be treated as future economic loss and assessed accordingly.

(d) Damages for inconvenience and discomfort (when not included in loss of amenity in a personal injury claim) are likely to amount to a modest sum.

6.2.5 Damages under the Human Rights Act 1998

This is, not surprisingly, a developing area, but the question of when damages should be awarded for breach of the Human Rights Act, and how such damages should be assessed, has now been considered in some depth by the Court of Appeal in *Anufrijeva v Southwark London BC* [2004] 1 All ER 833, and by the House of Lords in *R (Greenfield) v Secretary of State for the Home Department* [2005] 2 All ER 240.

Since the European Convention on Human Rights, incorporated into the 1998 Act, has objectives which go beyond merely compensating those whose human rights have been violated, an award of damages is not automatic where there has been a breach of the Act. Indeed in the vast majority of cases, a finding of violation is sufficient recompense in itself. Damages should only be awarded where actual loss has been caused by the breach. Damages should not be assessed by comparison with awards in tortious claims in the English courts, but rather by comparison with awards made by the European Court of Human Rights, which are more modest. Such awards are not precisely calculated, but are assessed on the basis of what is judged to be fair in each individual case. English courts should aim to be neither significantly more nor less generous in their awards than the ECHR. See also *Van Colle v Chief Constable of Hertfordshire Police* [2007] 3 All ER 122.

6.2.6 Damage to property

6.2.6.1 The two modes of assessing damages

Broadly speaking, wherever damage is done to the claimant's property a choice has to be made between two alternative modes of assessing damages. One is the cost of cure basis, ie, awarding the claimant the cost of repairing the damaged property or replacing the destroyed property; the other is the diminution in value basis, ie, awarding the claimant the value of the property destroyed or the difference between its value today and its value before it was damaged. There is no fixed rule as to which measure is correct; it depends on what is reasonable in all the circumstances. To recover damages for the cost of cure, the claimant must show that reinstatement of the damaged property, as opposed to the acquisition of a substitute, is what is required to make good his or her damage. He or she must show that he or she genuinely intends to reinstate and that it is reasonable to do so (subject to the duty to mitigate) (*Ruxley Electronics and Construction Ltd v Forsyth* [1996] 1 AC 344, HL).

6.2.6.2   Making the choice

Once the facts of a case are known it is not usually too difficult to make a choice. In the case of land, contrast the two cases mentioned above. In the case of goods, more than anything else the value of the chattel will be the deciding factor: a court, or an insurance company, will award whichever is the lesser of the cost of repairing a damaged motor car or its value just before it was damaged. Where property is kept for its value (eg, a painting), damages will usually be limited to its value. Where property is kept for use (eg, a ship), the claimant may well be able to recover its replacement cost (*Owners of Dredger Liesbosch v Owners of Steamship Edison* [1933] AC 449). However, a claimant whose working crane was destroyed was able to recover its resale value, not the cost of obtaining a replacement crane (*Southampton Container Terminals Ltd v Hansa Schiffahrts GmbH* [2001] 2 Lloyd's Rep 275). Where a chattel is merely damaged the choice may be three-way—cost of repairs, diminution in value, or cost of replacement less residual value. In such a case, particularly where the chattel is a ship, the decision depends on what is reasonable.

6.2.6.3   Consequential economic loss

Consequential economic loss can also usually be recovered. Where property is destroyed the claimant may recover damages for loss of its use until it is replaced: where it is damaged the claimant may recover damages for loss of its use while it is being repaired. This may include the cost of hiring an alternative, so long as this is reasonable.

Care must be taken where the chattel is a profit-earning chattel (eg, a ship available for charter). If damages are awarded on a cost of repair or replacement basis, then an additional sum can be recovered for loss of profit in the interim. But if damages are assessed on the basis of its market value at the date of destruction, this value would include its profit-earning potential and so damages cannot be awarded for loss of profit as well (though there have been cases where damages in respect of loss of profit on fixed future engagements have been recovered). If a profit-earning building is destroyed, similar care must be taken to avoid double recovery (see *Dominion Mosaics and Tile Co Ltd v Trafalgar Trucking Co Ltd* [1990] 2 All ER 246).

6.2.6.4   Negligent valuation of property

In cases of negligent survey reports, on the basis of which the claimant has bought property at a price above what he or she would have paid if the report were correct, the measure of damages is diminution in value, not cost of cure. The claimant can recover the difference between the price he or she paid and the actual value of the property, but not the cost of repairs, even if he or she has reasonably carried out those repairs (*Watts v Morrow* [1991] 1 WLR 1421). Consequential expenses may, however, be recovered (*Patel v Hooper & Jackson* [1999] 1 All ER 992).

6.2.7   Interference with property

6.2.7.1   Goods

Loss caused by interference with goods arises particularly in cases of conversion and trespass. If the claimant has been permanently deprived of goods, damages will be assessed on the same alternative bases as if they were destroyed: the claimant may either recover the value of the goods lost, or the cost of replacing them, whichever is reasonable. He or she may also recover consequential damages for loss of use. If the deprivation is temporary, damages are likely to be simply for loss of use. The rules of mitigation may well require the claimant to replace lost goods within a reasonable time in order to minimise loss. However, he or she will probably not be required to do so if he or she cannot afford to: see *Lagden v O'Connor* [2004] 1 All ER 277 and **5.9.3** above.

The date of assessment is also within the court's discretion. The general rule, reaffirmed in *BBMB Finance (Hong Kong) Ltd v Eda Holdings Ltd* [1990] 1 WLR 409, is that the value of goods lost is to be assessed at the date of loss or conversion. However, the rule is not absolute, and in other cases, particularly where damages are being awarded under the Torts (Interference with Goods) Act 1977, s 3, as an alternative to return of the goods, a later date may be appropriate (*IBL Ltd v Coussens* [1991] 2 All ER 133).

6.2.7.2   Land

Where the case involves trespass to land, damages are recoverable without proof of loss. If the claimant can show financial loss deriving from the loss of use of his or her land, damages are likely to be assessed on that basis. Otherwise they may be assessed on the basis of what would have been a fair rent for the land (*Swordheath Properties Ltd v Tabet* [1979] 1 WLR 285) or a fair sum for granting an easement (*Bracewell v Appleby* [1975] Ch 408). Where a nuisance has caused loss of enjoyment of land, damages are likely to be assessed on a loss of amenity basis. If the nuisance cannot be stopped by injunction, damages in lieu may well be quantified on a diminution in value basis.

6.2.8   Pure economic loss

Pure economic loss is by nature measurable, even if only with difficulty, and so can be quantified on a financial basis. Where there is an element of future loss, a degree of informed speculation may be required. Some of the possible approaches to this are dealt with in **Chapter 11**. It may also be necessary for a court to quantify a chance in order to award damages for lost opportunity.

6.3   Reduction of damages

6.3.1   Contributory negligence

6.3.1.1   Statutory basis

The power of the court to reduce damages to take account of the claimant's contributory negligence derives from the Law Reform (Contributory Negligence) Act 1945, s 1(1), which reads:

> *Where any person suffers damage as a result partly of his own fault and partly of the fault of any other person or persons, a claim in respect of that damage shall not be defeated by reason of the fault of the person suffering the damage, but damages recoverable in respect thereof shall be reduced to such extent*

as the court thinks just and equitable having regard to the claimant's share in the responsibility for the damage.

'Fault' is defined in s 4 as:

negligence, breach of statutory duty, or other act or omission which gives rise to a liability in tort or would, apart from this Act, give rise to the defence of contributory negligence.

Contributory negligence is therefore a partial defence, and accordingly a factor which reduces damages where the claim is made in tort. It appears to be applicable to all torts, except deceit (see **7.6**) and conversion (Torts (Interference with Goods) Act 1977, s 11). Contributory negligence is for the defendant to raise and prove. Once established, the court is obliged to apportion responsibility in some way.

6.3.1.2 Apportionment of responsibility

How apportionment is to be made is entirely within the court's discretion and depends on the facts of each case. The court will take into account not only negligence by the claimant which was a partial cause of the accident, but also negligence which was a partial cause of the injury, or which exacerbated the injury (such as failure to wear a seat belt). It is not just the extent to which the claimant caused his or her own injury that is relevant, but the extent to which he or she is blameworthy. Two claimants, both injured in the same accident and both guilty of the same omission, may not necessarily have to bear the same degree of responsibility for their own injury. The more culpable the defendant, the less responsibility on the claimant's part.

What is being measured is the extent to which the claimant is responsible for his or her own damage as opposed to anyone else. So if, for example, the claimant and two companions lawfully enter the defendant's premises, where the claimant is injured as a result of negligence attributable partly to the defendant, partly to his or her own companions and partly to himself or herself, it is nonsense to say contributory negligence cannot be more than 25% simply because three other people are involved. Contributory negligence may be 50% or more. In *Fitzgerald v Lane* [1989] AC 328 the judge found the claimant and two defendants in a road accident 'all three equally at fault', and assessed damages on the basis of one-third contributory negligence. The House of Lords held that the judge's finding of fact meant that contributory negligence was 50% as against each defendant.

6.3.1.3 The form of assessment

Contributory negligence is always assessed as a percentage or fraction and is a round number, eg, 20%, 25% (one-quarter), one-third, 40%, one-half, etc. The normal minimum is 10%—anything below that is likely to be ignored by the court.

6.3.2 Apportionment of liability

6.3.2.1 Apportionment between two defendants

Where a court has found two defendants to be liable to the claimant, or when the defendant has successfully claimed a contribution from a third party, a decision has to be made as to what proportion of the claimant's damages each should pay.

It must be remembered, however, that liability in tort is joint and several. So if the court holds two defendants equally liable, either of them is liable for 100% of the claimant's loss and will have to pay the full amount if the other cannot (see *Barker v Saint-Gobain Pipelines plc* [2005] 3 All ER 661). But if both defendants are able to pay, the court will apportion damages as it sees fit, considering the different degrees of fault, blameworthiness and causation. If there is more than one claimant, apportionment may be different in respect of each claimant (see, for example, *Wright v Lodge* [1993] 4 All ER 299).

6.3.2.2 Apportionment between two defendants and a claimant

Care needs to be taken in the apportionment of liability between defendants when there has also been a finding of contributory negligence by the claimant. The proportion of contributory negligence must be dealt with first, and only then is apportionment made between the defendants. That is why the net result in *Fitzgerald v Lane* [1989] AC 328 (see **6.3.1.2**) was that the claimant had to bear 50% of his or her loss himself or herself, and each defendant was liable for 25%.

If a court holds the claimant 10% to blame and apportions liability two-thirds to the first defendant and one-third to the second defendant, the first defendant will pay 60% of the claimant's loss (ie, two-thirds of 90%) and the second defendant will pay 30%.

If a court holds the claimant 20% to blame and the second defendant 25% to blame, the second defendant will pay 20% of the claimant's loss (ie, one-quarter of 80%). Similarly if a court orders a third party to make a 25% contribution.

Sometimes a court apportions liability between the parties in such a way as to produce a total of 100%. If, for example, the court holds the claimant 10% to blame, the defendant 50% and the third party 40%, the claimant will recover 90% of his or her loss from the defendant, who will then receive a contribution of four-ninths from the third party.

6.3.2.3 Apportionment between two causes

Where the claimant's injury is the result of more than one cause, and he claims against a defendant who can be shown to be liable for some, but not all of that injury, then the court must make an apportionment, attempting to assess what proportion of the claimant's injury the defendant can be said to be responsible for. This may be a difficult task, but it must be undertaken as best it can (*Holtby v Brigham & Cowan (Hull) Ltd* [2000] 3 All ER 421).

6.3.3 Mitigation

6.3.3.1 The positive requirement

The claimant has a duty to mitigate. This does not mean that he or she is required to minimise his or her loss at all costs, rather that he or she must take all reasonable steps to do so. If the claimant fails to do what he or she could reasonably have done to minimise his or her loss, damages will be assessed on the basis of what the loss would have been had he or she taken those reasonable steps. Any reasonable expense incurred in order to be able to mitigate may be recovered as damages. Indeed, if it was reasonable for the claimant to incur that expense in an attempt to mitigate, it will be recoverable even if, in fact, no mitigation is achieved.

6.3.3.2 The negative requirement

The claimant is also under a duty not to do anything unreasonable subsequent to the damage which might exacerbate it, and not to incur any unreasonable expense which increases the extent of his or her loss. If he or she does so, damages will be assessed on the basis of what the loss would have been had he or she not taken that action or incurred that expense. However, a claimant is not deemed to have the benefit of hindsight: the test is simply whether it was reasonable for the claimant to have behaved as he or she did at the time.

6.3.3.3   The test is subjective

When dealing with mitigation the courts apply the test of what is reasonable subjectively, ie, the question is whether it was reasonable for this claimant in all the circumstances to have behaved as he or she did, not whether a reasonable person would have behaved in that way. The courts are particularly lenient in cases of personal injury. There is a willingness, for example, to hold that it is reasonable for the parents of an injured child to give up their jobs in order to stay at home to care for their child, even though their financial loss would have been far less had they employed a nurse and a nanny.

6.3.3.4   The burden of proof

The burden of proof is on the defendant to show that the claimant has failed to take reasonable steps to mitigate, not on the claimant to show that he has done so. Any suggestion that the claimant should have to show his actions or decisions were reasonable is probably bad law (see *Geestplc v Lansiquot* [2003] 1 All ER 383).

6.3.4   Interest on damages

Interest can be awarded on damages recovered in tort under SCA 1981, s 35A. By s 35A(1), the award of interest is discretionary; but it becomes prima facie mandatory in cases of personal injury and death, unless there are special reasons why it should not be awarded (s 35A(2)). Because of this there are particular rules for claims for personal injury (see **11.16**) and fatal accidents (see **12.2.6** and **12.9**).

In other cases, both the rate of interest and the period for which it is awarded are within the court's discretion. However, the discretion to award interest is generally exercised in cases of financial loss; the rate will usually be based on current market rates—the usual maximum being the current Judgments Act 1838 rate. The period will usually be date of loss to date of trial.

6.4   Exemplary damages

Exemplary, or punitive, damages can be awarded in tort in the three situations laid down in *Rookes v Barnard* [1964] AC 1129, and confirmed in *Cassell & Co Ltd v Broome* [1972] AC 1027. These are:

(a) Where there has been oppressive or unconstitutional action by the servants of the government. These can include, for example, civil servants, politicians, local government officers, county councillors, and the police.

(b) Where the defendant's conduct has been calculated to make a profit which may well exceed the compensation payable to the claimant. This is not confined to strictly financial profit, but may include other benefits, eg, the eviction of a tenant.

(c) Where such damages are expressly authorised by statute. There do not appear to be any major examples of this.

Exemplary damages are recoverable for trespass, false imprisonment, malicious prosecution, assault, defamation, private nuisance, interference with business, intimidation, misfeasance in public office and possibly breach of copyright, but not for negligence, public nuisance, breach of statutory duty or deceit. The view that exemplary damages

8.2.2   Adequacy damages

8.2.2.1   Basic rule

The first and principal hurdle for a claimant to overcome is to show that *damages would not be an adequate remedy*. In most cases, damages are adequate and so specific performance will not be ordered. In order to show that they are not adequate, the claimant will usually have to demonstrate either the uniqueness of the thing contracted for, and/or the financial ineffectiveness of damages.

8.2.2.2   Uniqueness

Contracts, broadly speaking, are for the sale of property or the performance of services.

In contracts for the sale of property, the adequacy of damages may well depend on the uniqueness of the thing which the claimant contracted to buy. It may be unique either because there is no other thing in existence like it, or because, however ordinary the thing is, the claimant if awarded damages would be unable to obtain another thing like it from anywhere else.

Commodities and shares are usually considered not to be unique; they are readily available on the market. So, a contract for the sale of shares will not be specifically enforced (*Cuddee v Rutter* (1720) 1 P Wms 570) because damages would enable the claimant to buy other identical shares. But it would be different if substitute shares were not available (eg, where the breach deprived a claimant of a majority shareholding) (*Harvela Investments Ltd v Royal Trust Co of Canada (CI) Ltd* [1986] AC 207).

Land is, on the other hand, considered unique, however ordinary a simple house and garden may appear to be, and contracts for the sale of land are routinely enforced by specific performance. This tradition is so deeply rooted that the remedy may be regarded as virtually automatic, unless any of the other bars arises.

Goods and chattels fall somewhere in the middle of the uniqueness spectrum. Ordinary goods are not unique and specific performance will not be granted where substitutes can readily be obtained. But if the goods have some special or rare quality, an order may be granted: however, the courts are reluctant to recognise sentimental value as rendering goods unique. Ordinary goods may become unique if in all the circumstances no substitute can in fact be obtained: in *Sky Petroleum Ltd v VIP Petroleum Ltd* [1974] 1 WLR 576 an order was made requiring the defendants to deliver petrol to the claimants at a time of petrol shortage. Section 52 of the Sale of Goods Act 1979 gives the court a discretion to order specific performance of a contract for the sale of specific or ascertained goods, but does not seem in effect to have made such orders any more common than they would have been at common law.

Contracts for the performance of services are likely to be unique only where there is a personal service involved, in which case they are unlikely to be enforced for other reasons (see **8.2.3.4**). Where the services could be performed by anyone, damages are likely to be an adequate remedy.

8.2.2.3   Financial ineffectiveness

There are various ways in which damages may not provide effective compensation, but that fact does not necessarily mean that the court will deem damages to be an inadequate remedy.

The fact that damages would be difficult to assess does not necessarily mean that damages would be an inadequate remedy. Older cases accepted the idea that difficulty in assessment of damages should point towards specific performance being granted, but later cases have shown reluctance on the part of the courts to follow this line. In this respect courts are more lenient in granting injunctions than specific performance.

The defendant's inability to pay may be a relevant consideration.

Damages may not be adequate where the defendant's obligation is a continuing one, lasting beyond the date of judgment, such that an award of damages now will only compensate the claimant for his or her loss so far and a further action might be required in the future.

Where damages, if awarded, would be purely nominal, they may be considered to be an inadequate remedy, on the ground that specific performance would in such circumstances be the more appropriate remedy (eg, *Beswick v Beswick* [1968] AC 58).

Although a contract requiring the defendant to pay money will normally not be specifically enforceable, because damages would be an adequate remedy, *Beswick v Beswick* shows that it may be enforceable where payment is to be made to a third party or where the payment is in the form of an annuity or other periodical payment, which is a continuing obligation.

8.2.3   Other bars

8.2.3.1   Contracts requiring supervision

Traditionally, the court would not order specific performance where the enforcement of the order would require the court's constant supervision (eg, *Ryan v Mutual Tontine Association* [1893] 1 Ch 116). More recent authority suggests that this principle is exaggerated (eg, *Posner v Scott-Lewis* [1987] Ch 25).

Arguably, the difficulty of supervision is no longer a bar to specific performance, but rather a factor going to the court's discretion (*Tito v Waddell (No 2)* [1977] Ch 106). It may be that the need for supervision, even constant supervision, will not prevent specific performance being granted where it is important to protect the claimant's interest and where it is clear from the contract and/or order what the defendant is required to do.

8.2.3.2   Contract too vague

Specific performance will not be granted where the terms of the contract are so vague that it is impossible for the order to state exactly what the defendant is required to do, or for the defendant to know what should be done to comply with the order, or for the court to say whether the defendant has complied with the order or is in contempt.

8.2.3.3   Building contracts

The court will not normally make an order requiring a builder to erect or complete a building, on three grounds:

- Damages would be adequate if another builder could do the work.
- It is likely to be difficult to specify exactly what the builder must do.
- Constant supervision may be required.

However, in modern conditions, particularly where the contract is in a detailed form, specific performance may be granted if three conditions are satisfied:

- The work is precisely defined by the contract.
- Damages will not adequately compensate the claimant.
- The defendant is in possession of the land on which the building is to be done (*Wolverhampton Corporation v Emmons* [1901] 1 QB 515; *Carpenters Estates v Davies* [1940] Ch 160).

8.2.3.4   Contracts involving personal services

It is well established that the court will not order specific performance of a contract involving personal services, or service contracts which are personal in nature. The prime example is the contract of employment. With regard to the employee's services, the rule is now statutory and absolute (Trade Union and Labour Relations (Consolidation) Act 1992, s 236). In all other circumstances the rule remains discretionary, but is nevertheless well entrenched. The rule applies not only to contracts of personal service in the strict sense, but also to contracts involving the performance of services of a personal nature.

The greater the personal element involved in the contract, the less likely it is that specific performance will be ordered. However, the rule is not absolute and the courts are unwilling to make it so (eg, *C.H. Giles & Co Ltd v Morris* [1972] 1 WLR 307). Modern conditions of employment may make it possible for an employee to get an order against an employer (*Hill v C.A. Parsons & Co Ltd* [1972] Ch 305). Where the contract requires the performance of services which are not personal in nature, there is no bar, even if the services are to be performed by a particular individual.

8.2.3.5   Contracts to carry on a business

The court will not normally specifically enforce a contract in such a way as to require a person to carry on a business. This long-standing principle was recently affirmed by the House of Lords in *Co-operative Insurance Society Ltd v Argyll Stores (Holdings) Ltd* [1997] 3 All ER 297. This will be so even where damages may strictly not be an adequate remedy. The original reason was because such an order would require the constant supervision of the court, but it probably exists now as a principle in its own right, justified on the basis that it is against the public interest to require someone to carry on a busines at a loss if a plausible alternative exists.

8.2.3.6   Equity will not act in vain

Specific performance will not be granted where it would be in vain to do so, for example, where once the order was made the defendant could still lawfully terminate the contract at any time (*Sheffield Gas Consumers Co v Harrison* (1853) 17 Beav 294); or where the defendant would be incapable of fulfilling his or her obligations (*Castle v Wilkinson* (1870) LR 5 Ch App 534).

8.2.3.7   Coming to equity with clean hands

A claimant will not be granted specific performance of a contract unless he or she has performed all his or her obligations under the contract hitherto and remains ready and willing to perform any future obligations. This willingness must be pleaded and proved. A claimant who is himself or herself in breach of contract will not normally be granted specific performance of it, though this bar may not arise if the breach is trivial (*Dyster v Randall and Sons* [1926] Ch 932). How clean the claimant's hands are is a matter of the court's judgment and goes to its discretion.

8.2.3.8   Delay

There is no statutory limitation period barring claims for specific performance, but unreasonable delay will amount to a bar in equity. This is known as the doctrine of laches, and is again a matter of the court's discretion. How long a delay is unreasonable depends on the facts of the case, but in most circumstances not long is allowed. It was generally thought that one year was the upper limit for most cases, but this may be too strict. A delay of over two years was held not unreasonable in *Lazard Bros v Fairfield Properties* (1977) 121 SJ 893.

8.2.3.9 Want of mutuality

The doctrine of mutuality traditionally required an order for specific performance to be refused against a defendant where the defendant could not have enforced the contract by specific performance against the claimant. However, it is now clear that the doctrine can be waived by the court, which must judge mutuality at the time of judgment as opposed to the time of the contract (*Price v Strange* [1978] Ch 337).

8.2.3.10 Hardship

Specific performance will be refused where it would cause severe hardship to the defendant. This is simply part of the court's overriding discretion to refuse specific performance where it would be unjust to grant it. However, in a case of hardship, the hardship must be severe, not be brought about by the defendant's own acts, and lead to injustice. See, for example, *Patel v Ali* [1984] Ch 283.

8.2.3.11 Contract only partly specifically enforceable

Where the court cannot grant specific performance of the contract as a whole, it will not grant specific performance only of that part of the contract which is specifically enforceable (*Ryan v Mutual Tontine Association* [1893] 1 Ch 116). However, where a contract can be divided into one or more separate agreements, one part of the contract can be specifically enforced while the others are not.

8.2.4 Damages in lieu of specific performance

Damages originally obtainable in lieu of or in addition to specific performance under Lord Cairns' Act can now be obtained by virtue of SCA 1981, s 50. Such damages will be assessed on the same basis as damages at common law (*Johnson v Agnew* [1980] AC 367).

8.3 Rescission

8.3.1 What is rescission?

Rescission is an equitable remedy whereby a contract made between two parties is set aside, and they are restored to the position they would have been in had the contract never been made. The contract is in effect voidable: valid until it is rescinded, and thereafter treated as if it had never taken effect. Rescission is the equitable equivalent of damages in respect of the claimant's reliance loss.

8.3.2 When is rescission available?

There are three main situations in which rescission is available as a remedy:

- misrepresentation;
- undue influence; and
- duress.

Its availability as a remedy for misrepresentation is dealt with in **Chapter 7**. Rescission is the only effective remedy where a contract has been obtained by improper pressure amounting to undue influence.

For many years it was believed that rescission could sometimes, though rarely, be a remedy for mistake. However, in *Great Peace Shipping Ltd v Tsavliris Salvage (International) Ltd* [2002] 4 All ER 689 it was held that where a contract is valid and enforceable at common law, it cannot be rescinded in equity. Where a contract has been entered into as a result of a mutual mistake, it may in certain circumstances be unenforceable at common law, but then it is void—the remedy of rescission plays no part.

8.3.3   The act of rescission

Rescission is not just a judicial remedy: a party to a contract may rescind it for misrepresentation, mistake or undue influence by giving notice to the other party, and, if accepted by the other party, the contract will be at an end with no recourse to the courts necessary. However, a court order either for rescission or to declare the validity of the claimant's act of rescission may be necessary where there is a dispute between the parties, and an order for enforcement may also be required and involve application to the court.

8.3.4   Repudiation distinguished from rescission

Rescission is not to be confused with repudiation of a contract (which is a breach of contract) or with the claimant's right to accept a defendant's repudiatory breach as a discharge from the contract (which is sometimes referred to as 'rescission').

Where there has been a breach of contract, repudiatory or not, the claimant is entitled to seek damages to put him or her into the position he or she would have been in had the contract been performed. Where the claimant seeks rescission, he or she is asking to be put into the position he or she would have been in had the contract not been made: this may involve a claim for damages for consequential loss, but there can be no claim for damages in respect of the claimant's expectation loss.

8.3.5   Equitable bars to rescission

Rescission is a discretionary remedy and there are equitable bars that will prevent its being granted. There are four bars in particular.

8.3.5.1   *Restitutio in integrum* is not possible

Restitutio in integrum is the process by which the parties return and recover benefits gained under the contract. The contract will cease to be capable of rescission if the parties can no longer be restored to their original positions. The most likely reason for this is that the subject matter has changed so much that the party who gave it will not get back the same thing that he or she originally had (for example, goods have been destroyed or seriously damaged, or business assets have been disposed of). If the subject matter has merely diminished in value, this will not bar rescission, unless the loss is due to the acts of the buyer.

Nevertheless, equity does not require that restitution should be precise. There will be no bar, so long as it can be achieved substantially and fairly, so that a party gets back substantially the same thing he or she parted with and the change does not result in injustice. This will be so particularly if a financial adjustment can be made to take account of the alteration of the subject matter (*Erlanger v New Sombrero Phosphate Co* (1878) 3 App Cas 1218). The court will not apply the bar too strictly in cases of undue influence involving a breach of fiduciary relationship (*O'Sullivan v Management Agency and Music Ltd* [1985] QB 428). It has been held at first instance that the impossibility of *restitutio in integrum* is also a bar to rescission for duress at common law (*Halpern v Halpern* [2006] 3 All ER 1139); however the Court of Appeal in the same case ([2007] 3 All ER 478) reversed this decision so as to allow the point to remain open.

8.3.5.2 Third party acquiring rights

The right to rescind is lost if an innocent third party has acquired an interest under the contract for value before the claimant seeks to rescind. This is an application of the basic principle that equity will not defeat the bona fide purchaser for value without notice ('equity's darling'). There is, of course, no bar if the third party is a volunteer or the defendant's trustee in bankruptcy.

8.3.5.3 Affirmation

If the claimant, with knowledge of his or her right to rescind, nevertheless affirms the contract, his or her right to rescind is waived. He or she may affirm either expressly, by informing the defendant that he or she intends to proceed with the contract, or by conduct, for example, by continuing to take the benefit of it or by doing something which would suggest an intention not to rescind or seek rescission. However, the claimant can affirm only after he or she has discovered the truth. This means not only that the claimant must be aware of the facts of which he or she was previously unaware (for example, that the defendant's representation was false), but that he or she must also be aware of his or her legal rights and his or her option to rescind (*Peyman v Lanjani* [1985] Ch 457).

Failing to give notice of rescission within a reasonable time after discovering the truth may amount to affirmation. On the other hand, once notice has been given, continuing to perform the contract until trial, where there is no real alternative, does not constitute affirmation.

8.3.5.4 Delay

Delay between discovery of the truth and seeking to rescind may also evidence affirmation. An intention to rescind must always be communicated to the defendant. As a matter of practice a claimant should be advised to communicate this intention at the earliest moment. If the first notice of rescission is the service of proceedings, there is a good chance the claimant will be held to have affirmed.

Delay between the date of the contract and seeking rescission may, however, amount to a bar in itself, even where there is no question of affirmation. It will never do so in a case of fraud or breach of fiduciary duty, but it may do so in other cases (*Leaf v International Galleries* [1950] 2 KB 86).

8.3.5.5 Damages in lieu of rescission

Damages in lieu of rescission may be recovered for misrepresentation under the Misrepresentation Act 1967, s 2(2). See **Chapter 7.**

8.4 Rectification

8.4.1 What is rectification?

Rectification is a discretionary equitable remedy for mistake in contract. Where two parties have agreed the terms of a contract, but they are then incorrectly set down in or excluded from a document which purports to contain the full terms of the contract, the court may order the rectification of that document. It is the *writing* which is being put right, not the contract itself.

8.4.2 What is required?

The mistake must be the mistake of both parties. If the mistake is that of one party only, or one party was indifferent as to the detail that the claimant wants rectified, rectification will not be ordered. The exception is where the omission or error is due to the defendant's fraud. If terms are omitted from a document, it will be rectified to include them only if they were expressly agreed by the parties or are customary terms which could be implied in any event. A document which accurately records an oral agreement made by mistake cannot be rectified.

8.4.3 Standard of evidence required

Clear evidence is required before rectification will be ordered; there must be strong and convincing evidence that the document failed accurately to record the intention of the parties. It is most unlikely that rectification will be ordered solely on the claimant's oral evidence.

8.4.4 Bars to rectification

Rectification is barred by delay; where a third party has acquired rights for value; and where judgment has been obtained in an action in which rectification could have been sought, but was not.

8.5 Account of profits

It was established by the decision of the House of Lords in *Attorney-General v Blake* [2000] 4 All ER 385 that there is another equitable remedy available for breach of contract: an account of profits. In an exceptional case, the court is not limited to the remedies of damages, specific performance and injunction, but may order the defendant to account for all or some of the profits he or she has made through his or her breach of contract. The case is likely to be exceptional where the contractual obligation is very close to being a fiduciary obligation. The remedy will be granted where the court thinks it just in all the circumstances.

It remains to be seen whether the remedy will be granted in other cases. Although not limited in principle, it may be that the exceptional circumstances required will arise only in cases of the kind in *Blake,* which involved a convicted spy.

9 Injunctions

9.1 Introduction

An injunction is an equitable remedy by which the court makes an order to the defendant telling him or her to do or not to do a specific act. It is widely available in contract, tort and family law, subject to certain requirements established by case law.

9.2 Prohibitory and mandatory injunctions

An injunction may be prohibitory or mandatory. A prohibitory injunction restrains the defendant from doing something; a mandatory injunction requires the defendant to do something. Whether an injunction is mandatory or prohibitory is strictly speaking a matter of substance, not of the form of words used. So, an order restraining the defendant from not doing something is 'mandatory'; an order requiring the defendant to stop doing something is 'prohibitory'. The distinction may be significant, because a claimant is supposed to couch a mandatory order in positive terms; but a mandatory order is generally harder to obtain than a prohibitory order. In practice, therefore, the almost invariable tendency is to phrase injunctions prohibitively wherever possible, eg, an order restraining the defendant from allowing a state of affairs to continue.

In contract, a mandatory injunction to stop a breach is very rare, because in most cases it is to all intents and purposes an order of specific performance and will be sought as such. However, there is no such thing as interim specific performance, and in the pretrial stages of a claim an interim mandatory injunction may occasionally be sought.

9.3 Final and interim injunctions

A final injunction, sometimes known as a perpetual injunction (even if limited in time), is an order made at trial. However, most injunctions are sought as a matter of some urgency: the claimant cannot wait until trial. It may be that the defendant's alleged wrongdoing will cause the claimant irreparable continuing damage pending trial or the damage will have been done by the time the case comes on for trial. The claimant will then seek an interim injunction, which will last only for a temporary period, until trial at the latest. Such an injunction, in cases of extreme urgency, may be sought without notice to the defendant, but if sought without notice will usually only be granted with permission to the defendant to apply to set it aside, or for a short time.

The principles applicable to the grant of interim injunctions are basically procedural rather than equitable and are very different from the principles governing the grant of final injunctions.

9.4 Injunction for breach of contract

9.4.1 Support of contractual rights

An injunction can only be granted in support of a legal or equitable right. If the claimant has no such right which needs protecting, or has no *locus standi* to bring the action to protect the legal rights of others, no injunction can be granted. In contract, it is the claimant's contractual rights which are being supported. The claimant must therefore show a valid contract and a breach by the defendant.

9.4.2 Actual or threatened breach

Where the breach is actual, it will be relatively easy to prove. An injunction can readily be granted to restrain a continuing breach or to prevent the repetition of a breach. But sometimes the breach is merely threatened and lies in the future. In such circumstances a *quia timet* injunction may be granted to restrain the apprehended breach, but a high degree of proof is required. The claimant will have to prove a high probability of the breach occurring, and the likelihood of substantial damage resulting (*Attorney-General v Manchester Corporation* [1893] 2 Ch 87; *Fletcher v Bealey* (1885) 28 ChD 688).

Take care not to confuse an anticipatory breach (which is actual) and a threatened breach (which is not).

9.4.3 Prevention of breach of a negative stipulation

As explained in **9.2**, injunctions to restrain a breach of contract are almost always prohibitory unless interim. It follows that the need for an injunction arises where the defendant has done or threatens to do something he or she promised in the contract not to do: the injunction will be in support of a negative stipulation in the contract. Such a stipulation will normally be express, but an injunction can be granted to prevent a breach of an implied negative stipulation, provided that it does not amount to specific performance by the back door (see **9.6**). An injunction will not, however, be granted in support of an implied negative stipulation in a contract of employment or personal service (*Mortimer v Beckett* [1920] 1 Ch 571).

9.4.4 When is a final mandatory injunction appropriate?

The only circumstance in which a final mandatory injunction may be appropriate for breach of contract is where it is necessary to undo the effects of a breach by the defendant of a negative promise. For example, the claimant sells the defendant part of his or her land and the contract contains a covenant that the defendant will not erect a building on the land which is out of keeping with the houses in the neighbourhood. The defendant builds a Japanese pagoda and the claimant seeks a mandatory injunction requiring it to be pulled down.

9.4.5 The terms of the injunction

The terms of any injunction for breach of contract must be carefully drawn. The claimant's rights are defined by the contract and so the claimant cannot get an order any wider in scope than that which the contract entitles him or her to, unless the defendant's acts amount also to a tort or some other wrong.

9.5 The grant of an injunction

9.5.1 In general

Being an equitable remedy, an injunction will only be granted in the discretion of the court, and the usual equitable bars apply. However, the hurdles are not on the whole as difficult to overcome as they are for an order of specific performance. A prohibitory injunction to restrain a breach of an express negative stipulation will normally be granted, the important exception being where this would indirectly amount to specific performance of a contract which would not be specifically enforced in equity (see **9.6**).

9.5.2 Inadequacy of damages

The claimant must, of course, show that damages would not be an adequate remedy, but this is a much lower hurdle where he or she seeks to prevent the defendant doing something rather than where he or she requires him or her to do something: in the case of a prohibitory injunction to restrain a breach of contract, damages are not likely to be considered adequate (*Doherty v Allman* (1878) 3 App Cas 709). However, damages may be adequate where the likely harm would be trivial, and a much stiffer test will be applied where the claimant seeks a mandatory injunction (*Shepherd Homes Ltd v Sandham* [1971] Ch 340).

9.5.3 Other bars

Other bars will prevent the grant of an injunction in the same way as they prevent an order for specific performance:

(a) *Contract too vague.* An order will not be made if it does not allow the defendant to understand precisely what he or she may or may not do (see **8.2.3.2**).

(b) *Equity will not act in vain.* An injunction will not be made if it would have no effect (see **8.2.3.6**).

(c) *Clean hands.* An injunction will not normally be granted to prevent a breach of contract by the defendant if the claimant is also in breach; and the claimant must show himself or herself ready and willing to perform all his or her future obligations (see **8.2.3.7**).

(d) *Delay.* Delay may lead to an injunction being refused, but this is by no means as serious a bar as it is to specific performance. Where, however, the claimant's delay effectively amounts to acquiescence in the defendant's breach, an injunction may not be granted (eg, *Sayers v Collyer* (1884) 28 ChD 103) (see **8.2.3.8**).

(e) *Hardship.* See **8.2.3.10**.

9.6   Back-door specific performance

9.6.1   Ground for refusal of an injunction

An important additional ground for the refusal of an injunction arises where a prohibitory injunction, if granted, would in effect amount to an order for specific performance of the contract, but an order for specific performance would not be made. In other words, a claimant who is not entitled to specific performance cannot get it by the back door of an injunction. Where the injunction would have the same effect as an order for specific performance, the decision whether to grant it will be made on specific performance criteria, eg, *Sky Petroleum Ltd v VIP Petroleum Ltd* [1974] 1 WLR 576, *Hill v C.A. Parsons & Co Ltd* [1972] Ch 305.

9.6.2   Contracts of personal service and back-door specific performance

The issue arises most commonly in cases involving a contract of personal service, which cannot be specifically enforced and so cannot be indirectly enforced by an injunction restraining the defendant from withdrawing his or her services. However, where there is an express negative stipulation in the contract, typically a restraint of trade clause, this may be enforced by an injunction. So, although the claimant may not be able to compel the defendant to perform services for him or her, he or she may be able to prevent him or her performing services for someone else (*Lumley v Wagner* (1852) 1 De G M & G 604).

However, even an order restraining the defendant from working for someone else may still in effect amount to specific performance if the defendant would have no other means of earning a living. Accordingly, an injunction will not be granted in support of an express negative stipulation in a personal service contract if the end result will be that the defendant is still compelled to work for the claimant (*Rely-a Bell Burglar Alarm Co v Eisler* [1926] Ch 609) or is given the stark choice of working for the claimant or being unemployed (*Warner Bros Pictures Inc v Nelson* [1937] 1 KB 209). Some alternative means of earning a living must be open to the defendant before an injunction will be granted. The same principle applies where the contract is one of personal service by the claimant to the defendant (*Page One Records Ltd v Britton* [1968] 1 WLR 157).

If a claimant is prevented by this rule from obtaining an injunction against the person to whom he or she is contracted, he or she cannot get round it by instead seeking an injunction to restrain a third party from inducing a breach of the contract (*Warren v Mendy* [1989] 3 All ER 103).

An injunction will never be granted in support of an implied negative stipulation in a contract of personal service.

9.7   Injunctions in tort

9.7.1   Introduction

An injunction can only be granted in support of a legal right. Since a tort is a legal wrong the claimant has a right to prevent that legal wrong if it has caused, is causing or will cause damage to him or her or if he or she has *locus standi* to prevent damage to the public at large. Injunctions are particularly useful in tort to restrain trespass, nuisance, defamation, inducing breach of contract, and all the torts involving intellectual property. Except in cases of trespass and nuisance, interim injunctions are likely to be sufficient.

9.7.2 Prohibitory injunctions

9.7.2.1 The primary remedy

Although, strictly speaking, an injunction can only be granted where damages would not be an adequate remedy, when the claimant seeks to prevent a tort the granting of an injunction is more or less automatic. Injunction has become the primary remedy. Unless the claimant is barred, once his or her legal right is established an injunction will be granted, unless:

- the injury to the claimant's legal rights is small;
- the injury is assessable in money;
- small money payment would be adequate compensation; and
- it would be oppressive to the defendant to grant an injunction (*Shelfer v London Electric Lighting Co* [1895] 1 Ch 287; *Kennaway v Thompson* [1981] QB 88).

However, where these conditions are made out, damages are likely to be awarded in lieu (*Jaggard v Sawyer* [1995] 1 WLR 269).

9.7.2.2 Appropriateness of an injunction

An injunction has in effect become a right to which the claimant is entitled unless there are special circumstances (*Pride of Derby and Derbyshire Angling Association Ltd v British Celanese Ltd* [1953] Ch 149). This is because an injunction is so obviously appropriate and because damages will rarely be adequate. Damages can only compensate a claimant for past damage; they will never prevent future recurrence. And if damages are relatively small, a defendant might simply regard them as the price to be paid for the right to commit a tort.

9.7.2.3 Refusal of injunctions

The equitable bars to the granting of an injunction have the same meaning in tort as in contract. Injunctions may be refused where the conditions set out in **9.7.2.1** above are satisfied and/or the claimant is barred in equity by delay, acquiescence, or his or her own conduct. But in a serious case, injunctions are rarely refused. This is so, even if considerable hardship may be caused to the defendant (*Redland Bricks Ltd v Morris* [1970] AC 652), or if the interest of the public at large is overwhelmingly greater than the private interest of the claimant (*Attorney-General v Birmingham Borough Council* (1858) 4 K & J 528).

9.7.3 Mandatory injunctions

9.7.3.1 Nature

In tort, a mandatory injunction orders the defendant to undo the wrong. It will usually be sought in a case of trespass, to require the defendant to remove something from the claimant's land, or which causes a nuisance. The leading case is *Redland Bricks Ltd v Morris* [1970] AC 652.

9.7.3.2   Difficulty of obtaining a mandatory injunction

Mandatory injunctions are much harder to obtain than prohibitory injunctions. Their grant is certainly not automatic. Damages in lieu will usually be regarded as the primary remedy, and the adequacy of damages hurdle is not easy to cross.

A mandatory order will not be made where hardship may be caused to the defendant. The bars are similar to those to specific performance; or arguably stricter. A mandatory injunction may be refused not only where serious hardship would be caused to the defendant, but simply where the hardship suffered would on balance be greater than that suffered by the claimant if the order were refused.

9.7.4   *Quia timet* injunctions

Either prohibitory or mandatory *quia timet* injunctions may be granted to restrain a tort, usually nuisance. A high degree of proof is required: the claimant must show, on good evidence, that the tort is highly likely to occur and to occur imminently (*Attorney-General v Manchester Corporation* [1893] 2 Ch 87; *Fletcher v Bealey* (1885) 28 ChD 688).

9.8   Interim injunctions

9.8.1   Jurisdiction

Jurisdiction to grant interim injunctions in the High Court derives from the SCA 1981, s 37.

County court jurisdiction to grant interim injunctions derives from the CCA 1984, s 38(1), which allows the court to make any order which could be made by the High Court if the proceedings were in the High Court. See *Civil Litigation* manual, **Chapter 14.**

9.8.2   Principles

As stated earlier, the principles applicable to the granting of interim injunctions are largely procedural. A summary of the relevant principles is set out below. A more detailed explanation may be found in the *Civil Litigation* manual, **Chapter 14.**

9.8.2.1   The *American Cyanamid* guidelines

While the granting of an injunction lies within the discretion of the court, the guidelines applicable to such applications are found in the leading case of *American Cyanamid Co v Ethicon Ltd* [1975] AC 396. Generally the factors which the court will consider may be approached as a series of steps and the case for an injunction may fall at any point in the sequence:

(a) *Is there a serious question to be tried?* If the answer is yes (and it is often a fairly easy threshold to meet):

(b) *Would damages be an adequate remedy, ie, if the claimant succeeds at trial would he or she be adequately compensated by a (monetary) award?* If damages would be inadequate:

(c) *If the defendant succeeded at trial, ie, he or she demonstrated a right to do the act(s) which the claimant sought to enjoin, would he or she be adequately compensated by the claimant's undertaking as to damages?*

(d) *Where does the balance of convenience lie?* The factors which the court will take into consideration and the weight attached to each will vary with each case.

(e) Where factors appear to be evenly balanced the court will consider preserving the status quo. This means the state of affairs immediately before the issue of the writ, unless the claimant has delayed, in which case the status quo will be that existing immediately before the application. See *Garden Cottage Foods Ltd v Milk Marketing Board* [1984] AC 130, HL.

In some established areas the *American Cyanamid* approach is not strictly adhered to in determining whether to grant the injunction. Various factors may be of more or less importance depending on the nature of the dispute or third parties who may be affected by the granting of the injunction. Some of these areas are industrial disputes, defamation cases, actions against public authorities (where the public interest is an important factor in determining the balance of convenience), and covenants in restraint of trade.

9.8.2.2 Where granting an interim injunction would dispose of the action

It is important to distinguish between injunctions intended to be temporary in nature, ie, effective until later trial, and those which would, in effect, dispose of the dispute because there are no further issues between the parties which need to be determined at a later trial. If this is the case, the *American Cyanamid* guidelines on the balance of convenience are not applied. Rather it is appropriate for the court to consider the degree of likelihood that the claimant would have succeeded in establishing his or her right to an injunction at a trial on the merits. An injunction will only be granted if the claimant's case is overwhelming. See **Civil Litigation** manual, **Chapter 14**, and *Cayne v Global Natural Resources plc* [1984] 1 All ER 225, CA.

9.8.3 Procedure

Applications for interim injunctions are governed by CPR, Parts 23 and 25. An application must be made by application notice, supported by written evidence, usually in the form of a witness statement. This evidence should set out the facts on which the applicant relies. Under normal circumstances the application notice should be served not less than three clear days before the hearing. However, in urgent cases applications can be made without notice, even before the issue of a claim form. In these circumstances an injunction can be made without the respondent being heard. However, the order made will only last until a return date, when there will be a further hearing.

A more detailed explanation of the relevant procedure will be found in the **Civil Litigation** manual, **Chapter 14** and a more detailed explanation of the relevant documents will be found in the **Drafting** manual, **Chapter 19**.

Bailment and interference with goods

10.1 Definition

We can define bailment as being the delivery of goods on an express or implied condition that they shall be restored by the bailee to the bailor (or dealt with according to the bailor's directions) as soon as the purpose for which they are bailed has elapsed or has been performed.

Bailment is an area of law which combines elements of property law in addition to those of contract and tort.

10.2 When does bailment arise?

Bailment arises whenever one person (the bailee) is voluntarily in possession of goods belonging to another person (the bailor).

Although bailment is usually created by a contract, this does not necessarily have to be the case, as the legal relationship of bailor and bailee can arise independently of any contractual agreement.

The element common to all types of bailment is the imposition of an *obligation*. This arises when the bailee takes goods into his or her possession and thereby assumes responsibility for their safe keeping.

For bailment to arise, the actual or constructive possession of the goods must be relinquished by:

- the owner of the goods, or
- the bailor, or
- an agent who is duly authorised for the purpose,

to the bailee, who then either keeps the goods or performs some act with them.

Every bailee has a common law duty to take reasonable care of the bailor's goods and not to convert them to his or her own use (*Morris v C.W. Martin and Sons Ltd* [1966] 1 QB 716). The standard of care to be applied is the standard demanded by the circumstances of each particular bailment.

10.3 Classification

Bailment has in the past been categorised in many ways, with fine distinctions between them. However, for present purposes, there are two basic types: gratuitous bailment and bailment for reward.

10.3.1 Gratuitous bailment

Gratuitous bailment arises when a chattel is deposited with the bailee, who simply retains it until its return is demanded. Because the bailee does not receive any reward for his or her services, neither party acquires any rights or assumes any obligations until there is actual delivery and acceptance of the chattel. It is only then that the bailee becomes obliged to carry out his or her promise.

This category includes situations where property is lent to another for a specific purpose, without charge.

EXAMPLES

(a) Joe asks Fred, as an unpaid favour, to look after his hi-fi for him whilst he goes on holiday. Fred agrees. If Fred was to change his mind at any time prior to receiving the hi-fi, there is nothing that Joe can do about it. However, once Fred accepts delivery of the goods, he is bound to look after them, and to return them to Joe upon demand.

(b) Joe lends Fred his hi-fi to use at his birthday party. Fred is entitled to use it for that purpose only, and then is obliged to return it.

10.3.2 Bailment for reward

Bailment for reward covers situations where a chattel is pawned or pledged as security for a loan, or the performance of an obligation; or where goods are hired for reward.

EXAMPLES

(a) Anna borrows £100 from Tim, to be repaid in six months' time together with 10 per cent interest. She leaves her watch with Tim as security. Tim is the bailee of the watch.

(b) Sue hires a motor mower from Gardenhire Ltd, for seven days, at a cost of £20. She becomes a bailee of the mower.

10.3.3 Termination of bailment

Bailment will usually determine at the end of the period agreed between the parties. At the conclusion of the bailment, the bailor has the right to immediate possession of the goods. When this arises will depend on the circumstances of the individual case or on the terms of the contract if there is one.

10.4 Torts (Interference with Goods) Act 1977

Bailment, and the remedies available in respect of breach by bailor or bailee as well as the rights of third parties are now governed by the Torts (Interference with Goods) Act 1977, which basically protects the right to possession of and title to the goods.

Apart from a new tort of statutory conversion under s 2(2), the 1977 Act does not create any new torts and so previous case law regarding pre-existing torts is still relevant.

10.4.1   Causes of claim

Section 1 of the 1977 Act defines the torts for which a defendant may be liable if he or she wrongfully interferes with a claimant's chattels or goods. These are:

- conversion (s 1(a)),
- trespass (s 1(b)),
- negligence (so far as it results in damage to goods or to an interest in goods) (s 1(c)),
- any other tort as far as it results in damage to goods (s 1(d)).

These subdivisions are not mutually exclusive: conduct by a particular defendant may fall into one or more of the above categories.

Conversion is the most common tort and the main textbooks should be consulted for detailed guidance on this complex subject. However, some of the basic principles are set out below.

10.4.2   Conversion

10.4.2.1   Definition

Anyone who, without authority, takes possession of another person's goods, with the intention of asserting some right or dominion over them, is prima facie guilty of a conversion, provided that there is an intention on the part of the person so dealing with them to assert a right inconsistent with the rights of the owner. This can include (but is by no means limited to) wrongfully taking or parting with possession of goods, wrongfully retaining them, denying the title of the person entitled to possession, or, when acting as a bailee, so neglecting them that they are destroyed or totally lost. More particular examples are set out below.

The general rule is that the right to bring a claim for conversion belongs to the person who can prove that he or she had, at the time of the conversion, either actual possession or the immediate right to possess the goods.

The injury suffered by the claimant in such a case is twofold:

- an injury to the claimant's right to possession,
- an injury to the claimant's title in the goods.

10.4.2.2   An alternative definition

Conversion is a deliberate act of dealing by a defendant with a chattel in a manner inconsistent with the claimant's right which deprives the claimant of the use and possession of the chattel. One exception to the proposition that conversion is a deliberate act is contained in s 2(2) of the 1977 Act, namely, where a bailee is in breach of his or her duty to his or her bailor and thereby allows the goods to become lost or destroyed.

10.4.2.3   Conduct amounting to conversion

For liability to be established in conversion it is sufficient that the conduct of the defendant is inconsistent with the rights of the claimant. It follows that a whole range of acts can amount to conversion, from total abrogation of the claimant's rights in the goods to lesser conduct which may or may not amount to deprivation of the claimant's right in the goods depending upon the particular circumstances.

The following are the most common situations when conversion may arise:

(a) *Conversion by wrongful taking.* Peter wrongfully takes a watch belonging to Mary. Peter's intention must be either to deny Mary's rights or to assert a right which is inconsistent with her ownership. In the latter case the assertion of the right need not be that of full ownership: it is sufficient if assertion of the right is inconsistent with Mary's true entitlement.

(b) *Conversion by transfer.* This occurs when the defendant purports to give the claimant's goods to a third party along with some right over the goods which actually belongs to the claimant. To extend the above example, Peter gives Mary's watch to Antonia as a present.

(c) *Conversion by wrongful sale.* When property is wrongfully sold so that the property and the title to it are passed to a third party, irrespective of whether or not the goods are actually delivered to the buyer. Thus, if Peter sells Mary's watch to William, who buys it in good faith, Peter is guilty of conversion.

(d) *Conversion by taking.* There must be detention of the goods which is adverse to the rights of the true owner. A demand by the claimant and a refusal by the defendant must be shown. If Mary lends Peter her watch, but he thereafter refuses to return it when asked, Peter has committed an act of conversion.

(e) *Conversion by destruction.* Conversion will occur when the chattel is dealt with in such a manner that its original identity is destroyed. The destruction must be wilful. If Peter accidentally drops and treads on Mary's watch, no act of conversion is committed. If, however, he deliberately throws it into the river, the tort has been committed.

(f) *Conversion by loss.* Loss of someone else's chattel may amount to an abuse of possession (and therefore to conversion) if it is other than purely accidental.

(g) *Conversion by denial of right.* This can be considered to be a residual category embracing activities which do not fall into any of the above categories. This form of conversion occurs when a defendant deals with goods in a manner which amounts to denial of the true title. However, even absolute denial of title is not *per se* sufficient to amount to conversion because there must in addition be some further dealing with the goods; in other words some positive conduct on the part of the defendant, such as actively barring the claimant access to his or her goods whilst also repudiating the claimant's right to his or her goods.

The essential element in conversion is dealing with the goods in a manner which is altogether inconsistent with the title of the true owner. Therefore a defendant may be liable for conversion of goods notwithstanding the fact that he or she has never been in possession of them or physically handled them. However, the categories of conversion are not closed and in many cases it will be a matter of judicial discretion whether to treat the act as sufficiently inconsistent with the true owner's rights for a conversion to have taken place.

10.4.3 Subject matter of conversion

By s 14(1) of the 1977 Act:

> . . . *unless the context otherwise requires . . . 'goods' includes all chattels personal other than things in action and money.*

The definition does not purport to be exhaustive or all-embracing.

It is generally considered that the exclusion of money is limited to money in the sense of currency, so that valuable or antique coins can be converted (*Moss v Hancock* [1899] 2 QB 111).

10.4.4   Who may bring a claim for conversion and against whom?

10.4.4.1   Claimant

The right to bring a claim for conversion belongs to the person who is able to establish that at the time of conversion he or she either had:

- actual possession of the goods, or
- the immediate right to possess the goods.

It is doubtful whether an equitable right is sufficient to ground a claim in conversion (*The Future Express* [1993] 2 Lloyd's Rep 542).

10.4.4.2   Defendants

(a) *The immediate tortfeasor.* This should be self-explanatory.

(b) *Agents.* In order for an agent to be liable in conversion, it is necessary to consider the agent's actual or constructive knowledge of the true ownership of the goods. This is a detailed area of law beyond the scope of this chapter.

10.4.5   More than one claimant

The policy behind the 1977 Act is that a claimant should only recover his or her own actual loss and no more, and that multiplicity of actions should be avoided.

10.4.5.1   Double liability

Section 7(1) defines the scope of double liability which may arise where:

(a) two or more rights of claim for wrongful interference are founded on a possessory title (s 7(1)(a)), or

(b) the measure of damages in a claim for wrongful interference founded on a proprietary title is or includes the entire value of the goods, although the interest is one of two or more interests in the goods (s 7(1)(b)).

Section 7(2) provides that where there are two or more claimants in the same claim against one defendant the relief granted will be such as to avoid double liability of the defendant towards the claimants.

Section 7(3) provides that if there are two claimants but only one claimant is a party to the claim and that claimant receives more than he or she would have if s 7(2) applied then that claimant must account to any other person having a claim for that excess.

Section 7(4) protects a defendant who overpays in the event of double liability by permitting a defendant to recover overpayment from a claimant to the extent that that claimant has been unjustly enriched by the overpayment. Therefore if a bailor and bailee both have the right to sue for conversion they cannot both exercise such rights and thereby obtain double recovery from a defendant. Either bailor or bailee may sue and whoever is the first person to obtain damages will conclude the case (*Nicolls v Bastard* [1825–42] All ER Rep 429 at p 430). The successful claimant must then account to the other party for the proportion of damages representing his or her interest in the goods.

10.4.5.2   Competing rights to the goods

Section 8(1) of the Act permits a defendant to plead by way of a defence to the claimant's claim that a third party has title to the goods which is equal to, or superior to, that of the claimant.

10.4.5.3   Co-owners

If two or more people own a chattel then one co-owner cannot bring a claim against another co-owner for interference with his or her right to possession because each co-owner has a right to possession which is lawful. However, if one co-owner goes further and performs an act which could only be permitted if he or she alone had exclusive possession of the goods then a claim by the other co-owner or co-owners will be permitted. Such a claim is only allowed if there has been 'a destruction of the particular chattel or something equivalent to it' (s 10(1)).

Section 10(1) of the 1977 Act affirms the well-established proposition that one co-owner cannot maintain an action against another co-owner.

10.4.6   Forms of remedy

10.4.6.1   Nature of the remedy

The appropriate remedy is often prescribed by the state of the goods. If the goods have been destroyed or disposed of then the claimant's remedy will be confined to judgment for a sum of money. However, if the goods are still in the possession or control of the defendant then the remedies available to an aggrieved claimant are somewhat wider.

10.4.6.2   Available remedies

Where the goods are in the possession or control of the defendant, s 3(1) of the 1977 Act provides the following remedies:

(a) An order for specific delivery of the goods and payment of any consequential damages (s 3(2)(a)).

(b) An order for delivery of the goods but also giving the defendant the option of paying damages by reference to the value of the goods in addition to payment of any consequential damages (s 3(2)(b)).

(c) Damages, including the assessed value of the goods in addition to any consequential loss (s 3(2)(c)).

A remedy may only be given under one of these heads (s 3(3)(a)) and furthermore a remedy under s 3(2)(a) is at the discretion of the court whereas a remedy under s 3(2)(b) or s 3(2)(c) is at the election of the claimant (by virtue of s 3(3)(b)).

(d) On application by any person the court has a discretionary power to make an order for delivery up of the goods which either are or may become the subject matter of subsequent proceedings (for example, see *Howard E. Perry & Co Ltd v British Railways Board* [1980] 1 WLR 1375 and s 4 of the 1977 Act). Such an application may be made under the court's power to grant interim remedies under CPR, r 25.1(1).

We will examine each of the above remedies in turn.

10.4.6.3   Specific delivery

Section 3(2)(a) of the 1977 Act. This order is made at the discretion of the court and thus will not usually be made in respect of ordinary articles which have no special value either intrinsically or for the claimant, because in such cases damages would provide adequate compensation.

If the court makes an order for specific delivery, a duty is imposed on the defendant to ensure that the goods are ready for collection by the claimant. The order may contain conditions regarding delivery of the goods. The order may be enforced by writ of specific delivery to recover the goods or their assessed value.

If it can be shown to the court that an order for specific delivery has not been complied with then the court may proceed to revoke that order or any relevant part of the order and instead order payment of damages which will be assessed on the value of the goods.

10.4.6.4   Judgment for delivery or damages

Section 3(2)(b) of the 1977 Act. Here the claimant has an election between delivery or damages together in either case with payment of any consequential damages.

Damages will be assessed by reference to the value of the goods.

The provisions allowing the court to impose conditions on specific delivery under s 3(2)(a) apply equally under s 3(2)(b). Such order may be enforced as under s 3(2)(a).

10.4.6.5   Damages

A claimant may recover all such damages as are the direct and natural result of the conversion.

The 1977 Act is silent as to the time when damages should be assessed apart from a reference in s 6(1) regarding improvements to the goods. We must therefore rely on previously established rules.

A claimant who seeks damages for conversion based upon the value of the goods will be limited to the value of the goods at the time of conversion. If the value of the converted goods decreases after conversion, the claimant is still entitled to their original value and consequently receives a windfall (*Solloway v McLaughlin* [1938] AC 247).

A subsequent rise in the value of goods since the time of conversion is recoverable as consequential damages provided the increase in value was foreseeable at the time of conversion (*The Playa Larga* [1983] 2 Lloyd's Rep 171, CA).

10.4.6.6   Basis of assessment

If there is a market price for the goods, the value of the goods is to be taken as the market price at the time of conversion. However, if there is no market price, the basis for assessing damages will be the cost of replacement as determined by the evidence.

If the value of the goods is fluctuating, the measure of damages may depend upon the claimant's awareness of the conversion.

10.4.6.7   Taxation

When considering damages for conversion, the principles in *British Transport Commission v Gourley* [1956] AC 185 are thought to be applicable. Therefore, any tax liability which would have accrued to the claimant had the claimant's goods not been converted should be taken into account in the quantification of damages.

10.4.6.8   Aggravated and exemplary damages

Aggravated damages may be awarded if the court considers they are justified by the circumstances of the conversion (*Owen and Smith v Reo Motors (Britain) Ltd* (1934) 151 LT 274).

The availability of exemplary damages was severely curtailed by the judgment of Lord Devlin in *Rookes v Barnard* [1964] AC 1129. Essentially such damages will only be awarded in cases where the court considers that the tortfeasor should be taught a lesson and are generally reserved for exceptional cases of misconduct.

10.4.6.9   Special damage

Where a defendant is aware that the chattel converted by him or her is required by the claimant for a particular purpose (for example, to be hired out for profit), the defendant may be liable to pay special damage for failure of that purpose by reason of his or her conversion. See, for example, *Bodley v Reynolds* (1846) 8 QB 779, in which a workman deprived of his tools recovered loss of wages.

10.4.6.10   Effect

If a defendant satisfies a judgment for damages for conversion of goods, the claimant's title is transferred to the defendant (*Ellis v John Stenning & Son* [1932] 2 Ch 81).

10.4.7   Improvement of goods

Section 6(1) of the 1977 Act restates the common law rules and provides that a person who improved goods, honestly believing that he or she had good title to them, is to be entitled to the value of the goods attributable to the improvement. This is known as the principle of allowance and is based upon the fact that the true owner should not be compensated for more than the value of the goods which he or she originally lost. Generally, any expenditure of work or materials which enhances saleability will constitute an improvement.

Section 6(2) extends the availability of the allowance from the original wrongdoer who effects the improvement to a bona flde purchaser who has obtained his or her supposed title from the improver who is in this case the defendant.

Section 6(4) applies the principle of allowance to any person who acquires a limited interest in goods by way of bailment or otherwise.

10.4.8   Limitation

The Limitation Act 1980 provides that once the period of limitation, namely six years from the date of first conversion, has expired, the right to bring proceedings expires. This is an absolute bar, which is different from the basic limitation rule, which does not expressly bar the *right* to sue, but merely affords a complete defence to anyone taking the limitation point.

10.4.9   Defences

Liability in conversion is strict (*Marfani & Co Ltd v Midland Bank Ltd* [1968] 1 WLR 956 at p 971). However, if a defendant can invoke any of the exceptions to the *nemo dat quod non habet* rule, he or she may escape liability for conversion.

10.4.10   Trespass

10.4.10.1   Definition

Trespass may be defined as an intentional or negligent direct interference with goods in the possession of the claimant. It is concerned with *direct and immediate* interference with the claimant's possession of a chattel.

The tort of trespass includes not only the taking away, or removal out of the claimant's possession, of his or her goods but also any unpermitted contact with or impact upon another's chattel. Mere touching is sufficient as long as it causes damage.

10.4.10.2 Elements

Whilst a claim in conversion can be founded by a claimant who has the right to possession, though not actual possession, by contrast, a claim in trespass can only be brought by the claimant if he or she is actually in possession at the time of the interference. There are exceptions to this rule as regards executors and administrators and trustees, but these are beyond the scope of this chapter.

10.4.10.3 Nature of the interference

The interference must be of a direct nature and in addition there must be a blameworthy state of mind in the trespasser. Accidental interference of a non-negligent nature will not constitute a trespass.

10.4.10.4 Remedies

Damages and/or an injunction are available if the defendant is no longer in possession or control of the goods. If the defendant is in possession or control of the goods, the same remedies are available as for conversion.

Where the goods are damaged by trespass but the claimant is not actually deprived of them, the claimant will only be entitled to damages which represent the loss actually suffered as a direct result of the trespass.

10.4.11 Negligence resulting in damage to goods

This covers negligent damage to goods and the usual remedies for negligence apply, namely damages and/or an injunction, irrespective of whether the defendant has the goods in his or her possession or control. Orders for specific delivery or delivery and damages are not available.

10.4.12 Other torts

Section 1(d) of the 1977 Act applies the Act to any other tort so far as it results in damage to goods or to an interest in goods. This would cover, for example, non-natural user under the rule in *Rylands v Fletcher,* slander of title to goods and passing off. The scope of s 1(d) is not precisely defined, although it is considered to embrace negligent damage, loss or destruction of goods not covered by s 1(c).

10.4.13 Contributory negligence

Section 11(1) precludes contributory negligence as a defence in proceedings for wrongful interference which are founded on conversion or intentional trespass. However, there is internal inconsistency in the 1977 Act because such a defence is permitted for negligence and other torts, in other words, for proceedings brought under s 1(c) or (d) of the Act.

10.4.14 Reversionary injury

A person who is entitled to goods, but has neither immediate possession nor the right to possession, is unable to sue a wrongdoer for conversion or for trespass. However, a claim will lie if the wrong committed deprives the person, either temporarily or permanently, of the benefit of his or her reversionary interest. The act must affect the person's reversionary interest in the goods.

The remedy for reversionary injury is confined to damages and the claimant cannot obtain an interim order for delivery up of the goods. Apart from these distinctions the procedural provisions relating to conversion contained in the 1977 Act apply.

10.5 Exercises

10.5.1 Exercise 1

PROBLEM

Ben is a supplier of fresh fruit and owner of two fruit stores from which Pamela often buys fruit. Ben hires a motor car to Pamela for six weeks whilst he goes on holiday. He normally uses the car for fresh fruit deliveries to his two shops on a daily basis. Pamela collects the motor car and signs a contract whereby she will hire the car from Ben for six weeks at £120 per week. After four weeks Pamela can no longer afford the rent and decides to sell the car at an auction. James buys the car at the auction.

(a) Discuss liability and remedies.
(b) What difference would it make if Pamela had not signed a contract to hire the motor car but instead just borrowed it from Ben's premises with his permission?

SOLUTION

By hiring the motor car to Pamela a situation of bailment is created whereby Ben is the bailor and Pamela is the bailee. Because a contract of hire is signed between Pamela and Ben, the conditions of bailment are contained in a contract. If Pamela had not signed a contract, a situation of bailment between Pamela and Ben would still exist because Ben has entrusted goods (his car) to Pamela upon condition that she return them in the original state after six weeks. However, bailment would only exist when Pamela took delivery of the car from Ben.

By selling the motor car at an auction, Pamela has committed the tort of conversion because she has only hired the car from Ben. The ownership of the car vests in Ben.

By selling the car, Pamela is asserting a right which she does not have, namely that of ownership of the car, and secondly she is also asserting a right which is inconsistent with the right of the true owner, namely Ben's right to possession of the car.

The remedies for conversion are contained in s 3 of the 1977 Act. An order for specific delivery under s 3(2)(a) of the 1977 Act is only granted at the discretion of the court and will generally only be granted where the court considers that damages are inadequate as a remedy. However, Ben may seek an order under s 3(2)(b) of the 1977 Act for delivery of the goods and also giving the defendant the option of returning the goods any time before execution of the judgment. Because Pamela has sold the car at an auction to James, recovery of the car may be difficult if not impossible from James, who bought the car in the belief that the car once sold was his. The most appropriate remedy for Ben would be damages, which would be assessed by reference to the value of the goods lost. Furthermore because Ben uses the car for his occupation as a fruit supplier, he will be able to claim special damages from Pamela for loss of business. However, for such damages to be recoverable, Pamela must have been aware that the car was used by Ben for this purpose. Because she shops regularly at Ben's shop this requirement would be met.

Furthermore, Ben would have a claim for damages for breach of contract, namely the two weeks' rent that Pamela has failed to pay.

10.5.2   Exercise 2

PROBLEM

Frank and his wife Mary jointly own a computer, which they lend to Tracey for six weeks. Tracey does not return the computer to Frank and Mary because she threw it against a wall in a fit of rage when she lost some work stored on the hard disk. The entire computer is smashed and has been assessed by a computer specialist as being beyond economical repair.

(a) What remedies are available to Frank and Mary and which is the most appropriate in this case?

(b) What steps should they take to obtain such remedy?

(c) If Frank alone recovers the value of the computer what steps can Mary take to recover her share of the value of the computer?

Quantum of damages
for personal injury

11.1 The barrister's involvement

When representing a client in a claim for damages for personal injury a barrister will be closely involved, not only with the issues of liability, but also with the process of quantifying damages. If the issue of quantum goes to trial, you will present evidence on and argue the question of 'how much' before the court. If a settlement is reached you are likely to be involved in, or even to conduct, the negotiation. Even at the earliest stages of your involvement in the case you are likely to be asked to advise on quantum, ie, to state how much in your opinion a judge would be likely to award. A preliminary view on quantum needs to be taken before the claimant can decide whether to bring his or her claim in the High Court or County Court. By virtue of CPR, PD 7, para 3.6, if a claim for personal injury is started in the High Court, the claim form must state that the claimant expects to recover £50,000 or more

It follows that you must understand the principles on which damages are quantified, the process by which a court would arrive at a final figure, and the practical steps to be taken in advising on quantum.

11.2 The law

11.2.1 Basis of the law

The law in this area is largely judge-made, with occasional legislative assistance or interference. It has grown up in a piece-meal fashion over the last 80 years or so and has no overall coherence, logic or rationale. It is not very scientific, and its overall effect tends to be to undercompensate those who have suffered serious injuries. In *Lim Poh Choo v Camden and Islington Area Health Authority* [1980] AC 174 Lord Scarman said:

> Lord Denning MR in the Court of Appeal declared that a radical reappraisal of the law is needed. I agree . . . I would suggest to your Lordships that such a reappraisal calls for social, financial, economic and administrative decisions which only the legislature can take. The complexities of the present case . . . emphasise the need for reform of the law.

Few lawyers would disagree with this. Several statutory reforms have been made since 1980, but none of them constitutes the radical overhaul suggested. However, some recent legislation, and the decision of the House of Lords in *Wells v Wells* [1998] 3 All ER 481 have made some very significant steps towards a more scientific calculation of damages, which should lead to claimants being more properly compensated in future. For a fuller explanation see **11.10.3** and **11.18**.

11.2.2   The rationale of the law

There is no force of law behind most of the rules for the quantification of damages. In theory, at least, a court may assess damages in any way it sees fit in order to do justice to the parties. However, there are two very important constraints:

(a) The method of assessment is limited by the powers of the court. In particular, except where there is a claim for provisional damages (for which see **11.5**), the court can only ever make one order, at the date of trial, which cannot later be varied in the light of subsequent developments. So the court cannot adopt a wait-and-see approach to future uncertainties. It must assess damages in a way that will so far as possible do justice today for the claimant tomorrow. This will almost always be by the payment of a single lump sum. The only exceptions are that the court can now make an order for periodical payments under s 2 of the Damages Act 1996 (see **11.18**), and that it can approve a structured settlement agreed by the parties themselves (see **11.19**).

(b) There is a vital principle behind the assessment of damages, which is that parties must be able to predict as closely as possible the damages that a court would award. If they cannot do so, there is little chance of their agreeing on a sum in settlement of a claim, and every case would have to go to trial. Such a result would be most undesirable. So, if parties are to be able to predict the likely damages, courts must be consistent in their approach. That is why the rules for assessment that follow are universally applied by the courts, however unsatisfactory they may seem to individual judges or in particular cases.

11.2.3   Sources

The practitioner's 'bible' is Kemp & Kemp, *The Quantum of Damages*. Also useful is *Butterworths Personal Injury Litigation Service;* also essential is regular reference to *Current Law*. Valuable on-line services are Lawtel–PI Quantum Reports and Personal Injury Interactive; and Butterworths PI Online.

11.3   Basic principles

11.3.1   Application of the compensatory principle

The aim of an award of damages is to compensate the claimant for the loss caused to him or her by his or her injuries and to place him or her, so far as it is possible to do so, in the position he or she would have been in had those injuries not been suffered. The claimant must be compensated, therefore, not only for the injuries themselves, but also for the effect they have had on him or her emotionally, intellectually and financially. This cannot be done, of course, simply by the payment of money; but money is all the law has to give, and so some arbitrary yet fair relationship has to be found between the injury and the compensation.

Not all loss can be measured in money, but it still has to be assessed in financial terms.

11.3.2   Measurement of loss

Such loss as *can* be measured in money, is so measured. Loss that can only partially be measured in money is assessed arithmetically to a certain extent. Wholly non-financial loss is assessed according to conventional guidelines.

11.3.3   Time of assessment

Although the cause of action accrues at the date of the injury, and all damage that flows from the injury is deemed to have been suffered at that time, nevertheless to all intents and purposes damages are assessed as at the date of the trial.

In the case of financial loss already incurred, the court will take the total amount so far; and in the case of future financial loss, the court will give any item recoverable the value it bears at the date of trial. The court will also take account of all facts about the extent of the claimant's injury or its effect on him or her that are known at the date of trial, and of any supervening events, such as the claimant's death or redundancy, or the onset of some disease, even if these facts or supervening events were unpredictable at the time of the injury (see *Jobling v Associated Dairies Ltd* [1982] AC 794).

11.4   Two broad heads of damages

Damages are either special or general. In any ordinary case there will be a claim for both special and general damages.

11.4.1   Special damages

11.4.1.1   Nature and proof of special damage

Special damages represent the claimant's actual pecuniary loss between the date of injury and the date of trial; in other words, those losses that are strictly measurable in money and susceptible to precise calculation.

Every item of special damage must be specifically pleaded and specifically proved. This does not mean that every item can be given a value which is certain; rather, that every item can be given a value which is ascertainable, either by proof, by agreement between the parties, or by decision of the court. A schedule of loss and expenses, setting out the special damages claimed, must be served with particulars of claim for damages for personal injury (CPR, PD 16, para 4.2).

11.4.1.2   Examples of items of special damage

There is in principle no limit to the range of items that can be recovered as special damages, provided they are within the rules of causation, remoteness and the duty to mitigate, but the following list shows those items most commonly recovered:

(a) Incidental damage to property, eg, damage to a motor vehicle, damage to clothing, a broken wrist watch.

(b) Medical expenses. All reasonable medical expenses may be recovered. A claimant is not obliged to mitigate his or her loss by having treatment under the National Health Service (Law Reform (Personal Injuries) Act 1948, s 2(4)).

(c) Associated expenditure, eg, cost of travel to and from hospital, prescription charges.

(d) Cost of nursing care, whether in a residential institution or at home. The type of care (in a residential home or in a private arrangement), the cost of which should be awarded, depends on what is reasonable in all the circumstances, not necessarily what is in the claimant's best interests (*Sowden v Lodge* [2005] 1 All ER 581).

(e) Cost of other paid help, eg, housekeeper, nanny, baby sitter, gardener, etc.

(f) Reasonable necessary expenditure: eg, special equipment (crutches, wheel-chair); purchase of special car, or conversion of car to hand controls; purchase of new house, special accommodation; cost of converting present or new home for claimant's special needs (eg, building extension, enlarging bathroom, putting in a lift, ramps instead of steps, lowering work surfaces in kitchen).

(g) Increases in ordinary expenditure: eg, additional transport costs, heating costs, holiday costs, cost of employing someone to do work the claimant previously did on a D-I-Y basis.

(h) Loss of earnings from date of injury to date of trial. This is usually the major item of special damages.

(i) Loss of other fringe benefits from the claimant's employment, eg, free goods, services, use of company car for private purposes, private health scheme, etc.

(j) Loss of social security benefits. A claimant who was unemployed at the date of the accident and in receipt of social security benefits can recover the benefits he or she would have received but for the accident (*Neal v Bingle* [1998] 2 All ER 58).

(k) Other miscellaneous losses, eg, cancellation of a holiday.

(l) Costs incurred by members of the claimant's family visiting him or her in hospital, looking after him or her, etc, including their lost earnings. These are recoverable as part of the claimant's own loss (*Kirkham v Boughey* [1958] 2 QB 338).

(m) The value of unpaid care provided by a friend or relative. Surprising as it may seem at first sight, a reasonable sum can be recovered by the claimant for the notional cost of employing someone to care for him or her, even where that care is being provided gratuitously, irrespective of any legal liability to pay (*Cunningham v Harrison* [1973] QB 942; *Donnelly v Joyce* [1974] QB 454). This is so whether or not the relative has given up paid employment to look after the claimant; and even where the relative has given up paid employment and the claim is valued on that basis, the loss is still viewed as the claimant's, not the relative's, loss. However, the loss is not recoverable where it is the defendant himself or herself who is providing the voluntary care (*Hunt v Severs* [1994] AC 350). In order for damages to be recovered under this head, the amount of care required must go beyond the normal call of everyday life, but it is not necessary to show that but for the gratuitous care professional care would have been required (*Giambrone v JMC Holidays Ltd* [2004] 2 All ER 891).

(n) The above principle does not however apply to a relative who does gratuitous work for the claimant in his or her business. No damages are recoverable for the value of such work (*Hardwick v Hudson* [1999] 3 All ER 426).

(o) A claimant may also recover damages for the value of care which he used to provide gratuitously to a member of his family, but which as a result of his injury he is no longer able to provide (*Lowe v Guise* [2002] 3 All ER 454).

(p) Court of Protection fees; costs of administering a trust fund. Where the claimant is unable to look after his or her own affairs, a receiver will need to be appointed and remunerated; where the claimant is a minor a trust fund may be required. Such administrative costs are recoverable.

11.4.1.3   The schedule of loss and expense

CPR, PD 16, para 4.2, requires the claimant to 'attach to his particulars of claim a schedule of details of any past and future expenses and losses which he claims'. Note that what is required is a full setting out of the sums claimed, not only by way of past, but also of future loss and expense. Do not be confused into thinking that future losses and expenses are special damages.

11.4.2   General damages

11.4.2.1   Nature and proof of general damages

General damages represent the loss to the claimant that cannot be precisely quantified, that is, past and future non-financial loss and future financial loss.

General damages do not have to be specifically pleaded, though any material facts giving rise to a claim for general damages should be pleaded (eg, the injuries, loss of employment, handicap on the labour market). Nor do general damages need to be specifically proved: they can be implied to a certain extent. However, evidence is required, and in practice as much evidence as is available should be presented. A medical report must be served with the claimant's particulars of claim (CPR, PD 16, para 4.3).

11.4.2.2   Heads of general damages

Heads of general damages are as follows:

- Pain and suffering.
- Loss of amenity.
- Hybrid heads.
- Future loss of earnings.
- Loss of earning capacity.
- Loss of pension rights.
- Future expenses (including value of future unpaid help).

A further head of general damages, loss of expectation of life, was abolished by the Administration of Justice Act 1982 (AJA 1982), s 1.

Heads of damages may occasionally overlap, and where this happens care must be taken to avoid double recovery. There are various rules that have been developed by the courts to deal with overlap situations, which are explained below, where they arise.

11.5   Provisional damages

11.5.1   When may a claimant claim provisional damages?

A claimant may in certain circumstances claim provisional damages rather than damages. Section 32A of SCA 1981 (inserted by AJA 1982, s 6) provides:

> *(1) This section applies to a claim for damages for personal injuries in which there is proved or admitted to be a chance that at some definite or indefinite time in the future the injured person will, as a result*

of the act or omission which gave rise to the cause of action, develop some serious disease or suffer some serious deterioration in his physical or mental condition.

(2) Subject to subsection (4) below, as regards any action for damages to which this section applies in which a judgment is given in the High Court, provision may be made by rules of court for enabling the court, in such circumstances as may be prescribed, to award the injured person—

(a)   damages assessed on the assumption that the injured person will not develop the disease or suffer the deterioration in his condition; and

(b)   further damages at a future date if he develops the disease or suffers the deterioration.

(3) Any rules made by virtue of this section may include such incidental, supplementary and consequential provisions as the rule-making authority may consider necessary or expedient.

The same provisions appear as s 51 of the County Courts Act 1984, for actions in the County Court.

The relevant rules mentioned in s 32A(3) are to be found in CPR, Part 41.

The circumstances in which a court will make an award of provisional damages were considered in *Willson v Ministry of Defence* [1991] 1 All ER 638. The judge held that:

(a) the chance of serious disease or deterioration must be measurable rather than fanciful;

(b) the 'serious deterioration' must be something distinct and beyond the ordinary deterioration that is a normal part of the claimant's condition;

(c) the risk of further injury in the future will not give rise to a provisional award where that risk of injury and its likely consequences are purely speculative.

11.5.2   Effect of a claim for provisional damages

A claim for provisional damages will result in an initial award which will be lower than an award of damages on a once-and-for-all basis, but with the possibility of a further award in the future which, when taken together with the initial award, will produce a total sum greater than an award of damages on a once-and-for-all basis would have been. The reasons for this will be explained when we see how damages are quantified.

A claim for provisional damages affects only the general damages, not the special damages. A claimant may claim provisional damages or damages in the alternative. If a claimant claims damages, it is not open to a defendant to argue that the claimant should be awarded provisional damages.

11.5.3   Provisional damages are not interim payments

Be sure not to confuse provisional damages with interim payments in respect of damages under CPR, Part 25. See the *Civil Litigation* manual, **Chapter 13**.

11.6   Quantification of damages—introduction

The quantification of damages is a five-stage process:

Stage 1:   Quantify special damages.
Stage 2:   Quantify general damages.
Stage 3:   Make any necessary deductions.
Stage 4:   Contributory negligence.
Stage 5:   Add interest.

11.7 Stage 1: quantify special damages

11.7.1 A matter of arithmetic

Since special damages represent the claimant's quantifiable financial loss, this is basically just a matter of arithmetic. The claimant has to prove both the item of loss and its value. The court will therefore award such losses as are proved. If the claimant fails to prove that an item of expenditure is reasonable, the court will either not award it, or will award such sum as would have been reasonable.

11.7.2 Advising on quantum

If you are advising on quantum, look at the special damages that have been incurred, decide whether in your opinion they are reasonable, exclude what you think the claimant cannot prove or what is unreasonable, and take the result. Where the claimant is claiming the value of voluntary services, a reasonable figure for this must be claimed and proved.

   Do not look into the future with special damages. Although the cut-off point for a court is the date of trial, when negotiating a settlement or advising on quantum, take the cut-off date as today, calculate special damages so far, and treat the continuing expenditure in the future as general damages. Do not invent a notional date of trial.

11.7.3 Assessing special damages

The assessment of most items of special damage is straightforward once the figures are known: medical expenses, damage to property, costs of nursing care, paid help, items of expenditure, items of increased expenditure, value of fringe benefits, miscellaneous losses, costs incurred by, and lost earnings of, claimant's relatives, Court of Protection fees—all these can simply be added up taking the exact figures that have been ascertained.

   Some items of special damages are a little more complicated to assess, however, and the method for such items is as follows.

11.7.4 Assessing lost earnings

11.7.4.1 Basis of assessment

Except where the claimant is very seriously injured and the cost of caring for him or her is expensive, the major item of special damages is likely to be lost earnings. These are assessed not just on the basis of what the claimant was earning at the date of the accident, but on the basis of what he or she would have earned between accident and trial. So if, for example, the claimant is able to show that, but for his or her injuries, he or she would have had a chance of an increase in earnings, or promotion, or moving on to better paid employment, or advancing his or her career, or building up his or her business, etc, then damages will be awarded taking account of these increased earnings. The claim is for the loss of a chance. This means that the claimant does not have to show that he or she probably would have had an increase in earnings, only that he or she has lost the chance of such an increase; but damages will be assessed in accordance with the chance, so if the chance was 75%, the claimant will recover 75% of what the increase would have been.

Similarly, any likely decreases in income must be taken into account (eg, because of retirement, redundancy, ailing business).

11.7.4.2   Methods of calculation

Where the claimant was a regular wage earner, the lost earnings can be calculated by reference to someone else doing the same job. If he or she received regular amounts of commission, bonuses, overtime, then again his or her loss can be assessed in this way. Where, however, his or her earnings fluctuated, then an average will be taken over an appropriate period. The norm is to average the last six pay-packets, though a longer period may need to be taken (if, for example, he or she had overtime in summer but not in winter).

11.7.4.3   Taxation to be taken into account

The claimant's lost earnings are always calculated net, not gross. That is to say, you base the calculations on what the claimant earned or would have earned after deductions of tax and national insurance. This is the rule in *Gourley's* case (*British Transport Commission v Gourley* [1956] AC 185).

Since the claimant will not be liable to tax on the award of damages (Income Tax (Earnings and Pensions) Act 2003, s 406), tax must be taken off the amount received in compensation for lost earnings, otherwise the claimant will be better off than he or she would have been but for his or her injury. Both basic rate and higher rate tax is taken into account. Where the claimant's claim is for a partial, rather than total, loss of earnings, the earnings lost are deemed to be the top slice of his or her income.

11.7.4.4   The *Gourley* principle and pension contributions

The *Gourley* principle also applies to an employee's compulsory contributions to a pension scheme, and earnings are taken net of such contributions, if no pension rights have been lost (*Dews v National Coal Board* [1987] 2 All ER 545). If the non-payment of pension contributions has led to a diminished pension, then usually the claimant will claim damages for lost pension rights (see below **11.12**) and so must deduct his or her pension contributions to avoid double recovery.

11.7.4.5   Expenses incurred in connection with employment

On the same principle, it is necessary to set against the claimant's lost earnings any expenses he or she would have incurred in order to be able to earn that income but which have been saved, eg, the cost of travel to and from work, special clothing, etc. Obviously no such deduction needs to be made if the claimant still incurs these expenses in order to earn a lesser income.

11.7.5   The cost of a new home

There is no difficulty where the claimant is simply paying more in rent for his or her new accommodation: the measure is simply the increase in rent.

But where the claimant purchases new accommodation, the process is not as simple as might have been thought. The claimant cannot be awarded the capital cost of the new house less the sale value of his or her old house, because there will be a windfall effect for his or her family, dependants and heirs. What he or she has actually lost is the use of his or her capital tied up in the new house, and so he or she should be awarded the interest he or she could have gained by investing that sum (*Roberts v Johnstone* [1989] QB 878). It was decided in *Wells v Wells* [1998] 3 All ER 481 that this should be taken as 3% per year; but since a discount rate has been set under the Damages Act 1996 (see **11.10.3.4 to 11.10.3.9** below), it should now be taken as 2.5% per year. So calculate the loss by taking the difference in capital value (cost of new house less sale price of old) and award the claimant 2.5% of this sum per year. No deduction needs to be made for the 'Rolls-Royce' effect—the fact that the claimant may incidentally be enjoying better amenities (larger garden, closer to shops), or improved quality of life ('better' area, quieter neighbourhood) than he or she otherwise would, providing the new house was a reasonable purchase.

Costs involved in the purchase, eg, estate agent's fees, conveyancing costs and removal costs and any increased outgoings on the new house are also recoverable.

11.7.6   The cost of converting a home

The claimant may not only have had to purchase new accommodation, but may also have had to convert it, or his or her existing home, for his or her special needs. Such a cost is therefore recoverable additionally to the cost of any new home. However, an adjustment must be made to take account of any change in the value of the house brought about by the conversion work (*Roberts v Johnstone*).

Not all the money spent on conversion will have had an effect on house value. Ignore any expenditure which has not, and consider only the expenditure which has had an effect. Suppose the claimant has spent £30,000 on conversion, £20,000 of which has had no effect on the value of the house, and £10,000 of which has had the effect of increasing its value. He or she will recover £20,000 in any event. If the value of the house has increased by £10,000 or more, he or she cannot recover the £10,000 conversion cost. If the value has increased by less than £10,000, deduct the increase in value from the £10,000 and award the difference.

If the conversion work has decreased the value of the house, then the loss in value can be recovered as well as the conversion cost.

11.7.7   Loss of use of company car

The value of this item will depend on the extent to which the claimant was permitted to and did use the car for private purposes, and what sort of car it was. Figures provided by motoring organisations can be found in *Butterworths Personal Injury Litigation Service*, section XIV[86]–[90]. Expect a sum in the area of £2,000–£7,000 per year, even substantially more if the claimant did a high mileage in a large car. Take care to establish whether the claimant or the company paid for petrol for private use. Be careful to avoid any overlap with a claim for increased travel costs.

11.7.8   Value of unpaid care

The method of assessing this item is discretionary, and will depend to some extent on who the relative providing the care is and what he or she has given up in order to be able to do so. One common approach is to award the cost of employing a professional or professionals to provide the services being valued. If the claimant's spouse nurses him or her round the clock, then the value will be the cost of 24-hour nursing attendance, less an allowance for the amount of care he or she would have provided in any event as a spouse. Alternatively damages may be assessed on the basis of the relative's lost earnings, if he or she has given up work to look after the claimant. If the relative has reasonably given up work to care for the claimant, the lost earnings are likely to be recoverable in full, even if the care is strictly less valuable. There may even be an added value if the relative is providing services over and above those that giving up work has enabled him or her to provide.

The courts frown upon artificial 'contracts' between the claimant and the carer, and will not take the amount in the contract as reliable evidence of the value of the services.

Although this item of damages is not precisely quantifiable in financial terms and is a matter of assessment, nevertheless it is strictly part of the special damages.

11.7.9   Agreement on quantum

The quantum of special damages will usually be agreed between the parties, subject to liability. Certainly, the court will expect special damages to be agreed and, if they are not, will want to know why not. Even if there is a dispute as to an item of special damages, the quantum can still be agreed on an either/or basis. See *Practice Direction (Damages: Personal Injury Actions)* [1984] 1 WLR 1127.

11.8   Stage 2: quantify general damages

11.8.1   Introduction

Each head of damages is quantified in an entirely different way, so we must look at them separately. However, the first two heads can be taken together.

11.9   Heads 1 and 2: pain and suffering and loss of amenity

11.9.1   A single award

These are usually quantified together; that is to say, a single award will be made for pain and suffering and loss of amenity as a composite, without any indication from the court as to how much is awarded under each head.

This award will simply be a round sum, apparently plucked out of the air. Pain and suffering and loss of amenity are by their nature wholly non-financial losses, and the compensation cannot possibly be calculated, it can only be evaluated on some basis. The basis chosen for evaluation is basically convention, coupled with comparison with previous awards, experience, and sheer intuition. The process is not as arbitrary as it may sound, however. Before we look at it, we should distinguish pain and suffering and loss of amenity, which are closely connected, and sometimes overlap, yet which are not quite the same thing.

11.9.1.1   Damages for pain and suffering

Damages for pain and suffering compensate the claimant for the physical pain and the emotional and intellectual suffering caused by the injury. Shock is included, as are anxiety, embarrassment and emotional injury. It is strictly speaking not the injury itself for which the claimant is being compensated, so a claimant who suffers multiple injuries, and is thereby rendered immediately and permanently unconscious, recovers nothing under this head, because although he or she has been injured, he or she feels no pain and is not experiencing any mental suffering as a result of his or her injuries. Nevertheless, it is the injury itself which will form the starting point for evaluating pain and suffering, so the exact nature and extent of the injury is important. The more serious the injury, the longer it lasts, the greater the award. A claimant who makes a complete recovery gets less than one who is permanently handicapped or disfigured.

Emotional distress, eg, fear, horror, anguish and grief, which is not connected to physical or psychiatric injury, does not by itself give rise to a claim under this head.

It is necessary to look at the particular claimant and his or her individual circumstances. A claimant who is distressed by a scar on his or her face suffers more than one who is not. The claimant's age and life expectancy are relevant. The shorter his or her expected life, the shorter the period of pain and suffering and the less he or she will recover in damages, even where it is the injuries themselves that have reduced his or her life expectancy. However, the claimant's suffering may be increased by knowledge that his or her life expectancy has been reduced, and this must be taken into account (AJA 1982, s 1(1)(b)).

11.9.1.2   Damages for loss of amenity

Damages for loss of amenity compensate the claimant for his or her lost or reduced enjoyment of life. Loss of amenity can be general—for example, where the injuries have affected the claimant's general sense of well-being or cheerful disposition; or specific—for example, where the claimant is no longer able to enjoy a game of football or play the piano. Other examples of loss of amenity include loss of brain function, loss of any of the five senses, loss of sex-life, loss of mobility, loss of ability to do one's job, loss of job satisfaction, loss of ability to form friendships or relationships, loss of marriage prospects, breakdown of marriage, and loss of enjoyment of a holiday. In this case it is the loss of amenity itself for which the claimant is being compensated, not the suffering caused by awareness of it, so a claimant who is in a coma or so severely brain-damaged as to have realisation of his or her plight can recover damages under this head (*Wise v Kaye* [1962] 1 QB 638; *Lim Poh Choo v Camden and Islington Area Health Authority* [1980] AC 174).

Loss of amenity, even more than pain and suffering, is highly subjective and specific to the claimant. As with pain and suffering, the claimant's age and life expectancy will make a difference, and the shorter the life expectancy the *shorter* the loss of amenity. But it does not follow that the shorter the life expectancy the less the loss of amenity. An injury may diminish the quality of life of an older claimant far more than it does that of a younger claimant. You must look to see precisely how each claimant has been affected by his or her injuries. For example, loss of hearing may be more serious for a musician than a painter; a permanent limp may be more serious for an athlete than a bank manager; a broken nose may be more serious for a model than a builder.

11.9.1.3   The difficulty of separating the two heads of damage

In the end pain and suffering and loss of amenity have to be taken together because it is usually impossible to say where one ends and the other begins. If, for example, a claimant has an injured leg and can walk only half a mile before it starts to hurt, there is pain, there is suffering, and there is loss of amenity, but one cannot say they are three separate items of loss. The pain causes loss of mobility; inability to enjoy a walk produces suffering. It is necessary for the court to award a single lump sum.

11.9.2   Arriving at a figure for pain and suffering and loss of amenity

11.9.2.1   The first stage

The starting point for the court in selecting that figure is the evidence presented to it—medical evidence and the evidence of the claimant. A barrister's starting point in advising on quantum will be the medical reports and information contained within the claimant's statement. The first stage is to ascertain as accurately as possible the nature and extent of the injuries, the degree of pain and suffering and the loss of amenity. Where the evidence is contradictory, the court will have to decide what evidence to accept; in advising all you can do is bear that conflict in mind.

11.9.2.2 The second stage

The next stage is to look up the awards that have been made in past cases of a similar nature. These are found in *Kemp & Kemp,* volumes 3 and 4, in *Butterworths PILS* and in *Current Law,* categorised according to the broad nature of the injury; also on Lawtel and Butterworths LexisNexis, where you need to search for keywords. There is a conventional tariff or a guideline range for each type of injury. The tariffs used by judges are published by the Judicial Studies Board and can be found in *Kemp & Kemp* and *Guidelines for the Assessment of General Damages in Personal Injury Cases,* 8th edn, Oxford: OUP, 2006. They are also available online at Lawtel. You should certainly make use of these, but they are not sufficient by themselves. First try to ascertain the correct range for the type of injury you are dealing with, then try to ascertain whereabouts in the range your case falls, by comparing the facts of your case with those reported and making such value judgments as seem right, taking particular account of your claimant's individual circumstances, suffering and losses of amenity. It is not a precise art, but it is possible to get quite close. This is what a judge will do, and it is what you do in negotiating a settlement or advising on quantum.

11.9.2.3 Example

Compare the awards made to the claimants in the following two cases. Do you think they were about right? What factors do you think explain the difference? The relevant *JSB Guidelines* (5th edn) were: moderate whiplash injuries where the period of recovery has been fairly protracted and where there remains an increased vulnerability to further trauma—£3,750 to £7,000; minor soft tissue and whiplash injuries and the like where symptoms are moderate and a full recovery takes place within at most two years—up to £3,750.

Case A—November 2000—Damages £6,750

Female, aged 38 at the time of the accident and 42 at trial, sustained injury when her car was struck from behind with some force by the defendant's vehicle. She was taken to hospital where a whiplash type injury was diagnosed. She was given a collar and painkillers and was off work for six weeks. She saw her GP on a couple of occasions and was referred for physiotherapy. Although her symptoms improved over time, they never disappeared. At the date of trial she continued to experience intermittent pain at the base of her neck radiating into her left shoulder. Although she had been able to resume aerobics after a short break she now avoided exercises requiring her to raise her left arm above the horizontal. Heavier housework or a change in weather would also bring on symptoms in her shoulder. The opinion of the joint expert was that she had sustained a classic whiplash with partial tearing of the ligaments of the neck. The expert anticipated further gradual recovery until about five years after the accident. Thereafter she would be left with intermittent symptoms which, although permanent, would be no more than a minor nuisance.

Case B—November 2000—Damages £3,000

Male, aged 32 at the date of the road traffic accident and 33 at trial, sustained injury in a head-on collision. He struck his head on the car door pillar suffering a mild head injury and sustained a whiplash type injury to his neck and back. He visited his GP who referred him for four sessions of physiotherapy. He also took painkillers and was off work for three weeks. Thereafter he had headaches at work when concentrating on his computer screen. He was unable to go swimming for several months due to neck and back pain and had not returned at all to playing football. At the date of trial, his back problems had resolved. However, he was still experiencing a dull ache in his neck associated with certain activities and headaches, albeit with decreasing frequency. Medical opinion was that there would be a full resolution of symptoms within 12 months of the accident.

11.9.2.4   *Heil v Rankin*

The process of comparing awards in previous cases must be performed in the light of the decision of the Court of Appeal in *Heil v Rankin* [2000] 3 All ER 138. In that case (and seven others considered at the same time) the Court took account of a recent Law Commission Report to the effect that awards for pain, suffering and loss of amenity were too low, and decided that an increase was required in all awards that would previously have been over £10,000. Awards under £10,000 did not need increasing. The increase should be on a sliding scale, with the highest (those over £150,000) increasing by a third. By way of indication, the Court increased an award of £40,000 by 10%, an award of £45,000 by 11%, an award of £80,000 by 19%, an award of £110,000 by 25% and an award of £135,000 by 30%. This has become known as the *Heil v Rankin* uplift.

The 8th edition of the JSB Guidelines (June 2006) takes this adjustment into account, and so no uplift needs to be made when using the Guidelines as a starting point for assessing damages. Nor will there be any need to add an uplift when using a case decided after 23 March 2000 as a comparison. But when looking at a case before that date, in which damages were more than £10,000, it will be necessary to add a *Heil v Rankin* uplift to see what would have been awarded today.

This may be done approximately, using the Court of Appeal's examples as a guide; or it may be done rather more precisely, using this formula, explained in *Quantum,* 18 April 2000:

If £A is the value of an award in March 2000, immediately prior to Heil v Rankin, then the award after the uplift will be £A + [(£A—10,000)/420,000 × £A]. The part in square brackets is the uplift.

But this will only be one part of a calculation which also has to take account of inflation: see below.

11.9.2.5   Inflation

It is particularly important to look at recent awards and take account of the effect of inflation on the value of money. The tariffs for each type of injury, and the actual sums awarded, gradually increase more or less in line with inflation. The need to take accurate account of inflation was recognised by the Court of Appeal in *Housecroft v Burnett* [1986] 1 All ER 332. Before that decision, awards had been lagging behind inflation for some years.

The most accurate assessment can be made when one can find a comparable very recent award. *Current Law* and Lawtel are particularly helpful here, but *Kemp & Kemp* and *Butterworths PILS* are also updated regularly. In the absence of a recent comparable award, one needs to look at earlier awards and multiply them by the appropriate inflation factor. A table of such multipliers can be found in *Kemp & Kemp,* volume 2, chapter 36–001, 36–002. Alternatively, Lawtel has a very useful inflation calculator. Be very cautious, however, of adopting this approach to awards prior to *Housecroft v Burnett*, since an inaccurate result may be obtained. Generally speaking, awards more than ten years old are of little practical help.

Additional account will need to be taken of the *Heil v Rankin* uplift where the value of the award was over £10,000 in March 2000. This can lead to some fairly complex calculations, and so not surprisingly wherever possible reliance should be placed on the *JSB Guidelines* and recent cases. But not all types of injury are covered by the Guidelines, and there is not always a comparable recent award, so such calculations will sometimes be necessary. As the years pass, and more and more recent awards are reported, it will be possible in due course to forget about the uplift. Some sample calculations follow.

11.9.2.6   Sample calculation—inflation only

Suppose you want to find out what the value of an award of £7,500 made in June 1998 is in March 2008. The size of the award is such that no *Heil v Rankin* uplift will be involved. So the adjustment needs to be made for inflation only. There are three ways of doing the calculation, two manual and one automatic.

The shorter, less accurate, manual method is to use the table in *Kemp & Kemp*, 36–001. At the time of writing, this was up to date only to January 2007. You will see that if you apply a multiplier of 1.26 to an award made in January 1998, you will get the value in January 2007. You can be a bit more accurate if you look also at the multiplier for January 1999, which is 1.23, and make a rough and ready guess that for June 1997 the multiplier might be about half way between the two, so 1.245. You can also notice that in recent years the multiplier has increased by about 0.035 a year, so you can estimate that this should be added on to give you the value of the award up to January 2008, which is close enough to March 2008. Then £7,500 × 1.28 gives you £9,600. This calculation will usually do for advisory purposes where only an approximate sum is required.

A fuller, more accurate calculation can be made using the monthly Retail Prices Index tables in *Kemp & Kemp* 36-002. First look up the RPI for June 1998, which is given as 163.4. Then look up the RPI for March 2007. You may find that the table in *Kemp & Kemp* does not go that far (it is usually several months behind), so go online to <http://www.statistics.gov.uk/instantfigures.asp>, where you will find that the RPI for February 2008 (the most recent figure) was 211.4. You then do the calculation £7,500 × 211.4 ÷ 163.4, which gives you £9,703.18, which you would round off to £9,700.

The quickest and easiest method, however, is to use *Lawtel's* inflation calculator. Simply put in the amount of the award you wish to update and the month and year of the award, and with one click you get the answer. It also tells you what the relevant RPI figures used were. You will not be able to check the calculation above, because it can only update to the present day, which by the time you read this will no longer be January 2007, but rest assured that when tested it matched the £9,703.18 figure given above.

11.9.2.7   Sample calculation—inflation and *Heil v Rankin* uplift

Suppose you want to find out what the value of an award of £60,000 made in June 1998 is in March 2008. You will need to do the calculation in three stages.

First you must update the award for inflation to March 2000. Using the RPI tables and the method explained above (RPI in March 2000 was 168.4), the sum will be £60,000 × 168.4 ÷163.4 = £61,836. Alternatively, slightly less accurately, there is a table in *Kemp & Kemp* at 36–190, which gives multipliers to update awards from any month to March 2000. The multiplier for June 1998 is 1.031. This gives you the result £61,860, which is near enough.

Next you must give this sum the *Heil v Rankin* uplift. Using the formula set out in **11.9.2.4**, the sum is £61,836 + [(£61,836—10,000) ÷ 420,000 × £61,836]. This produces an uplift of £7,632 and so an adjusted sum of £69,468. Alternatively, again you can use a table in *Kemp & Kemp* at 36–191, which tells you that £62,000 plus the uplift is £69,676. Subtract the odd £140 and you have £69,536, which is again close enough to £69,468.

Finally, you must update this sum for inflation between March 2000 and March 2008. Using the RPI table again, the sum is £69,468 × 211.4 ÷168.4 = £87,206, which you would round to £87,200. This then is your answer.

But once again, the quickest and simplest method is to use Lawtel's inflation calculator, which automatically includes a *Heil v Rankin* uplift in its calculations. The answer for March 2008 was £87,206. It is very accurate!

11.9.2.8   Criminal Injuries Compensation Board awards

Awards made by the Criminal Injuries Compensation Board were in the past assessed in the same way as awards made by courts. However, from 8 November 1995, the Criminal Injuries Compensation Act 1995 introduced a new scheme of compensation, based not on common law damages but on fixed tariffs laid down by the Home Secretary. Such awards are not likely to be reliable or helpful and should not be used.

11.9.2.9   The final figure

In the end the figure arrived at is chosen by judgment based upon careful research and informed experience. When advising on quantum, a barrister will frequently, having formed a preliminary view, test it out on other members of chambers before setting down his or her final conclusion. That opinion may be expressed as a range—'in the range £25,000–£30,000—or as an approximate figure—'about £12,000'. It is probably better to give an approximate figure if you can, especially if an attempt at settlement is to be made. If you give a range, indicate what circumstances will put the award at the bottom and the top end of the range.

11.9.3   The problem of future uncertainty as regards pain and suffering and loss of amenity

A particular problem arises in quantifying damages for pain, suffering and loss of amenity where the prognosis is uncertain. This will in fact almost always be the case to some extent, except where the claimant has wholly recovered from his or her injury. It is to the claimant's advantage usually to try and delay trial or settlement until the future is as certain as it is going to be, but this may not be possible. For example, it may not be certain whether the claimant's condition will deteriorate; whether he or she has recovered as far as he or she is going to or whether he or she will continue to improve; whether osteoarthritis will set in in ten years' time; whether an apparent obstacle has been overcome permanently or temporarily; whether a female claimant will be able to give birth to children or not. In such circumstances the court has to assess the chance and value it. Broadly speaking, if there is a 10% chance of an unfavourable development, the court will award 10% of any increase in damages that that development would attract.

Alternatively, where the uncertainty is as to whether the claimant's condition will seriously deteriorate, or whether some serious disease will set in (but *not* in the case of any other uncertainty) the claimant has the option of claiming provisional damages under SCA 1981, s 32A and CCA 1984, s 51. This will result in a lower award now, but with the certainty of a further award in the future if the serious deterioration or disease occurs.

This has to be balanced against the advantages of a once-and-for-all settlement which evaluates the chance, produces a greater sum now and brings the litigation to an end. It is a tactical decision.

11.9.4   Hybrid heads

11.9.4.1   Overlap between loss of amenity and financial loss

There are certain miscellaneous heads of damages which are sometimes seen as losses of amenity and sometimes as financial losses. Occasionally there is an element of both loss of amenity and financial loss, and care must be taken to avoid overlap. Some common examples of hybrid heads follow. This list is not exhaustive.

11.9.4.2   Loss of congenial employment

Awards are increasingly often being made under this head. Such damages compensate the claimant for his or her loss of job satisfaction. If the claimant was previously employed or earning his or her living in a way which brought him or her particular pleasure, enjoyment, pride or responsibility, and as a result of his or her injury is now employed in a more boring or mundane job, even if there is no loss of earnings, there is a recoverable loss under this head. It ought strictly to be part of the claimant's loss of amenity, but has come to be treated as a separate head of damages for which a lump sum of up to about £5,000 might be awarded. If there is also a claim for loss of earnings, care must be taken not to take account of loss of job satisfaction twice. A table in *Kemp & Kemp* (para 36–180) shows some sample awards.

11.9.4.3   Loss of housekeeping ability

This head was established by *Daly v General Steam Navigation Co Ltd* [1981] 1 WLR 120. It is strictly a claim for financial loss. If a claimant has suffered an impairment of his or her ability to do housework, to the extent that this has diminished his or her happiness, it can be taken account of as part of the general loss of amenity. But otherwise it is essentially a claim for the cost of a housekeeper and is valued on that basis, both for special damages and general damages (see **11.13.3**).

11.9.4.4   Loss of marriage prospects

Under this head there is truly an element of both loss of amenity and financial loss. It arises where a young claimant's injury has diminished or destroyed his or her chances of marriage. To the extent that this affects his or her happiness, it is a loss of amenity. But there is also a financial loss. Only female claimants have in the past succeeded in claiming this financial loss, which is the financial support a husband would probably have provided. However, such a loss could in theory be established by a man who was engaged to a wealthy woman at the time of the accident. How a female claimant is compensated under this head is dealt with in **11.10.5.2**.

11.9.4.5   Breakdown of marriage

Sometimes a claimant's injuries can lead to his marriage breaking down. This is something to be taken account of in the award for loss of amenity, but there may also be a financial loss. Provided it is not too remote, an award can be made under this head, for example, for the loss of a spouse's services. The breakdown of the marriage may also result in significant extra expenditure, particularly if there is a divorce. Unfortunately there are conflicting authorities on whether such loss is recoverable: *Jones v Jones* [1985] QB 704; *Pritchard v J.H. Cobden Ltd* [1988] Fam 22.

11.10 Head 3: future loss of earnings

This head of damages arises where there is at the date of trial or settlement an annual loss of earnings which is measurable at today's values, and evidence that it will continue into the future. If at the date of trial there is no measurable annual loss, but nevertheless evidence that some loss is likely to accrue in the future, then an award under the next head, loss of earning capacity (see **11.11**) may be more appropriate.

11.10.1 The multiplier and the multiplicand

Damages are calculated on a multiplier/multiplicand basis. This means that two separate figures must be arrived at in turn and then multiplied together to produce the result. The multiplicand represents the aspect of the claimant's loss that is reasonably certain and measurable in financial terms, ie, his or her current annual loss. The multiplier represents that aspect of the loss that is uncertain and not precisely ascertainable, ie, how long into the future such a loss will continue.

11.10.2 Calculating the multiplicand

This is basically the claimant's net annual loss of earnings as at the date of trial, or as at the date on which you are advising on quantum. In calculating special damages, account has already been taken of any likely pay increases, promotion, career moves, business developments etc, and these factors obviously also affect what the claimant would have been earning today. The *Gourley* principle again applies and all calculations should be done using net sums. The calculation is simply, what the claimant would have been earning net annually, minus what he or she is now earning net annually (if anything), minus annual expenses saved. What you are left with is the multiplicand.

This calculation of the multiplicand is straightforward where the claimant's loss of earnings is likely to continue at more or less the same level until the age at which he or she would have retired. But what if there is evidence that the claimant was likely to have been promoted, or that his or her earnings would have increased for some other reason, for example a new job, or the expansion of his or her business; or alternatively evidence that he or she would have been likely to lose his or her job or suffer a decrease in earnings at some point in the future? The traditional approach to these problems was to make no adjustment to the multiplicand, but rather to make an adjustment to the multiplier to take account of any future uncertainties. But as we shall see in **11.10.3** when we look at multipliers, the approach these days is likely to be more scientific, and there may well be a reluctance to make speculative adjustments to the multiplier. If so, then the court has two alternative approaches open to it. One is to decide on a multiplicand which represents not the annual loss of earnings today, but the average annual loss of earnings over the period to be measured, applying a single multiplier. The other approach will be for the court to look at the evidence, and find as a fact, for example, that the claimant's earnings would probably have increased by £x in about five years' time, and make a split award, using two or even three, multiplicands, and a multiplier divided into two (or three) parts. See **11.10.4.**

11.10.3 The multiplier

11.10.3.1 What is the multiplier?

The multiplier represents the number of years for which the claimant is to be awarded his or her net annual loss of earnings. It is sometimes known as the 'number of years' purchase'. It is important to realise that the multiplier is *not a real number of years.* If a claimant were to be given his or her loss for a real number of years, the effect of accelerated receipt (ie, the fact that he or she receives the money earlier than he or she would have done had he or she earned it) would be to over-compensate him or her massively. Think, for example, of a male claimant aged 25 at the date of his accident, with a net annual loss of £10,000. He would have retired at 65 and so has lost 40 years of income. But a multiplier of 40 produces a lump sum of £400,000, from which the claimant would be able to derive an annual income far in excess of £10,000.

The multiplier is therefore an artificial figure. It takes account of accelerated receipt. It also takes account of all the variables and uncertainties with regard to the future. It is specific to the individual claimant.

11.10.3.2   The old approach to selecting the multiplier

Until recently, multipliers were selected in a rather artificial way. The starting points were the claimant's age, sex, state of health before the accident and the nature of the employment lost. The more secure the job, the higher the retirement age, the higher the multiplier would be. There was then an assumption made that the claimant, when investing his or her lump sum award of damages, would be able to achieve a net rate of return on his or her investment of 4 to 5% per year. To take account of accelerated receipt, therefore, the total lump sum needed to be reduced by about 4.5% a year, and the multiplier would be arrived at on this basis. This was not generally done by accurate calculation, but rather by reference to tables in *Kemp & Kemp* which showed the multipliers used in other cases, and conventional wisdom, which told us that the appropriate multiplier, for example, was 13 for 20 years of real time, 15 for 25 years of real time, etc. The multiplier selected was almost always a whole number of years, and the court would move the figure first arrived at up or down by a year or so to take account of contingencies like promotion, unemployment etc.

11.10.3.3   The development of a new approach

This method had, however, become rather out of date. The 4.5% discount rate assumed that the claimant would invest his or her damages to a substantial extent in higher-risk investments, such as equities, or at least ought to. If he or she invested in a safer way, for example in Index-Linked Government Securities (ILGS), he or she would probably only achieve an annual net rate of return of 2 to 3%. Very few claimants actually invested their damages in anything more adventurous than a deposit account, and so ended up under-compensated. Further, the method ignored the existence of what are called the 'Ogden Tables'. These are actuarial tables compiled by a working party under Sir Michael Ogden and first published in 1983. The 6th edition (2007) can be found in *Kemp & Kemp*, 36-010, *Butterworths PILS* Part [XIV] 161, and on Lawtel. The tables set out the multipliers that should be adopted to measure various periods of the future for claimants of every age, at different discount rates, based on statistical evidence of the population's life expectancy and mortality rate. These tables make it possible to select multipliers in a much more accurate way.

The Law Commission in 1994 made two recommendations: that the Ogden Tables should become admissible in evidence, and that multipliers should be based on an annual discount rate of 3% rather than the conventional 4.5%. Parliament accepted these recommendations and enacted s 10 of the Civil Evidence Act 1995, and the Damages Act 1996. However, case law intervened.

11.10.3.4   Civil Evidence Act 1995, s 10

This section provides that the Ogden Tables should be admissible in evidence. This obviates the need to call expert evidence to prove them in every case. Section 10 has never been brought into force, but in the light of the decision in *Wells v Wells* (see **11.10.3.7),** this is no longer of any importance. It may now never be brought into force.

11.10.3.5   Damages Act 1996

Section 1 of the Damages Act 1996 reads:

> *(1) In determining the return to be expected from the investment of a sum awarded as damages for future pecuniary loss in an action for personal injury the court shall, subject to and in accordance with rules of court made for the purposes of this section, take into account such rate of return (if any) as may be prescribed by an order made by the Lord Chancellor.*
>
> *(2) Subsection (1) above shall not however prevent the court taking a different rate of return into account if any party to the proceedings shows that it is more appropriate in the case in question.*
>
> *(3) An order under subsection (1) may prescribe different rates of return for different classes of case.*
>
> *(4) Before making an order under subsection (1) above the Lord Chancellor shall consult the Government Actuary and the Treasury; and any order under that subsection shall be made by statutory instrument subject to annulment in pursuance of a resolution of either House of Parliament.*
>
> *(5) . . .*

The effect of this section is to enable the Lord Chancellor to prescribe a rate of return lower than 4.5%. It also enables the parties to argue for any rate of return they think is appropriate in the light of the current state of the market and the facts of the case. Once the appropriate rate of return on investment is prescribed, it becomes possible to find the correct multiplier to be taken as a starting point by reference to the Ogden Tables.

The Damages Act 1996 came into force on 24 September 1996, but it was not until June 2001 that the Lord Chancellor prescribed a rate. He was initially waiting for the decision of the House of Lords in *Wells v Wells* [1998] 3 All ER 481, but nearly two years passed before a consultation paper was issued by the Lord Chancellor's Department in March 2000, which stated that the Lord Chancellor intended at last to prescribe a rate, and at the same time to bring s 10 of the Civil Evidence Act 1995 into force. Responses to the consultation were invited by June 2000, and on 27 June 2001 the Lord Chancellor prescribed a rate. But before we consider the effect of this order, we need to look at what happened in the meantime.

11.10.3.6   *Wells v Wells*—the background

In 1994 and 1995 several claimants were successful in persuading judges to assume a rate of return on investment of damages of 3% or even less, thus obtaining a multiplier substantially greater than that which would have been applied using the conventional discount. They were able to do so with expert evidence on investment and the use of the Ogden Tables. Several of these cases went to the Court of Appeal and were reported under the name of the first, *Wells v Wells* [1997] 1 All ER 673.

The Court of Appeal came down emphatically in favour of retaining the conventional approach to multipliers, and assuming a rate of return on investment of about 4.5%, thus putting the common law in clear conflict with the intention of the Law Commission and the Damages Act 1996. There was then more than a year's delay before the case went to the House of Lords.

11.10.3.7   The House of Lords decision in *Wells v Wells*

The House of Lords decided that the conventional rate of discount of 4.5% should no longer be used when selecting multipliers, and that a rate reflecting the likely rate of return when investing in ILGS should be used instead. This rate should be a standard rate, to be applied in every case until a new rate was set. This would facilitate the settlement of claims, and avoid the need to call expert evidence at trials. The rate should for the time being be 3% until either there was a very considerable change in economic circumstances and/or the Lord Chancellor set a different rate under s 1(3) of the Damages Act 1996. The House of Lords invited him to do this as soon as possible, to avoid uncertainty. Thereafter the rate should always be set by the Lord Chancellor under the Act, so as to avoid the need for the courts to reconsider the issue. The rate should always be set to within 0.5 of a percentage point (ie 2.5%, 3%, 3.5% etc), so as to make it possible for the Ogden Tables always to be used in practice.

The standard rate should not, however, be regarded as absolutely fixed. It was accepted by the House of Lords in *Hodgson v Trapp* [1989] AC 807, and anticipated by s 1(2) of the Damages Act 1996, that there may be exceptional circumstances in which an argument can be made out for assuming a different rate of return on investment, particularly where higher rate tax is likely to be payable on income. But it is likely to be rare that such an argument will succeed.

The House of Lords also held that the correct approach in future to selecting a multiplier should be to use the Ogden Tables. Once the correct rate of discount (the assumed net rate of annual return of investment) is known, the tables will provide the correct multiplier, or at least the correct starting point. At this point therefore a new approach to selecting the multiplier came into effect, and the use of the Ogden Tables had official sanction, even though s 10 of the Civil Evidence Act 1995 was not yet in force.

11.10.3.8   After *Wells v Wells*

While the Lord Chancellor continued to delay setting a rate under the Damages Act 1996, pressure mounted for the courts to adopt a rate lower than 3%. Sir Michael Ogden argued in an article in The Times that the rate should be set at 2%, and in one case a judge decided to do so, but the Court of Appeal in *Warren v Northern General Hospital Trust* The Times, 10 April 2000, held that the courts could not alter the 3% discount rate until the Lord Chancellor made an order.

11.10.3.9   The rate set by the Lord Chancellor

In June 2001 the Lord Chancellor prescribed a rate of 2.5%. He accepted the need to have a single rate to cover all types of case, so he did not exercise his power under s 1(3) of the Damages Act 1996. He also accepted the view of the House of Lords that the rate should be set as a multiple of 0.5%, and that the rate of 2.5% should remain unchanged for the foreseeable future.

It remains the case under the Damages Act 1996, s 1(2), that a party may seek to persuade the court to adopt a different rate where appropriate on the facts of the case. However, following the decision in *Warriner v Warriner* [2003] 3 All ER 447, it is hard to envisage in what circumstances a party will succeed in doing so. In that case the Court of Appeal held that the different rate must be more appropriate in the light of the reasons given by the Lord Chancellor for setting the rate at 2.5%. So, in effect, it must be shown that there are circumstances to the case which were not considered by the Lord Chancellor. A very long life expectancy and very large damages are not such circumstances.

We therefore now have a settled approach to the selection of multipliers, which is explained in the next paragraphs. Remember that if the rate does change in the future, this will make very little difference to the process of calculation of damages. The principles by which multipliers are selected will remain unchanged; it is only the appropriate column in the Ogden Tables which will alter.

11.10.3.10   Selecting a multiplier—the new approach

The starting point in finding the multiplier for a loss of future earnings claim will be the appropriate Ogden Table (6th edition).

For loss of earnings Tables 3–14 are the relevant ones. Choose the table appropriate to the claimant's sex and likely retirement age, then all you need to know is the claimant's age today, and the correct discount rate (2.5%) and the multiplier can be read off. In the event of non-standard retirement ages you need to adjust the claimant's age. If the claimant is a 35-year-old male but would not have retired until the age of 67, you can either use Table 9 (retirement age 65) but treat the claimant as aged 33, which gives you a multiplier of 21.46; or you can use Table 11 (retirement age 70) but treat the claimant as aged 38, which gives you a multiplier of 21.14. There is a method explained in paragraphs 13–14 of the Explanatory Notes to the Ogden Tables to produce an accurate multiplier between these two figures. You multiply 21.46 x 2 (because you have reduced the claimant's age by two years), giving 42.92, and multiply 21.24 x 3 (because you have added 3 years to the claimant's age), giving 63.42. Add these two sums together, a total of 106.34, and divide by 5 (the difference between the two retirement ages you have used), and you get a resulting multiplier of 21.27.

11.10.3.11   Discount for contingencies

As explained above, account has to be taken of uncertainties with regard to job security and any other contingencies other than mortality. The House of Lords in *Wells v Wells* recognised that this practice needed to continue in the case of multipliers for loss of future earnings. The unscientific approach of the past (add or subtract a year or two by guesswork) does not mix well with the actuarial approach and will doubtless be abandoned. There are two ways of dealing with contingencies.

The first is that advocated by the Ogden Working Party and explained in paragraphs 26–44 of the Explanatory Notes to the Tables. It is rather more complicated than the approach that has been proposed in the past. The contingencies that need to be taken account of are the claimant's age, sex and level of educational attainment, as well as whether the claimant was employed or unemployed and disabled or not disabled at the time of the accident. The multiplier that would be appropriate according to the main tables must then be reduced by the factor indicated in table A, B, C or D in para 42, So if you take a male aged 35, who would have retired at 65, Table 9 gives you a multiplier of 20.53. Now add the facts that he was employed and not disabled at the time of the accident, and that he had middling educational attainment (ie, up to GCSE or A level but not beyond) and Table A tells us that the multiplier should be discounted by a factor of 0.90. So multiply 20.53 x 0.90 and the final multiplier is 18.48.

The other way of dealing with contingencies is much more rough and ready. It is simply to reduce the multiplier by 10%. This was the conventional method before *Wells v Wells*, and it appears that it is still widely followed in practice. It is too soon to say whether it will die out.

There will not normally be any good reason to adopt any other approach to the discount for contingencies. In particular, it is not sound to make a larger discount on the basis that the claim is really a claim for the loss of a chance—*Herring v Ministry of Defence* [2004] 1 All ER 44.

11.10.3.12   Other contingencies

There are still circumstances in which the court will or may make further adjustments to the multiplier from that suggested by the Ogden Tables. If there are any contingencies unique to the claimant that have not been taken account of already by the tables mentioned above, for example, a particularly risky job, or ongoing ill-health short of disability before the accident it is still open to the court to decide that the multiplier should be further reduced, and the reduction is likely to be made in the old-fashioned, rather arbitrary way of deducting a certain number of years.

Previously, there were other contingencies that could affect the multiplier, particularly factors like the claimant's actual earning capacity following the accident, or prospects of improving his or her earnings in the future. It seems unlikely that such contingencies will affect the multiplier in future. If they are to be taken account of, they will affect the multiplicand, maybe giving rise to a split award.

11.10.3.13   Factors which do not affect the choice of multiplier

(a) Future inflation. It has often been argued that in times of high inflation multipliers should be adjusted upwards to take account of the fact that the lump sum awarded to the claimant will diminish in value in real terms more quickly. However, high inflation is usually accompanied by higher interest rates and so no adjustment needs to be made (*Lim Poh Choo v Camden and Islington Area Health Authority* [1980] AC 174). The theory is that inflation is already taken account of in the conventional multiplier selected. It was thought for a time that there was an exception where the award was so great that the income it produced when invested would attract tax at higher rates and not merely basic rate, but this exception was all but ruled out by the House of Lords in *Hodgson v Trapp* [1989] AC 807.

(b) Foreign tax. The fact that a foreign claimant is liable to pay tax in his own country at a higher rate than he would pay in this country is not a justification for altering the discount rate or the multiplier (*Van Oudenhoven v Griffin Inns Ltd* [2000] 1 WLR 1413).

(c) The period between injury and trial. The length of time between injury and trial is not to be taken into account in the selection of the multiplier (*Pritchard v J. H. Cobden Ltd* [1988] Fam 22), though of course the court looks to the number of working years lost at the date of trial, not at the date of the injury. The rule is the opposite to the rule that applies in claims under the Fatal Accidents Act (see **12.5.2.8**) and does operate slightly in favour of claimants who are slow in bringing their cases to trial.

11.10.4   Split awards

Split awards for loss of future earnings are those where more than one multiplicand is worked out, and a separate multiplier applied to each. Following *Wells v Wells* it is likely that such awards will become a lot more common in future. It is the most effective way of calculating loss where the claimant's earnings or losses are likely to change in the future. If for example there is evidence that the claimant would have been promoted in about 10 years, with a corresponding increase in salary, the court is likely to take two multplicands and split the multiplier. A method is described in paras 22–23 of the Explanatory Notes to the Ogden Tables.

For example, let us assume a female claimant aged 43, who would have been promoted at the age of 50 and retired at the age of 60. The judge calculates two multiplicands, one for her existing loss—£35,000 per year, the other for her loss after promotion—£42,000 per year. The multiplier according to Ogden Table 8 is 13.66. However you also need to use Table 28, which gives multipliers for fixed periods. The multiplier for her overall loss should measure a real period of 17 years. Ogden Table 28 tells us that for a fixed period of 17 years the multiplier is 13.88. But the period before promotion is a fixed period of 7 years, for which the multiplier is 6.43. The difference between 13.88 and 6.43 is 7.45, which represents the 10 year period after promotion. Now you work out 6.43 and 7.45

as percentages of 13.88. The answer is 46.33% and 53.67%. Next, you divide the correct multiplier, namely 13.66, into these percentages, which gives you 6.33 for the first 7 years and 7.33 for the remaining 10 years. Now apply the discount for contingencies other than mortality (let's say 0.89 in accordance with Table C) and you get multipliers of 5.63 and 6.52. Finally you can do the calculation: for the loss up to the date of promotion, she gets 5.63 x £35,000 = £197,050, and for the loss thereafter she gets 6.52 x £42,000 = £273,840, giving a grand total of £470,890.

It is even possible that in appropriate cases the court will split the multiplier into three or four periods, with three or four different multiplicands and multipliers, for example where the claimant is a young man in his early twenties who had a very long and promising career ahead of him. A split award will also always be necessary in lost years cases; see **11.10.7.3** below.

11.10.5   Female claimants and future loss of earnings

11.10.5.1   Possible lower awards

A female claimant may not recover damages for loss of future earnings assessed on the basis of the Ogden Tables. This is because the court must take account of the possibility that she would have given up or interrupted her employment at some time in the future in order to have children and raise a family. If she is able to satisfy the court that she would not have done so, then of course the multiplier will be unaffected. But in the absence of such evidence, the court must evaluate the chance, and it remains a statistical probability that an unmarried woman will get married, and will have children, and will give up or interrupt her employment for some years at least; so a reduced award will result.

11.10.5.2   Loss of marriage prospects

However, an unmarried female claimant may very well also have suffered a loss of marriage prospects. This is not just a loss of amenity, it is also a financial loss—she has lost the financial support her husband would have provided had she given up work to raise a family. Although to make an award for lost marriage prospects and loss of future earnings may amount to double recovery, one can cancel the other out. In *Moriarty v McCarthy* [1978] 1 WLR 155 the court reduced the award for loss of future earnings on the ground that the claimant might have given up work to raise a family, but made an award of an amount equal to the reduction for loss of marriage prospects. More simply, the court in *Hughes v McKeown* [1985] 1 WLR 963 made no award for loss of marriage prospects, but used the same multiplier in the claim for loss of future earnings as would have been applied in the absence of any loss of marriage prospects.

11.10.6   Child claimant and future loss of earnings

When the claimant is a child who has not yet started work or chosen a career, particular difficulties arise. There can never be a measurable annual loss and so damages assessed on a multiplier/multiplicand basis are not prima facie appropriate. Indeed, where the claimant is very young, and where his or her earning capacity has been reduced rather than destroyed by the injury, the court is likely to make an award for loss of earning capacity rather than loss of future earnings (eg, *Joyce v Yeomans* [1981] 1 WLR 549). But if the claimant has lost any chance of career or employment, the court may well assess damages on a multiplier/multiplicand basis (eg, *Croke v Wiseman* [1981] 3 All ER 852).

The court will first of all need evidence of what the child's likely earnings would have been. If there is good evidence that the child's background was such that he or she would have been a high earner, then the court may take quite a large multiplicand (or series of multiplicands, for a split award). In the absence of such evidence, national average earnings are likely to form the basis of the multiplicand.

The multiplier will depend on the age at which the child would probably have started work. Treat the child as if that were its age in looking up the appropriate multiplier in the Ogden Tables. Reduce it for contingencies in accordance with Tables A–D, and then turn to Ogden Table 27 to determine the extra effect of accelerated receipt before the age of 18. So if for example the claimant is a 5-year-old boy who would probably have started work at the age of 18 after taking A levels and retired at the age of 65, the multiplier will be 27.22 according to Ogden Table 9. This will be reduced by a factor of 0.90 in accordance with Table A, making 24.50. But the money will be received 13 years in advance, so Table 27 shows that the multiplier must be discounted further by a factor of 0.7254. 24.50 × 0.7254 gives a final multiplier of 17.77.

11.10.7   Lost years

11.10.7.1   Basis of assessment

What if, as a result of his or her injury, the claimant's life expectancy has been reduced? Is the multiplier in the claim for loss of earnings to be based on his or her actual, reduced, life expectancy, or on what his or her life expectancy would have been but for his or her injury? The answer, laid down in *Pickett v British Rail Engineering Ltd* [1980] AC 136, is that the claimant can claim loss of future earnings, not only for the period he or she will survive, but also for the years he or she has lost, unless that loss is too remote to be measurable. It was thought to be too remote to be measurable if, for example, the claimant was a very young child (*Croke v Wiseman* [1981] 3 All ER 852) or if the years that had been lost could have had only a negligible effect on the choice of multiplier (eg, a 20–year-old whose remaining life expectancy has been reduced from 50 to 40 years). However, following the adoption of the Ogden Tables as the normal starting point, it is now arguable that such a loss is always measurable, even if small.

11.10.7.2   Deduction for living expenses

But in a lost years case a deduction will have to be made from the multiplicand to take account of the claimant's living expenses over those lost years; living expenses which he or she will no longer incur and so which cannot be recovered. 'Living expenses' includes all that the claimant would have spent exclusively on himself or herself—both needs (food, clothing, travel etc) and pleasures (beer, cigarettes, entertainments etc)—but not what he or she would have saved or spent on the support of his or her dependants, or others, such as friends. Expenditure which would have been both for his or her own and his or her dependants' benefit (eg, rent, mortgage interest, council tax, heating, electricity, gas, TV rental, the cost of running a car) has to be apportioned and a share taken from the multiplicand as the claimant's living expenses (*Harris v Empress Motors Ltd* [1983] 3 All ER 561).

11.10.7.3   Two awards

It follows that in a lost years case there will usually be two awards for loss of future earnings, each with a different multiplicand and multiplier: one in respect of the period that the claimant is likely to survive, using a multiplicand from which living expenses have not been deducted; and one in respect of the lost years, using a reduced multiplicand. For the method of calculation, see **11.10.4**.

11.10.8   Provisional damages for future loss of earnings

The court may in appropriate cases make a provisional award for future loss of earnings under SCA 1981, s 32A or CCA 1984, s 51. Normally uncertainties with regard to the future are taken account of by evaluating the chance. But where the uncertainty is as to whether the claimant's condition will seriously deteriorate, causing him or her to lose their job, the court can assess damages initially on the basis that his or her loss of earnings will continue at its present level, and award a further sum in the future if the loss increases due to the deterioration in condition.

11.11   Head 4: loss of earning capacity

11.11.1   The nature of the award

This head of damages arises where there is clear evidence that the claimant will not earn as much in the future as he or she would have done but for the injury, but there is nevertheless no measurable annual loss to found an award for loss of future earnings on a multiplier/multiplicand basis. Instead an award for loss of earning capacity may be made. This is commonly known as a *'Smith v Manchester'* award, from *Smith v Manchester Corporation* (1974) 17 KIR 1. It compensates the claimant, not so much for lost earnings, but rather for lost earning capacity or the 'handicap on the labour market', and is assessed as a single lump sum.

11.11.2   When is an award of this kind appropriate?

It is possible to identify various situations in which an award of this kind is appropriate:

(a) Where the claimant is back in pre-accident employment, or in work of equal value, so that there is no immediate loss, but nevertheless, as a result of the injury, he or she will at some time in the future be forced into an early retirement or a less well paid job. If there is a real, or substantial, risk of this, a lump sum award can be made (*Moeliker v A. Reyrolle & Co Ltd* [1976] ICR 252).

(b) Where the claimant is back in pre-accident employment and is not likely to lose it, but nevertheless the injury has damaged prospects of promotion, ability to advance the career or chances of moving on to higher paid employment.

(c) Where the claimant is handicapped on the labour market by the injury. For example, he or she was not in settled employment or was unemployed at the date of the accident, or is not yet back at work but will be soon, and is now going to find work harder to come by, or will find that the range of jobs open to him or her is narrower than it was. In all these instances a *Smith v Manchester* award is appropriate.

(d) Where the claimant is a child who has not yet entered the labour market (see **11.10.6**).

11.11.3   Quantification of an award for loss of earning capacity

The award is quantified as a round lump sum which is chosen on a fairly arbitrary basis, with some reference to awards in previous cases. A table in *Kemp & Kemp,* para 36-182 gives some guidance and shows that awards under this head are generally not particularly high. A typical working basis for assessment is to take one to two years' net pay, but a higher sum may be appropriate; see, eg, *Foster v Tyne and Wear County Council* [1986] 1 All ER 567, where a lump sum of five times annual net pay was approved.

11.11.4 Awards combining heads 3 and 4

Judges do not always draw a clear distinction between damages for loss of earnings and loss of earning capacity, and occasional hybrid awards can be found where damages for future loss of earnings have been assessed as a lump sum, or where damages for lost earning capacity have been quantified by means of a speculative multiplicand and multiplier. It is likely that this tendency will be more marked following *Wells v Wells*, with judges seeking to use a multiplier/multiplicand basis whenever possible.

The two heads are normally alternative to each other, but there are cases where an award under each head is appropriate, eg, where the claimant has not yet gone back to work but is expected to do so in, say, a year's time; he or she will then resume pre-accident employment but will still be handicapped on the labour market or have lower prospects of promotion. In such a case the court would probably award one year's loss of earnings and a small lump sum. The courts are increasingly willing to recognise that there is a distinction between the two heads and to make an award both for future loss of earnings and for handicap on the labour market.

11.11.5 Provisional damages and loss of earning capacity

If the claimant has claimed provisional damages, this may well preclude an award being made under this head. If, for example, there is uncertainty as to whether the claimant's condition will deteriorate, but certainty that if it does, the claimant will be forced into early retirement, the court will assess damages initially on the basis that there is no loss of earning capacity, and any later award, if there is deterioration, is likely to be on a multiplier/multiplicand basis.

11.12 Head 5: loss of pension rights

11.12.1 Basis of the award

It is often the case that if a claimant has lost his or her employment as a result of their injury, or employment has been interrupted, he or she has also lost their employers' contributions towards a retirement pension, which will accordingly be reduced. Damages can be awarded to compensate for this loss.

11.12.2 Old method of calculating damages under this head

Damages used to be calculated as follows (see *Auty v National Coal Board* [1985] 1 All ER 930):

(a) Assuming no change in the value of money, what annual pension would the claimant have received on retirement had he or she not been injured and had there been no interruption to the pension contributions?

(b) What annual pension will the claimant in fact receive, again assuming no change in the value of money?

(c) The difference between (a) and (b) is the annual loss. Multiply it by an appropriate multiplier representing the number of years for which he or she is likely to receive the pension (or, in a lost years case, would have received it).

(d) Discount the lump sum arrived at by 4% or 5% per annum for accelerated receipt. This calculation is on a year-on-year basis.

11.12.3   New method of calculation

Following *Wells v Wells* it must now be appropriate to use an actuarial method of calculation, using the Ogden Tables. *Wells v Wells* did not actually deal with the assessment of damages for a lost pension, but exactly the same principles apply.

The multiplicand can be calculated as above—it is the difference between the annual pension the claimant would have received on retirement but for the injury and the annual pension that will now be received. The multiplier can be found from Ogden Tables 15-26. Choose the table according to the sex and retirement age of the claimant, and then read off the multiplier according to the claimant's age today and the appropriate rate of discount (2.5%). The tables take account not only of the element of accelerated receipt once the claimant reaches retirement age, but the further element of accelerated receipt, given that the claimant will receive a lump sum in respect of pension loss before reaching retirement age.

The multiplier will again need to be adjusted for contingencies other than mortality. The procedure is exactly the same as in multipliers for loss of future earnings—see **11.10.3.11.**

11.12.4   A simpler method of assessment

An alternative and simpler method of valuing a loss of pension rights, which can be agreed by parties negotiating a settlement, but which does not have the court's approval, is to obtain quotations from life assurance companies. If the claimant has had his or her pension right on retirement reduced from say £15,000 to £10,000 per year, find out the market price today of a £5,000 pa pension from age 65 for life, and take this as an appropriate sum.

11.13   Head 6: future expenses

11.13.1   Similarity to special damages

These are likely to be the same items or the same sort of items as were included in the claim for special damages; but where the expenditure has not yet been incurred, or will continue into the future for a number of years or indefinitely, the loss is future loss and forms part of the award for general damages. Anything that was reasonably recoverable as special damages is also recoverable for the future.

11.13.2   'One-off' items

Items of expenditure that are 'one-off', such as the cost of home conversion or the purchase of special equipment, are quantified on a lump sum basis. If the court takes the present day value, the advantage of accelerated receipt is cancelled out by inflation.

11.13.3 Recurring items

Recurring items, such as the cost of nursing care, the cost of a housekeeper, and the value of voluntary services, are quantified on a multiplier/multiplicand basis. The multiplicand is the annual cost or value of the service as at the date of trial. The multiplier, following *Wells v Wells,* will be selected from the Ogden Tables. If the item of expenditure will last only for a certain number of years, Table 28 will be appropriate; if the item of expenditure will last indefinitely, then the multiplier represents the claimant's life expectancy and Ogden Tables 1 and 2 will be used. The only contingency that is relevant is mortality, and so no further adjustment should be made to the multiplier found by reference to the tables. There may in occasional cases (but not as a general rule) be evidence that the claimant has a particularly low or high expectation of life, in which case the court may be persuaded to make an adjustment to the multiplier. This is likely to be done by assuming a different age for the claimant when reading the multiplier off the table. In the event that the claimant's injuries have substantially reduced life expectancy to a given number of years, then Table 28 will be the appropriate table.

The discount rate is that specified by the Lord Chancellor—currently 2.5%, as in claims for loss of future earnings. Attempts have been made to argue that the discount rate should be smaller in claims for the cost of future care, relying on s 1(2) of the Damages Act 1996, but the courts are extremely reluctant to depart from the standard rate. In *Cooke v United Bristol Healthcare NHS Trust* [2004] 1 All ER 797, several claimants tried to get round the convention by arguing that the multiplicand should increase in stages over future years (because the costs of care are increasing faster than the general rate of inflation). However, the Court of Appeal refused to adopt this approach. It is hard to see when, if ever, s 1(2) can actually be applied.

There may frequently be several items of recurring expense, and each will need to be calculated with its own multiplicand and multiplier. Note that not all future expenditure will last indefinitely. For example, if the claimant is claiming for the cost of a gardener, when he or she used to do their own gardening, it is arguable that he or she should not recover this loss for life, because even if the claimant had not been injured he or she would probably have given up doing the gardening at some stage before death.

A claim for the cost of nursing care may well have to be calculated on a split basis, because as the claimant gets older, the cost will increase. In such cases the court will allow one multiplicand for, say, 10 years, and a higher multiplicand thereafter. The multiplier will be split in the way explained in **11.10.4.**

The cost of purchasing a new house is a recurring item: the multiplicand is 2.5% of the increased capital value (see **11.7.5**) and the multiplier represents the claimant's life expectancy.

Where the item of recurring expenditure is not an annual expense, the easiest way to calculate the loss is to spread the multiplicand over a number of years. For example, if the claimant will need a new wheelchair every five years for the rest of his or her life, at a cost of £1,000 at present day values, take a multiplicand of £200 and a multiplier from Ogden Table 1 or 2.

11.13.4 The domestic element in the cost of care

Where there is a claim for the cost of future care of the claimant, as well as a claim for the claimant's lost earnings, care must be taken to avoid duplication or overlap of damages in the area of living expenses. It is quite likely that part of the cost of looking after the claimant in an institution will match what the claimant would have spent in looking after himself or herself (eg, food, clothing). If no deduction were made, the claimant would therefore be compensated for some of the loss twice over. Rather than deducting living expenses from the award for loss of earnings, instead the 'domestic element' is deducted from the claim for the cost of care (*Lim Poh Choo v Camden and Islington Area Health Authority* [1980] AC 174). This involves an adjustment to the multiplicand, not the multiplier.

The domestic element is narrower than living expenses as defined by *Pickett v British Rail Engineering Ltd* [1980] AC 136: it is merely that portion of the living expenses that is replaced by the cost of care, and does not include any portion of the joint expenditure or what the claimant would have spent on pleasures. (It is irrelevant that the claimant can no longer enjoy those pleasures.)

11.13.5   Cost of investment advice

If a claimant is to receive a large award of damages for future loss, he or she is very likely to need to pay for professional advice on how to invest it, and will also incur charges from fund managers investing the money. The question arises whether such sums can be recovered as future expenses. It was held in *Page v Plymouth Hospitals NHS Trust* [2004] 3 All ER 367 that these expenses are not recoverable as damages. In setting the discount rate to be used when selecting the multiplier, the Lord Chancellor has assumed that damages will be invested in index-linked gilt-edged stock, for which these expenses will not be incurred. The discount rate would have been greater if the kind of investment requiring advice and management had been contemplated, so it would be too generous to a claimant to take account of these expenses in awarding damages. In *Eagle v Chambers* [2005] 1 All ER 136, the Court of Appeal held that the same rule must apply to panel brokers' fees charged by the Court of Protection.

11.14   Stage 3: make any necessary deductions

11.14.1   Introduction

Following his or her injury, the claimant may have received benefits or made savings as well as suffered losses. On the compensatory principle, therefore, any gains made as a result of the injury should be deducted from any claim for losses suffered. However, the courts require a clear causative link between injury and benefit, and not all benefits received have to be deducted. There are various rules for different types of benefit. Some have been considered already: see **11.7.4.3, 11.7.4.4, 11.7.6, 11.10.7.2, 11.13.4.**

11.14.2   Social security benefits

Social security benefits may well have been received by the claimant, but will be recovered by the state on payment of damages: see **11.17** below. Therefore they should be disregarded in the assessment of damages (ie, no deduction should be made). This is expressly provided for in s 17 of the Social Security (Recovery of Benefits) Act 1997.

11.14.3   Contractual sick pay

Any sick pay received by the claimant from his or her employer under their contract of employment is equivalent to earnings and so must be deducted from any claim for lost earnings. For statutory sick pay see below in **11.17.**

11.14.4   Insurance

Where the claimant was insured against accidental injury and receives the benefits of that insurance policy, no deduction is to be made (*Bradburn v Great Western Railway* (1874) LR 10 Ex 1). The rule is the same even where the insurance premium was paid on the claimant's behalf by another (such as an employer). But where the claimant's employer runs a sick-pay scheme through an insurance policy, by which the claimant is contractually entitled to sick-pay under his or her contract of employment, such sick-pay is treated as part of his or her earnings and is to be deducted (*Hussain v New Taplow Paper Mills Ltd* [1988] 1 All ER 541). However, where the insurance premiums have been paid by the tortfeasor, the insurance benefit is to be deducted (*Gaca v Pirelli General plc* [2004] 3 All ER 348).

11.14.5   Pensions

Where the claimant receives a pension as a result of his or her injuries, no deduction is to be made, whether the pension was payable as of right or was discretionary, whether it was contributory or non-contributory (*Parry v Cleaver* [1970] AC 1, re-affirmed by the House of Lords in *Smoker v London Fire and Civil Defence Authority* [1991] 2 AC 502). State retirement pensions are also not deductible (*Hewson v Downs* [1970] 1 QB 73; *Hopkins v Norcros plc* [1992] ICR 338).

However, in *Longden v British Coal Corp* [1998] 1 All ER 289 the House of Lords allowed a small exception to this rule. Where the claimant had received an incapacity pension consisting of a lump sum as well as an annual payment, the proportion of that lump sum that related to the period after the claimant would have retired was to be deducted from any claim for lost retirement pension.

11.14.6   Redundancy payments

Where the claimant has been made redundant and received a redundancy payment, this will not normally be deducted since the payment has nothing to do with the injury or incapacity to work (*Mills v Hassall* [1983] ICR 330). However, where the claimant has been made redundant or has been offered and accepted voluntary redundancy, but would not have been made redundant or would not have accepted redundancy but for the injury, then the redundancy payment is deductible (*Colledge v Bass Mitchells and Butlers Ltd* [1988] 1 All ER 536).

11.14.7   Benevolent donations

It sometimes happens, particularly following well-publicised disasters, that the claimant has benefited from a fund created by voluntary donations. Any such benefits are not deductible (*Redpath v Belfast and County Down Railway* [1947] NI 167).

Similarly, no account is to be taken of gifts from family or friends, or an ex gratia payment by the claimant's employer (*Cunningham v Harrison* [1973] QB 942). A voluntary payment by an employer may be deductible, however, where the employer is the liable defendant (*Hussain v New Taplow Paper Mills Ltd* [1988] 1 All ER 541) and particularly where the payment is expressed to be treated as an advance against any damages that may be awarded (*Williams v BOC Gases Ltd* [2000] ICR 1181). Indeed, as a general rule, any redundancy payments made by the tortfeasor will be treated as deductible (*Gaca v Pirelli General plc* [2004] 3 All ER 348). No deduction is made in respect of voluntary services provided by family and friends (see **11.4.1.2(m)** and **11.7.8**).

11.14.8   Maintenance at public expense

If the claimant is being or has been maintained wholly or partly at public expense in a hospital, nursing home or other institution, any saving made must be deducted from any damages for lost earnings or earning capacity (AJA 1982, s 5). This deduction is roughly equivalent to the deduction of the domestic element (see **11.13.4**).

11.14.9   Foreign repayable benefits

If the claimant has received a foreign state benefit which he or she is by law obliged to repay if he or she recovers damages, then no deduction will be made from the damages to take account of this benefit, even if it would otherwise be deductible (*Berriello v Felixstowe Dock & Railway Co* [1989] 1 WLR 695). To do so would penalise either the claimant or the provider of the benefit.

11.14.10   Statutory compensation

Where a claimant has received compensation payable under the Pneumoconiosis etc (Workers' Compensation) Act 1979, and then recovers damages in respect of the same disease for which he or she received that compensation, those damages must be reduced by the full amount of the compensation received. By analogy, the same principle is likely to apply in respect of any other statutory compensation that may be payable for industrial injury or disease.

11.15   Stage 4: contributory negligence

11.15.1   Introduction

Damages may well have to be reduced to take account of the claimant's contributory negligence. The circumstances in which such a reduction is to be made are set out in **6.3.1**.

11.15.2   Quantification

If there has been a finding of contributory negligence, the total sum of damages quantified so far must be reduced accordingly. If the finding is 25% contributory negligence, reduce the total award by 25%. If advising on quantum, form an opinion as to whether there is likely to be a finding of contributory negligence and, if so, reduce your estimate of damages accordingly.

11.15.3   Reduction for contributory negligence is made last

Note that any reduction for contributory negligence is made after taking account of any other deductions.

This sequence of deductions operates in the claimant's favour. To take an example: Damages are assessed at £2,500. Contributory negligence is 50%. The amount to be deducted is £500.

If contributory negligence was taken account of first, the claimant would receive: £(2,500 × 50%)—£500 = £750.

In fact the other deductions are made first, and the claimant receives £(2,500—500) × 50% = £1,000.

11.16 Stage 5: add interest

11.16.1 Introduction

Interest will be awarded by the court under SCA 1981, s 35A or CCA 1984, s 69. By s 35A(2) and s 69(2), the award is prima facie mandatory, unless there are special reasons to the contrary. The sections give no guidelines as to interest rates or periods, which are in the court's discretion, but there are rules of practice.

11.16.2 Interest on special damages

Interest is awarded on special damages at half the 'appropriate rate' from the date of accident to the date of trial (*Jefford v Gee* [1970] 2 QB 130). The date of trial is the date of judgment on damages, not liability (*Thomas v Bunn* [1991] 1 AC 362).

The appropriate rate is the rate of interest allowed on the High Court Special Investment Account over the relevant period. This rate of interest is fixed from time to time by the Lord Chancellor, and can be found in Civil Procedure (the White Book) at 7.0.17 and *Blackstone's Civil Practice* at 62.12. At the time of writing it is 6%.

11.16.3 Interest on general damages

Interest is awarded on damages for pain and suffering and loss of amenity from the date of service of the writ to the date of trial (*Pickett v British Rail Engineering Ltd* [1980] AC 136). The rate was set at 2% a year by *Wright v British Railways Board* [1983] 2 All ER 698. It was thought that following *Wells v Wells*, the rate should be 3%, but this was ruled out in *Lawrence v Chief Constable of Staffordshire* The Times, 25 July 2000. The rate therefore remains at 2%.

No interest is awarded on any damages for future loss.

11.17 Recovery of benefits

11.17.1 Introduction

Since 1989 it has been government policy that when a claimant receives a compensation payment in respect of injuries, any social security benefits which he or she has received in the meantime should be repaid to the State. The scheme was first introduced by the Social Security Act 1989, amended a few times and consolidated into the Social Security Administration Act 1992. There were certain injustices in the scheme, notably that benefits could be recovered from a claimant's damages for pain, suffering and loss of amenity as well as loss of earnings, so that in some cases a claimant could be left with very little in the way of damages at all. A revised scheme was therefore introduced by the Social Security (Recovery of Benefits) Act 1997. A fundamental change is that benefits are no longer recovered from the claimant, but from the compensator.

11.17.2   How the scheme works

11.17.2.1   The basic outline

By ss 1 and 6 of the Social Security (Recovery of Benefits) Act 1997, a person who makes a compensation payment (whether on his or her own behalf or not) to any other person in consequence of any accident, injury or disease, must pay an amount equal to the total amount of the recoverable benefits to the Secretary of State.

By s 8 he or she may then deduct the amount paid to the Secretary of State from the compensation to be paid to the claimant under the appropriate head of damages, but not so as to reduce the amount payable to the claimant under that head below nil. So if the claimant has received more in benefits in respect of a particular type of loss than he or she is to receive by way of compensation, the claimant does not lose compensation under other heads to make up the difference.

On the other hand, the compensator must repay benefits in full to the Secretary of State, so if the benefits are greater than the compensation under the relevant head, he will pay more in total than would have been the case if there had been no recovery of benefits. However, by s 22, if he was insured in respect of liability to the claimant, then he is also insured in respect of liability to the Secretary of State.

11.17.2.2   Recoverable benefits

The recoverable benefits are the listed benefits which have been or are likely to be paid to the claimant during the relevant period (s 1(1) of the 1997 Act). The listed benefits are set out in Sch 2. The effect of s 8 is that each benefit is recoverable from compensation in respect of a particular type of loss only. The table in Sch 2 is:

Head of compensation	Benefit
1. Compensation for earnings lost during the relevant period	Disablement pension
	Incapacity benefit
	Income support
	Invalidity pension and allowance
	Jobseeker's allowance
	Reduced earnings allowance
	Severe disablement allowance
	Sickness benefit
	Statutory sick pay
	Unemployability supplement
	Unemployment benefit
2. Compensation for cost of care during the relevant period	Attendance allowance
	Care component of disability living allowance
	Disablement pension increase
3. Compensation for loss of mobility during the relevant period	Mobility allowance
	Mobility component of disability living allowance

By s 24 of the 1997 Act the Secretary of State can amend Sch 2 by statutory regulation.

11.17.2.3   The relevant period

The relevant period is defined by s 3 of the 1997 Act. In the case of accident or injury, it is five years from the date of the accident or injury. In the case of disease, it is five years from the date on which the claimant first claimed benefit in respect of that disease. In either case the relevant period comes to an end before the end of the five years when the defendant makes a compensation payment.

11.17.2.4   Certificates of recoverable benefits

How does the person making the compensation payment know how much to pay to the Secretary of State and how much to deduct from the compensation payment? He or she is given the necessary information by a certificate issued by the Compensation Recovery Unit. By s 4 of the 1997 Act, before the compensator makes any compensation payment, he or she must apply for a certificate of recoverable benefits which informs the compensator how much he or she must pay to the Secretary of State if they make the compensation payment within a specified time. If the compensator does not make the payment within that time, he or she must apply for a new certificate.

11.17.3   Court orders

The scheme applies in exactly the same way whether the compensation is paid by a court order, by agreement or voluntarily. But where the court makes an order for the payment of damages (other than a consent order), then by s 15 of the 1997 Act it must specify the amount awarded under each of the heads of compensation set out in Sch 2.

11.17.4   Other provisions

The above is only an abbreviated outline of the effect of the 1997 Act. There are other provisions dealing with reviews and appeals against the amounts of recoverable benefits, recovery of overpayments, payments by more than one person in respect of the same injury, and other matters. In particular, there is a power to make regulations exempting small payments (up to a specified sum) from the scheme, though no such exemption has been made.

11.17.5   Contributory negligence and recovery of benefits

Recovery bites into damages actually paid, after the assessment process is complete, so any reduction for contributory negligence will already have been made before the compensation payment is reduced to take account of the amount paid to the DSS.

11.17.6   Interest on damages to be recovered

A claimant is entitled to receive interest on all the special damages assessed, not just those damages which he or she will in fact be paid after the defendant has made a deduction in consequence of the recovery of benefits (*Wisely v John Fulton (Plumbers) Ltd* [2000] 2 All ER 545). However, the defendant can set off the benefits repaid to the DSS against both the damages and the interest on those damages (*Griffiths v British Coal Corporation* [2001] 1 WLR 1493).

11.18   Other ways of quantifying damages

The methods of quantifying damages set out above have been developed over the years by judges, practitioners and Parliament. To a very large extent the rules are rules of practice rather than rules of law; nevertheless, judges are bound to follow guidelines laid down by the Court of Appeal and House of Lords, and it is in nobody's interest if a judge decides to take a maverick approach to the quantification of damages, arriving at a figure which could not have been predicted by either side. Accordingly, the methods set out above are universally used by courts, even though the quantum of damages is, strictly speaking, wholly within the judge's discretion, so long as his or her decision is just. Hence the need for legislation if any major changes are to be made (see **11.2.1**).

But parties negotiating a settlement are not bound to follow the conventional methods if they agree not to do so. They may agree to use actuarial calculations; they may agree to take full notice of inflation. In particular, unlike a judge, they are not obliged to agree to a once-and-for-all lump sum.

There is now also s 2 of the Damages Act 1996, as substituted by s 100 of the Courts Act 2003, and in force from 1 April 2005. Here are the fundamental subsections:

2 Periodical payments

(1) *A court awarding damages for future pecuniary loss in respect of personal injury—*

   (a) *may order that the damages are wholly or partly to take the form of periodical payments, and*

   (b) *shall consider whether to make that order.*

(2) *A court awarding other damages in respect of personal injury may, if the parties consent, order that the damages are wholly or partly to take the form of periodical payments.*

(3) *A court may not make an order for periodical payments unless satisfied that the continuity of payment under the order is reasonably secure.*

. . .

(8) *An order for periodical payments shall be treated as providing for the amount of payments to vary by reference to the retail prices index . . . at such times, and in such a manner, as may be determined by or in accordance with Civil Procedure Rules.*

(9) *But an order for periodical payments may include provision—*

   (a) *disapplying subsection (8), or*

   (b) *modifying the effect of subsection (8).*

As an addition to its other powers, the court can now order damages to be paid wholly or partly by way of periodical payments. It had the power to do so previously with the consent of the parties, but it may now do so even without their consent. It also has a duty in every case to consider whether to make such an order.

So, for example, rather than making a lump sum award for future medical expenses, calculated on the basis of a multiplicand of £24,000 a year and an appropriate multiplier taken from the Ogden Tables, it may instead order the defendant to pay the claimant periodical payments of £2,000 per month for life. The figure of £2,000 will be automatically updated in line with inflation under subsection (8) or (9).

There are a lot more detailed provisions in ss 2A and 2B of the Damages Act, especially with regard to ensuring that continuity of payment is reasonably secure.

It is too soon to say how frequently and in what circumstances the court will exercise its powers under the new s 2. At first it was thought that periodical payments would only be likely to be more appropriate in high value cases, and that lump sum awards would continue to be the norm in ordinary low to average value claims. However, that was partly because claimants were reluctant to seek periodical payments, especially for the cost of care. Since it seemed likely that such payments would be index-linked to the RPI under ss (8), while all the indications are that medical and caring costs rise at well above the rate of inflation, such an order did not seem to be in the claimant's best interests.

However, in *Flora v Wakom (Heathrow) Ltd* [2006] 4 All ER 982 the Court of Appeal held that index-linking to RPI under ss (8) was merely a default position to be followed when the order for periodical payments did not name any other index. There was nothing in the Act to suggest that RPI would be the normal index, or that exceptional circumstances had to exist before any other index was used. The courts were therefore free under ss (9), if it was just to do so, to adopt any index that was consistent with the principle that the claimant should be fully compensated for his or her loss, only resorting to the RPI under ss (8) when there was no better or fairer alternative.

The matter was considered again by the Court of Appeal in *Thompstone v Tameside and Glossop Acute Services NHS Trust* [2008] All ER (D) 72 Jan. The CA reinforced the principle that the judge has an absolute discretion to depart from the RPI as a default index and adopt any other index that on the evidence is appropriate, giving overriding consideration to the claimant's needs (as opposed to preferences), giving very little weight to the defendant's preference and seeking to achieve as far as possible 100% compensation. It seems likely that as a result of this decision periodical payments orders will become a lot more frequent, certainly in high value cases.

11.19 Structured settlements

11.19.1 What is a structured settlement?

A structured settlement is an agreement between the parties that damages will not be paid as a conventional lump sum, but rather in the form of future annual payments and future lump sums. It is not so much an alternative way of quantifying damages, as an alternative way of paying them.

A structured settlement is not something that can be imposed by a court, but must be agreed between the parties. It can then be approved by the court and incorporated into a Tomlin order if necessary. The first case in which a judge approved a structured settlement was reported in July 1989 (*Kelly v Dawes*, reported as a news item in The Times, 27 September 1990, but see *Kemp & Kemp*, para 23-004); since then there have been several hundred and there will be more and more every year as the idea takes hold.

The result of an effective structured settlement is likely to be that the claimant's needs are better provided for, that the claimant actually receives more money over his or her lifetime than they would with a conventional award, and that the defendant's insurer actually pays less.

11.19.2 When is a structured settlement appropriate?

The cases in which structured settlements have been agreed are all ones in which the claimant has suffered serious or very serious injuries, which have resulted in substantial ongoing future loss for the rest of the claimant's life. A structured settlement is of little use where there has been a complete recovery, or when the claimant's injuries are relatively minor, or where the bulk of damages are to compensate the claimant for past losses.

But where the future losses are high, because the claimant will need continued care or incur significant expense throughout his or her life, there is a real advantage to be gained in a structured settlement, provided the extra cash generated is not outweighed by the costs of setting up and administering the settlement. At present, this is likely to be where the sum to be paid by way of future instalments is more than about £100,000, though this threshold has already come down from £200,000 and is likely to fall further as the various professionals involved in the implementation of structured settlements gain more experience.

11.19.3   How does a structured settlement work?

11.19.3.1   Investment of a conventional lump sum

When a seriously injured claimant receives a conventional lump sum award, it is intended to compensate not only for the expense already incurred, but also to pay for all future needs. The claimant will therefore doubtless invest a proportion of it and use both capital and income to provide for himself or herself for the rest of their life.

The most effective way of ensuring that the money does not run out before death, the time of which may be very uncertain, is to purchase an index-linked annuity from a life office. The claimant will then receive an annual sum representing both capital and interest which will rise in line with inflation. But he or she will receive the annual sum net of income tax.

11.19.3.2   The structured settlement

The essence of a structured settlement is that the defendant's insurers will pay some of the damages as an immediate lump sum, to provide for the claimant's past and present needs, and will use the rest of the sum available to purchase an index-linked annuity for the claimant. The life office will pay the insurers the annual sum net of tax, but the insurers can recover that tax from HM Revenue and Customs (HMRC), under an agreement made between the Revenue and the Association of British Insurers in 1987, and will then pay the claimant the gross value of the annuity. The claimant thus receives more.

Because the claimant receives more a year than he or she would if they were to receive a conventional lump sum, it is possible for the defendant's insurers to negotiate a lower sum to be invested in the purchase of the annuity. Both sides therefore gain from the arrangement. If the parties focus on the claimant's annual needs, and then find out how much it would cost to purchase an index-linked annuity at that annual value for the claimant's life, they may well then be able to agree on that sum as the lump sum to be invested (after making allowance for costs). That sum is likely to be lower than the sum that would otherwise have been awarded.

11.19.4   How is a structured settlement worked out?

The first step will be to work out or agree the value of the claimant's claim for damages on a conventional basis. Only if that sum is known can either side appreciate the benefits of a structured settlement, or whether those benefits will outweigh the costs.

There will then need to be a cooperative effort between a considerable number of people: the claimant's and the defendant's legal advisers, the defendant's insurers, a life assurance broker, an accountant with experience of structured settlements, a life office, and HMRC. If the claimant is a patient, the Court of Protection will also be involved, and if a claim has been commenced, the approval of the court is likely to be required.

Only if the scheme is in the correct form will HMRC agree to treat the future instalments as payments of capital, and so refund the tax deducted by the life office.

The costs and professional fees are what make the setting up and administration of a structured settlement more expensive than a simple payment of damages. However, provided the sum to be invested is large enough these are likely to be offset by the tax savings and lower capital sums involved.

11.19.5   The importance of maintaining flexibility

Although the central ingredient of a structured settlement is the purchase of an annuity on the claimant's behalf by the defendant's insurers, there are many other ingredients that may be appropriate in individual cases. The claimant's situation and likely future needs will be different in every case, and it is important that the settlement should be *structured* to cater for any possible or anticipated changes in the claimant's situation.

For example a structure which involves gradually increasing annual sums may be required if the claimant's condition is likely to deteriorate. Another way of dealing with this might be to purchase two annuities, one deferred. It may be wise to build in occasional future lump sums to enable the claimant to cope with specific anticipated events in the future.

The value of a structured settlement will be lost if it becomes an inflexible form of settlement revolving solely around the annuity.

11.19.6 Recovery of benefits

Structured settlements do not prevent recovery of benefits! Section 18 of the Social Security (Recovery of Benefits) Act 1997 enables regulations to be made setting out how benefits to be recovered will bite into sums paid by way of structured settlements and periodical payments ordered by the court under s 2 of the Damages Act 1996. The Social Security (Recovery of Benefits) Regulations 1997 make the necessary provisions.

12

Quantum of damages for a fatal accident

12.1 Rights of claim

12.1.1 Introduction

There are two rights of action that arise as a result of a fatal accident, both statutory. These are an action on behalf of the deceased's estate under the Law Reform (Miscellaneous Provisions) Act 1934 (LR(MP)A 1934); and a claim on behalf of the deceased's dependants under the Fatal Accidents Act 1976 (FAA 1976). These Acts were both amended by the Administration of Justice Act 1982 (ss 3, 4), as a result of which (except in the case of deaths occurring before 1983) the two *rights* of action are entirely separate from each other and there is no overlap between them, though both will be founded on the same *cause* of action.

12.1.2 The right of action under the LR(MP)A 1934

12.1.2.1 Section 1 of the Act

Section 1 of the LR(MP)A 1934 provides:

> *(1) Subject to the provisions of this section, on the death of any person after the commencement of this Act all causes of action subsisting against or vested in him shall survive against, or, as the case may be, for the benefit of, his estate. Provided that this subsection shall not apply to causes of action for defamation.*
>
> *(1A) The right of a person to claim under section 1A of the Fatal Accidents Act 1976 (bereavement) shall not survive for the benefit of his estate on his death.*
>
> *(2) Where a cause of action survives as aforesaid for the benefit of the estate of a deceased person, the damages recoverable for the benefit of the estate of that person—*
>
> > *(a) shall not include—*
> >
> > > *(i) any exemplary damages;*
> > >
> > > *(ii) any damages for loss of income in respect of any period after that person's death;*
> >
> > *(b) . . .*
> >
> > *(c) where the death of that person has been caused by the act or omission which gives rise to the cause of claim, shall be calculated without reference to any loss or gain to his estate consequent on his death, except that a sum in respect of funeral expenses may be included.*

12.1.2.2 The effect of the provision

The effect of this provision is that any cause of action which the deceased had at his or her death can still be pursued by his or her estate, so that if the deceased could have sued the defendant in negligence for damages for personal injury, his or her estate may step into his or her shoes and do so instead. The deceased's estate may claim damages in respect of any losses that had already accrued at the moment of death. So the estate will recover any damages that the deceased himself or herself could have recovered if he or she had instituted a claim for personal injury, pursued it, and obtained judgment, all in the instant before death; with the important exception of the damages the deceased could have recovered for loss of earnings in his or her lost years, which are not recoverable (s 1(2)(a)(ii)), and the further exception of any claim for bereavement the deceased may have had (s 1(1A)).

12.1.2.3   Dependants' losses not recoverable

The estate *cannot* recover damages in respect of any loss *resulting* from death, or which arises because of the death (s 1(2)(c)). Such loss is not the deceased's own loss, but is his or her dependants' loss, and can be recovered by them under the FAA 1976. The single exception to this is funeral expenses, where the funeral was paid for out of the deceased's estate.

12.1.2.4   Damages form part of deceased's estate

The claimant(s) will be the deceased's personal representative(s)—the executor(s) or administrator of the estate. Damages recovered under the LR(MP)A 1934 form part of the estate and will be distributed in accordance with the terms of the deceased's will or the rules of intestacy.

12.1.3   The right of action under the FAA 1976

12.1.3.1   Sections 1 to 5 of the Act

Sections 1-5 of the FAA (as amended) provide:

> ### 1 Right of action for wrongful act causing death
>
> *(1) If death is caused by any wrongful act, neglect or default which is such as would (if death had not ensued) have entitled the person injured to maintain an action and recover damages in respect thereof the person who would have been liable if death had not ensued shall be liable to an action for damages, notwithstanding the death of the person injured.*
>
> *(2) Subject to section 1A(2) below, every such action shall be for the benefit of the dependants of the person ('the deceased') whose death has been so caused.*
>
> *(3) In this Act 'dependant' means—*
>
> > *(a) the wife or husband or former wife or husband of the deceased;*
> >
> > *(aa) the civil partner or former civil partner of the deceased;*
> >
> > *(b) any person who—*
> >
> > > *(i) was living with the deceased in the same household immediately before the date of the death; and*
> > >
> > > *(ii) had been living with the deceased in the same household for at least two years before that date; and*
> > >
> > > *(iii) was living during the whole of that period as the husband or wife or civil partner of the deceased;*
> >
> > *(c) any parent or other ascendant of the deceased;*
> >
> > *(d) any person who was treated by the deceased as his parent;*
> >
> > *(e) any child or other descendant of the deceased;*
> >
> > *(f) any person (not being a child of the deceased) who, in the case of any marriage to which the deceased was at any time a party, was treated by the deceased as a child of the family in relation to that marriage;*
> >
> > *(fa) any person (not being a child of the deceased) who, in the case of any civil partnership in which the deceased was at any time a civil partner, was treated by the deceased as a child of the family in reltion to that civil partnership;*

(g) *any person who is, or is the issue of, a brother, sister, uncle or aunt of the deceased.*

(4) The reference to the former wife or husband of the deceased in subsection (3)(a0) above includes a reference to a person whose marriage to the deceased has been annulled or declared void as well as a person whose marriage to the deceased has been dissolved.

(4A) The reference to the former civil partner of the deceased in subsection (3)(aa) above includes a reference to a person whose civil partnership with the deceased has beenannulled as well as a person whose civil partnership with the deceased has been dissolved.

(5) In deducing any relationship for the purposes of subsection (3) above—

(a) any relationship by marriage or civil partnership shall be treated as a relationship by cosanguinity, any relationship of the half blood as a relationship of the whole blood, and the stepchild of any person as his child, and

(b) an illegitimate person shall be treated as the legitimate child of his mother andputed father.

(6) Any reference in this Act to injury includes any disease and any impairment of a person's phyical or mental condition.

1A Bereavement

(1) An action under this Act may consist of or include a claim for damages for bereavement.

(2) A claim for damages for bereavement shall only be for the benefit—

(a) of the wife or husband or civil partner of the deceased; and

(b) where the deceased was a minor who was never married or a civil partner—

(i) of his parents, if he was legitimate; and

(ii) of his mother, if he was illegitimate.

(3) Subject to subsection (5) below, the sum to be awarded as damages under this section shall be £10,000.

(4) Where there is a claim for damages under this section for the benefit of both the parents of the deceased, the sum awarded shall be divided equally between them (subject to any deduction falling to be made in respect of costs not recovered from the defendant).

(5) The Lord Chancellor may by order made by statutory instrument, subject to annulment in pursuance of a resolution of either House of Parliament, amend this section by varying the sum for the time being specified in subsection (3) above.

2 Persons entitled to bring the action

(1) The action shall be brought by and in the name of the executor or administrator of the deceased.

(2) If—

(a) there is no executor or administrator of the deceased, or

(b) no action is brought within six months after the death by and in the name of an executor or administrator of the deceased,

the action may be brought by and in the name of all or any of the persons for whose benefit an executor or administrator could have brought it.

(3) Not more than one action shall lie for and in respect of the same subject matter of complaint.

(4) The plaintiff in the action shall be required to deliver to the defendant or his solicitor full particulars of the persons for whom and on whose behalf the action is brought and of the nature of the claim in respect of which damages are sought to be recovered.

3 Assessment of damages

(1) In the action such damages, other than damages for bereavement, may be awarded as are proportioned to the injury resulting from the death to the dependants respectively.

(2) After deducting the costs not recovered from the defendant any amount recovered otherwise than as damages for bereavement shall be divided among the dependants in such shares as may be directed.

(3) In an action under this Act where there fall to be assessed damages payable to a widowin respect of the death of her husband there shall not be taken into account the remarriage of the widow or her prospects of remarriage.

(4) In an action under this Act where there fall to be assessed damages payable to a person who is a dependant by virtue of section 1(3)(b) above in respect of the death of the person with whom the dependant was living as husband or wife or civil partner there shall be taken into account (together with any other

matter that appears to the court to be relevant to the action) the fact that the dependant had no enforceable right to financial support by the deceased as a result of their living together.

(5) If the dependants have incurred funeral expenses in respect of the deceased, damages may be awarded in respect of those expenses.

(6) Money paid into court in satisfaction of a cause of action under this Act may be in one sum without specifying any person's share.

4 Assessment of damages: disregard of benefits

In assessing damages in respect of a person's death in an action under this Act, benefits which have accrued or will or may accrue to any person from his estate or otherwise as a result of his death shall be disregarded.

5 Contributory negligence

Where any person dies as the result partly of his own fault and partly of the fault of any other person or persons, and accordingly if an action were brought for the benefit of the estate under the Law Reform (Miscellaneous Provisions) Act 1934 the damages recoverable would be reduced under section 1(1) of the Law Reform (Contributory Negligence) Act 1945, any damages recoverable in an action under this Act shall be reduced to a proportionate extent.

12.1.3.2   Basis of the right of action and recovery

The right of action under the FAA 1976 arises because of, and only because of, the deceased's death. It belongs to the dependants, who can recover damages in respect of the loss they have suffered as a result of his or her death. They can recover nothing of what the deceased himself or herself could have recovered: such damages belong to the estate and are recoverable under the LR(MP)A 1934. They can recover nothing in respect of losses they would have suffered even if the deceased had survived: such damages could either have been recovered by the deceased, or the dependants will have a separate right of action in their own name (eg, in respect of their own personal injuries).

12.1.3.3   Who brings the claim?

Although the right of action belongs to the dependants, and damages will in the end be paid to them, the claim is prima facie brought by the executor or administrator of the estate (s 2(1)). Not every de facto dependant has a right of action, only those brought within the Act by s 1(3), (4) and (5).

12.1.3.4   Dependants must have a cause of action

The dependants must also have a cause of action. For the purposes of their claim they 'borrow' whatever cause of action the deceased had, the same cause of action which survives for the benefit of the estate under the LR(MP)A 1934. If the deceased had no cause of action, the dependants also have none.

12.1.4   The relationship between the two claims

There will almost invariably be a claim under both Acts, with the same claimant and using the same cause of action to establish liability. Beyond that there is no longer any connection between the claims. Each is for different damages on behalf of different persons. The only exception to this is funeral expenses, which can be recovered under either Act, depending on who paid for the funeral (LR(MP)A 1934, s 1(2)(c); FAA 1976, s 3(5)).

Before 1983 there was a symbiotic relationship between the two claims: the estate could recover damages in respect of the deceased's earnings over the lost years, which could only be assessed by reference to the FAA award; and damages awarded to the estate under the LR(MP)A 1934 usually had to be taken into account in quantifying the FAA award. This relationship was, thankfully, effectively severed by the AJA 1982, which inserted s 1(2)(a)(ii) into LR(MP)A 1934 and rewrote FAA 1976, s 4, but you need to be aware of this history to understand reported cases.

12.1.5 Where the deceased has commenced a claim for personal injury

It is not uncommon that an injured person commences a claim for personal injury, but dies before the claim is complete, or soon after damages are awarded. What is the position then of the estate and dependants?

12.1.5.1 Where the claim is still pending

In these circumstances, the estate has the right to continue the claim under the LR(MP)A 1934, but that will not be sufficient in itself because the estate cannot recover any damages in respect of the deceased's future loss of earnings (s 1(2)(a)(ii)). It is these damages which would have provided for the dependants after the deceased's death and so the dependants will need to recover their loss by a separate claim under the FAA 1976. This is a distinct claim, and may be pursued even when the deceased's personal injury claim has been discontinued (*Reader v Molesworth Bright Clegg* [2007] 3 All ER 107).

12.1.5.2 Where the deceased had recovered damages in full

The dependants' claim under the FAA 1976 is likely to be limited to bereavement and funeral expenses. The damages awarded to the deceased were intended to restore him or her to the position he or she would have been in had he or she not been injured (including, if necessary, damages for lost earnings in the lost years), and so they cannot show that they have suffered any additional loss of dependency as a result of the death.

12.1.5.3 Where the deceased had recovered provisional damages

The position is now governed by s 3 of the Damages Act 1996, which provides:

> *(1) This section applies where a person—*
> > *(a) is awarded provisional damages; and*
> > *(b) subsequently dies as a result of the act or omission which gave rise to the cause of claim for which the damages were awarded.*
>
> *(2) The award of the provisional damages shall not operate as a bar to a claim in respect of that person's death under the Fatal Accidents Act 1976.*
>
> *(3) Such part (if any) of—*
> > *(a) the provisional damages; and*
> > *(b) any further damages awarded to the person in question before his death,*
>
> *118 as was intended to compensate him for pecuniary loss in a period which in the event falls after his death shall be taken into account in assessing the amount of any loss of support suffered by the person or persons for whose benefit the claim under the Fatal Accidents Act 1976 is brought.*
>
> *(4) No award of further damages made in respect of that person after his death shall include any amount for loss of income in respect of any period after his death.*
>
> *(5) In this section 'provisional damages' means damages awarded by virtue of subsection (2)(a) of section 32A of the Supreme Court Act 1981 or section 51 of the County Courts Act 1984 and 'further damages' means damages awarded by virtue of subsection (2)(b) of either of those sections.*
>
> *(6) Subsection (2) above applies whether the award of provisional damages was before or after the coming into force of that subsection; and subsections (3) and (4) apply to any award of damages under the 1976 Act or, as the case may be, further damages after the coming into force of those subsections.*
>
> *(7) . . .*

Section 3 sorts out a problem that existed when a claimant commenced a claim for personal injury, and was awarded provisional damages, but then died. In such a case the dependants were precluded from suing for their lost dependency under the FAA 1976 and it was unclear whether the estate, under the LR(MP)A 1934, could continue the personal injury claim and seek a further award under s 32A of the Supreme Court Act 1981, including damages for lost earnings in the 'lost years'.

Section 3 adopts the sensible solution. In such cases, a barrier is brought down on the personal injury claim—the estate can only seek a further award under s 32A in respect of the deceased's losses up to the date of death. Instead, the dependants can bring a claim under the FAA 1976 for their lost dependency, but account must be taken of any damages the deceased received as compensation for losses in the period after death and which the dependants may have inherited.

12.2 Quantification of damages under the LR(MP)A 1934

12.2.1 General principles

Since the claim is basically a claim by the deceased for damages for personal injury, damages will be quantified upon the same principles and in the same stages as a personal injury claim. The total sum, however, is likely to be relatively small, since there is no claim for any future loss. It is only likely to be substantial if there was a significant delay between accident and death.

12.2.2 Special damages

Special damages are likely to be small, unless they include, for example, damage to a motor vehicle, lost earnings between accident and death, or funeral expenses. On the other hand, there will usually be some special damages sufficient to justify a claim under the LR(MP)A 1934, even if nothing else is recoverable under this Act.

12.2.3 General damages

The only head of general damages recoverable is pain and suffering and loss of amenity, and then only if there was a significant period of time between the accident and death. If death was instantaneous or nearly instantaneous, nothing is recoverable, since any pain and suffering is in reality part of the death (*Hicks v Chief Constable of South Yorkshire* [1992] 1 All ER 690). If the deceased was unconscious between the accident and death, damages for loss of amenity only are recoverable. The longer the deceased survived after the accident, the greater the award will be, but it is still going to be small compared to what would be given to an injured claimant with a life-time's pain, suffering and loss of amenity ahead of him or her.

12.2.4 Deductions

The award will be subject to any deductions that would have been made in a personal injury claim (see **11.14**).

12.2.5 Contributory negligence

The award will be subject to reduction for the deceased's contributory negligence (see **11.15**).

12.2.6 Interest

Interest will be added as in personal injury claims (see **11.16**).

12.2.7 Recovery of benefits

The compensator will be liable to repay benefits under the Social Security (Recovery of Benefits) Act 1997, but will be able to reduce the damages paid to the deceased's estate in the usual way (see **11.17**).

12.3 Quantification of damages under the FAA 1976

12.3.1 The sole head of damages

With the single and simple exception of damages for bereavement (s 1A), the loss recoverable under the FAA 1976 is wholly financial loss, and what is being assessed is the value of the 'dependency', which is the only head of damages. The dependency consists of:

- the amount the deceased would have applied to the benefit of his or her dependants;
- any additional expense the dependants have been put to as a result of his or her death; and
- any additional losses the dependants have suffered as a result of his or her death

over the period for which they would have remained dependent.

If the dependants have suffered loss of income, it does not matter what the source of that income was. So, for example, if the deceased's only source of income was state benefits, and as a result of his or her death those benefits are no longer payable, the dependants can recover their loss to the extent that the lost benefits were applied to their support (*Cox v Hockenhull* [1999] 3 All ER 577).

12.3.2 The seven-stage process

The quantification of damages is a seven-stage process:

Stage 1:   Calculate the pre-trial loss.
Stage 2:   Assess the future loss.
Stage 3:   Add lump sums.
Stage 4:   Add bereavement.
Stage 5:   Contributory negligence.
Stage 6:   Add interest.
Stage 7:   Apportion between dependants.

12.4 Stage 1: calculate the pre-trial loss

12.4.1 What is the pre-trial loss?

The pre-trial loss is the total value of the dependency so far, that is from the date of death to the date of trial (or the date of settlement or the date on which you are advising as to quantum). It is roughly equivalent to the special damages in a personal injury claim.

Like special damages it is, in theory at least, precisely ascertainable: in reality a great deal of estimation may be required, but it should still be quantified as accurately as possible.

12.4.2   The approaches that may be adopted

The basic principle of assessment is exactly the same in every case: the court is trying to put a value on each of the three aspects of the dependency (see **12.3.1**). However, the items that will be included within the dependency vary according to the relationship between the dependants and the deceased, and so the court's approach to the assessment tends to vary as well. There are three main approaches that may be adopted:

(a) The item by item approach—where each item of loss and expenditure is added up one by one.

(b) The earnings minus living expenses approach—where the court looks at what the deceased earned, takes away personal living expenses, and assumes whatever is left to be the dependency.

(c) The conventional percentage approach—where the court assesses the likely dependency as $x\%$ of the deceased's earnings.

These three approaches are not mutually exclusive: the court may use a little of each. Where the claim is for the death of a husband/father, however, the modern practice is to use the conventional percentage approach almost exclusively.

Whether an item is to be included or not is simply a matter of evidence. What approach the court adopts to assessment will also depend on the evidence, or the lack of it, and convenience. It is easiest to look at the assessment process according to certain, well established types of claim, but there is no rule that any item of dependency can only be recovered in certain types of claim; it is recoverable wherever it exists. Do not therefore be misled into generalisation: every case depends on its own facts.

12.4.3   Claims for the death of a husband/father

12.4.3.1   The item by item approach

This approach is only likely to be possible, but will be the most reliable, where there exist detailed household accounts. It is, however, difficult to persuade a judge to use this approach, rather than the quick and simple conventional percentage approach.

Where the husband was the breadwinner, and the dependants are his wife and children, or just his wife, the items likely to form a part of the dependency are:

- Housekeeping money.
- Rent, mortgage instalments.
- Council tax.
- Repairs, maintenance, decoration, cleaning.
- Fuel bills.
- Telephone.
- Clothing.
- School fees.
- Costs of running a car, travel and transport.
- Holidays and outings.

- Gifts, entertainments, sports and leisure, pets.
- Pocket money.
- Insurance.
- TV rental.
- One-off purchases, eg, furniture, luxury goods.

12.4.3.2 Deductions

From each of these any element of the deceased's own living expenses must be deducted (housekeeping money, for example, is likely to include an element of his food and keep). Expenditure which is joint, ie, where there is no saving as a result of death (eg, rent, fuel bills), does not have to be reduced. (Note the difference between this rule and the rule for living expenses in a lost years claim: see **11.10.7.2.**)

12.4.3.3 Other losses

To this add any other losses. For example, the widow may as a result of her husband's death have had to give up work for a while and so have lost earnings; the family may have lost other free perks from the deceased's employers. Also add any loss of benefits in kind, or additional expenditure the dependants have been put to. Common examples are:

(a) The value of D-I-Y work around the home, where the deceased used to carry out repairs and improvements, which can have considerable annual value. Take care to include only the value of the work, not the cost of materials.

(b) The value of fruit and vegetables grown by the husband in the garden or allotment.

(c) The loss of use of a company car for private purposes.

(d) The loss of other employee's perks: eg, health insurance; free goods or services; school fees.

12.4.3.4 Total the loss

If the evidence of the family's expenditure is on a weekly basis, calculate the amount per week and multiply by the number of weeks between death and trial. Similarly if the accounts are monthly. Some benefits in kind are more easily valued on an annual basis, in which case bring them in at that stage.

12.4.3.5 The 'earnings minus living expenses' approach

Where the evidence is not complete enough for the item by item approach, the court may use the quicker and easier earnings minus living expenses approach. Take the deceased's net earnings (weekly or monthly) and deduct his personal living expenses. His living expenses under the FAA 1976 include all that he spent exclusively on himself, both needs and pleasures, but *not* a portion of any expenditure for the joint benefit of himself and his dependants. What is left will be the prima facie value of the dependency, to which can be added any additional losses or benefits in kind. This approach is now almost entirely obsolete.

12.4.3.6 The conventional percentage approach

These days the court is likely to save time and trouble by going directly to a conventional percentage figure. This is 75% where the dependants are widow and child(ren), or 67% where the widow is the sole dependant; ie, the court assesses the dependency as 75% or 67% of the deceased's net earnings (see *Harris v Empress Motors Ltd* [1984] 1 WLR 212).

12.4.3.7   Arriving at a percentage

Whatever approach has been used, it is usually helpful to express the dependency as a percentage of the deceased's net earnings. This makes it easier to take account of any likely increases in pay over the pre-trial period.

12.4.3.8   Changes in the value of the dependency between death and trial

These must be taken into account—both actual changes and changes that would have occurred but for the husband's death. The most obvious example of an actual change is a child who becomes financially independent at some point during the pre-trial period. His or her dependency obviously comes to an end, or at least is very substantially reduced from that time.

But there is usually likely to be some evidence of changes that would have occurred as well. The deceased's earnings might well have increased during the pre-trial period through pay rises, promotion, career moves, building up a business, etc. If this is the case the question arises, would the dependency have increased as well? If there would have been no increase, simply value the dependency as at the date of death and multiply by the appropriate number of weeks or months. If the increase in the dependency would have been in proportion to the increased earnings, the percentage approach is helpful. The dependency continues to be the same fixed percentage of the increased net pay. But if there would have been an increase proportionally greater or smaller than the increase in earnings, then an adjustment will have to be made to the percentage. Similar considerations apply if the deceased's earnings would have fallen during the pre-trial period, for example as a result of retirement. In the absence of evidence to the contrary, assume that the dependency would have increased or decreased in line with the change in income, applying the fixed percentage.

12.4.3.9   Deceased's savings

If the deceased saved regularly, the money may or may not be part of the dependency, according to how he would eventually have spent it. If some of it would eventually have been applied to his dependants' benefit and he saved regularly, then a suitable portion of the savings can be added to the weekly or monthly dependency. If savings were irregular, it may be more appropriate to add a lump sum at Stage 3.

12.4.3.10   Widow's remarriage or prospects of remarriage

These are not to be taken into account in assessing her dependency (FAA 1976, s 3(3)). However, if the claim is for the death of a breadwinner wife, the husband's remarriage or prospects must be taken into account.

12.4.3.11   Widow's earnings or earning capacity

Where a widow has lost earnings as a result of the death, this loss forms part of the dependency. Where a widow was a working woman both before and after the death, clearly her earnings are irrelevant to her claim under the FAA 1976. A non-working widow's earning capacity can usually be ignored (*Howitt v Heads* [1973] QB 64). If she goes out to work after her husband's death her earnings should probably be ignored, even if she would not have worked but for her husband's death: the earnings are simply a realisation of her earning capacity, not a gain resulting from the death.

12.4.3.12   Family living beyond its means

It may be that the amount the deceased was spending on himself and his dependants was more than he was earning. If this was being paid for out of his capital, then the dependency can be valued at its actual rate but account must be taken of how long the capital would have lasted. If it was being subsidised by a loan, the value of the depend-ency will be reduced to take account of the amount the deceased would have had to repay.

12.4.4   Claim for the death of a wife/mother

12.4.4.1   The items forming the dependency

Where the wife was working, the value of her contribution to the family expenses can be quantified in much the same way as for a husband (see **12.4.3**). But whether the wife was working or not, the main item in the dependency is likely to be the value of her services as a wife and mother. There may also be a claim for lost benefits in kind—where the wife did D-I-Y work, or made clothes for her husband and children, for example.

12.4.4.2   Assessing the value of a wife's services

The value of a wife's services is not easily quantified, and is very much in the court's discretion. At the very least it is likely to be assessed as the cost of employing a home-help and/or a housekeeper. Nevertheless, there is a good argument for looking at a wife's services more broadly and valuing each service she performed for the family, not just those that a housekeeper can perform (*Regan v Williamson* [1976] 1 WLR 305). Where the wife was in full-time employment, the amount of time she had available to care for the family is less than it would have been if she were a full-time housewife, and so the value of her services is proportionally less (see, eg, *Cresswell v Eaton* [1991] 1 All ER 484). Where the wife was a poor mother, the value of her services will be lower (see *Stanley v Saddique* [1992] QB 1).

If the husband has reasonably given up his work in order to stay at home and look after the home and children, then the dependency may be assessed on the basis of the husband's lost earnings (*Mehmet v Perry* [1977] 2 All ER 529). Similarly if a relative has given up full-time work in order to be able to do so, the dependency may be based on that relative's loss of earnings. But if the relative's full-time care replaces only part-time care by the mother a discount will need to be made (*Cresswell v Eaton*).

Where a father is the defendant being sued in respect of his wife's death, and he has given up work to look after their children, the value of the services he is providing should be set off against the value of the mother's services lost, so as to reduce the children's claim (*Hayden v Hayden* [1992] 4 All ER 681).

12.4.5   Claims for the death of a parent

Where the dependants claiming are simply the children, either because both parents were killed simultaneously, or the family was a one-parent family, or because the surviving parent has no claim since he or she is the defendant being sued, some special considerations apply.

To the extent that the children's claim is for the death of their father who provided financial support, it can be quantified as in **12.4.3**. To the extent that the children's claim is for the death of their mother, it cannot be quantified simply on the basis of the cost of employing a housekeeper, for they have lost more than this. It may be appropriate to assess the cost of providing a full-time nanny for the children, if they are young, and this loss is recoverable even if no nanny in fact needs to be employed because the children are being looked after by a relative (*Hay v Hughes* [1975] QB 790). Alternatively, particularly when the children are older, it may be more appropriate to assess their loss on the basis of the cost of providing a foster home; at the very least some account must be taken of the fact that they will not need a nanny throughout the period of their dependency (*Spittle v Bunney* [1988] 3 All ER 1031).

If the children have been legally adopted since the death of their parents, their dependency from the date of adoption will be limited to any difference between the value of the dependency provided by their father (assuming he was the breadwinner) and that provided by their adoptive father. The care provided by the adoptive mother replaces that provided by the natural mother and so a claim for the value of their mother's services comes to an end on adoption (see *Watson v Willmott* [1991] 1 QB 140).

12.4.6   Claims for the death of a child

Where the claim is made by parents in respect of the death of their child, the dependency is likely to be assessed item by item and to be fairly small. If the child was adult, and was in fact supporting his or her parents at the date of death, account must be taken of the likelihood that this support would have diminished or ceased if he or she left home or got married. In the case of a minor child the parents have lost little more than the chance that they might have received some support in the future, plus the occasional gifts.

12.4.7   Claims by other dependants

A claim by a cohabitee or civil partner can be assessed in the same way as a claim by a husband or wife; claims by grandchildren or grandparents, if appropriate, in the same way as claims by children and parents. In the case of other relatives, the claim is likely to be very small and can be quantified item by item.

12.4.8   Funeral expenses

Having calculated all the rest of the pre-trial loss, add funeral expenses if they were incurred by the dependants.

12.5   Stage 2: assess the future loss

The future loss to the dependants consists of (a) the loss of dependency over the remainder of the deceased's working life, and (b) the loss of dependency flowing from the deceased's pension, where the dependants would have received any benefit from it. A widow cannot however recover in respect of her husband's retirement pension if she has instead received a widow's pension under the same scheme from her husband's employers (*Auty v National Coal Board* [1985] 1 All ER 930).

12.5.1   The multiplicand

The multiplicand is the annual value of the dependency as at the date of trial. It takes account of all the items dealt with under Stage 1, and includes the three aspects of the dependency (see **12.3.1**). It also takes account of any likely changes in the value of the dependency that would have occurred between the date of death and the date of trial. Everything that has been said in **12.4** with regard to the dependency applies equally to the future loss. The multiplicand is the answer to the question 'What is the annual loss as at today's date?'

Although a widow's earning capacity can usually be ignored, it may need to be taken into account where, for example, a widow has lost her job because of her husband's death, but can reasonably be expected to resume work soon (*Cookson v Knowles* [1977] QB 913). A widow's future earnings or earning capacity may also be taken into account in assessing the value of the children's dependency where they are claiming for the death of their father (*Dodds v Dodds* [1978] QB 543).

As with personal injury claims, there is likely to be a growing tendency to make split awards in the future. Where there is evidence that the deceased's earnings would have increased at some point after death, the court will achieve the most accurate assessment of the dependency by taking separate multiplicands for separate periods, and apportioning the multiplier. There may be a single multiplicand for the whole of the period of dependency (the deceased's and the dependants' joint lives), or the period may be divided into the years before retirement, and the pension years, with the first multiplicand being based on the deceased's net earnings and the second based on the annual value to the dependants of the deceased's pension.

12.5.2 The multiplier

12.5.2.1 Introduction

As in personal injury cases, the multiplier is not a real number of years, but is discounted to take account of accelerated receipt and contingencies. It represents the number of years for which the dependency would have lasted. This is prima facie the deceased's and dependants' joint lives. In the case of a deceased husband and widow, the dependency would have lasted until the first of them died.

Following the decision in *Wells v Wells* [1998] 3 All ER 481, it would seem incongruous not to take an actuarial approach to the quantification of damages. The conventional approach was even more intuitive and unscientific in fatal accident claims than it was in personal injury claims. But *Wells v Wells* was concerned only with personal injury claims, and no more modern approach has yet been approved by the Court of Appeal or House of Lords. Section D to the explanatory notes to the Ogden Tables explains how the tables can be used to quantify damages in fatal accident cases with reasonable accuracy. However, this approach results in a much more complicated calculation than that in personal injury cases. It cannot at present be stated with any confidence, therefore, that this is the correct approach to use.

12.5.2.2 The conventional approach

Before *Wells v Wells* the multiplier was selected in a manner very similar to that used in personal injury cases (see **11.10.3.2**). The period being measured was the period from the deceased's date of death (not the date of trial as in personal injury claims) and the end of the period of dependency. This had to be estimated taking into account the deceased's age, the age(s) of the dependant(s), the deceased's likely retirement age, the deceased's and dependants' life expectancy, and a large number of other variables such as job security, promotion prospects, health, etc. A fairly substantial discount was made for contingencies and uncertainties, and a discount for accelerated receipt based on a notional rate of return on investment of 4–5%. Tables in *Kemp & Kemp* enabled comparisons with previous cases to be made, and the final result was usually a rough and ready approximation.

12.5.2.3   The conventional approach today

Even without an approved new method of calculation, it seems that the conventional approach is too out of date to use. At the very least a discount rate of 2.5% should surely be used, which renders tables of multipliers in pre-*Wells* cases useless, and necessitates some reference to the Ogden Tables. This would suggest that the following method might be appropriate.

First decide whether to assess the dependencies for the pre-retirement years and the pension years together or separately. If they are to be taken together, then use Ogden Tables 1 and 2, looking under the 2.5% column. In the case of a husband and wife, look up the multiplier for a male of the age the deceased was at the date of his death, and the multiplier for a female of the age the widow was at that date: whichever is the smaller figure will be the correct multiplier to take as a starting point.

Alternatively, the working years and retirement years may be calculated separately. Use Tables 3–14 to find the multiplier for the dependency up to the deceased's retirement, and Tables 15–26 for the pension loss after that date. A widow is entitled to recover a sum in respect of her husband's retirement pension, where she would have derived benefit from it.

12.5.2.4   Discount for contingencies

The multiplier found by the above method must then be discounted to take account of contingencies other than mortality, as in personal injury cases. There is no easy guide as to how this should be done. It is necessary to take account of contingencies relating not only to the deceased, but also to all of the dependants. The result in the past was a rather bigger discount than might have been made in a personal injury case. This ought logically to continue to be the case. In the absence of anything better, since this is still a less than accurate method of selecting the multiplier, it is likely that the courts will continue to make the conventional discount of 10%, at least, making further adjustments as necessary.

12.5.2.5   Other contingencies

There are a large number of other contingencies which may have a specific effect, and cause the multiplier to be adjusted upwards or downwards:

(a) Evidence of the deceased's actual life expectancy. If this can be shown to be plainly lower or greater than average for a person of the deceased's age, an adjustment may need to be made.

(b) The possibility of divorce. The fact that at the deceased's death the marriage was showing signs of collapse does not mean that the dependency is automatically reduced: a dependant's right to financial support continues even after divorce, and so the dependency might well have been unaffected. However, the possibility also exists that after divorce the deceased would have remarried, which might have resulted in a diminished level of support for the first spouse, so the risk of divorce may be a relevant factor (*Martin v Owen* The Times, 21 May 1992).

(c) Children's ages and marriage prospects. The court should be aware of how long any children would have remained dependent on the deceased. The actual dependency of young children is obviously longer than that of adult or nearly adult children, and may be a factor affecting the multiplier. Similarly the age at which the children will cease full-time education and become financially independent is material. These matters will certainly make a difference when the children alone are the dependants. However, they will not normally do so when there is also a dependent spouse. When children cease to be dependent, the usual expectation is that the dependency of the spouse simply increases proportionately, so no adjustment needs to be made.

(d) The fact that a cohabitee had no enforceable right to financial support by the deceased (FAA 1976, s 3(4)). This must result in some reduction in the multiplier, since the cohabitee's dependency was less secure than a spouse's.

12.5.2.6   Factors which do not affect the multiplier

The following factors do not affect the choice of multiplier to be used in assessing future loss:

(a) A widow's remarriage or prospects of remarriage. This is expressly excluded from consideration by FAA 1976, s 3(3).

(b) The likelihood of future inflation (*Cookson v Knowles* [1979] AC 556). This is the same principle as for personal injury (see **11.10.3.10**). The decision in *Hodgson v Trapp* (see **11.10.3.6**) must by implication apply also to claims under the FAA 1976.

12.5.2.7   A single multiplier

Although there may be several dependants, nevertheless in the vast majority of cases the dependency has conventionally been assessed as a single sum, there being just one multiplier to take account of all the dependants' claims. This is because, if the deceased had a certain amount of money available to support any dependants, that sum would have been spread among them in some way or other, but would not have been affected overall by their individual needs. However, in a minority of cases, where it seems that the circumstances of the case demand it, the court has assessed the multiplier and multiplicand for each dependant separately, and it may be that after *Wells v Wells* it will do so more frequently.

12.5.2.8   Deduct the pre-trial period

The multiplier chosen by the above method runs from the date of death. Since the dependency for the pre-trial period has already been calculated separately, the actual multiplier to be applied to the annual future loss is therefore what is left after deducting the pre-trial period (*Graham v Dodds* [1983] 2 All ER 953). So if, for example, the multiplier selected is 16, and the period from death to trial is 3 years 9 months, the multiplier applied to the future loss is 12.25. (Distinguish the rule in personal injury claims (see **11.10.3.10**).) But where the pre-trial period has virtually swallowed up the multiplier, the court may take this into account and adjust the multiplier upwards to permit some future loss—see *Corbett v Barking, Havering and Brentwood Health Authority* [1991] 2 QB 408 (true dependency 18 years, multiplier prima facie 12, but pre-trial period $11\frac{1}{2}$ years, so multiplier increased to 15, allowing $3\frac{1}{2}$ years' future loss).

12.5.3   Split awards

As suggested above, it may become increasingly common for the court to make split awards when calculating the future dependency. It may value different periods of the dependency with a different multiplicand, it may take the working years separately from the pension years, it may take the dependency of each dependant separately. The manner of calculation will be as explained in **11.10.4**.

12.5.4 Taking Stages 1 and 2 together

When advising on the quantum of damage, if there is no evidence as to how the dependency would have increased after death, then there is little point in assessing the pre-trial loss and the future loss separately. Simply value the dependency as at the date of death and apply a suitable multiplier without deducting the pre-trial period.

12.5.5 The Ogden approach to future loss

As mentioned above, Sir Michael Ogden in his explanatory notes to the Tables proposed a more actuarial approach to the calculation of future loss. This has not yet had the approval of any higher court, and it is arguably in contradiction with the House of Lords decision in *Cookson v Knowles* [1979] AC 556 (though Ogden argued that it is not). It involves changing the rule that the multiplier runs from the date of death, and it involves calculating the dependency in three separate amounts: the pre-trial period, the pre-retirement period and the pension period. It also involves calculating the dependency of each dependant separately. It is fully explained in Section D of the Explanatory Notes, to which you should refer if you wish to use this method. Although it is lengthy, it is clearly explained and it is not any more difficult than the method of selecting and refining the multiplier in personal injury cases.

12.6 Stage 3: add lump sums

There can be added to the total sum arrived at so far any lump sums which it can be shown that the dependants would have benefited from in the future—for example, the deceased's savings or capital.

12.7 Stage 4: add bereavement

The spouse of the deceased or the parents of an unmarried minor (but no other dependants) can recover damages for bereavement, quantified as a fixed lump sum (FAA 1976, s 1A). The sum can be specified from time to time by the Lord Chancellor and is currently £10,000 (or £7,500 for causes of action accruing before 1 April 2002). The parents of an unmarried child cannot recover damages for bereavement where he or she was under 18 at the date of injury but over 18 on the date of death (*Doleman v Deakin* The Times, 30 January 1990).

12.8 Stage 5: contributory negligence

The total sum quantified so far must be reduced if there has been a finding of contributory negligence by the deceased. Take off the appropriate percentage.

Contributory negligence by a dependant must also be taken into account, but only as regards that dependant's share of the dependency (an example of a situation where the dependency for each dependant will have to be assessed separately).

12.9   Stage 6: add interest

Interest will be awarded by the court under SCA 1981, s 35A. By s 35A(2) the award is prima facie mandatory, unless there are special reasons for the contrary. The guidelines for the award of interest were laid down by *Cookson v Knowles* [1979] AC 556.

- Interest is awarded on the pre-trial loss from the date of death to the date of trial at half the 'appropriate rate'. For the meaning of 'appropriate rate' see **11.16.2**.

- Interest is awarded on damages for bereavement at the full appropriate rate from the date of death to the date of trial (*Prior v Hastie* [1987] CLY 1219).

- No interest is awarded on damages for future loss.

When advising on the quantum of damages it is not usual to make any attempt to calculate interest.

12.10   Stage 7: apportion between dependants

Although there is usually only one multiplier and damages are awarded as a single lump sum, the court must indicate how that sum is to be divided up between the dependants (FAA 1976, s 3(2)). The apportionment must bear some relationship to the comparative value of each dependant's dependency, but does not have to be exact.

The only difficulties arise when apportioning between a widow and child(ren). The widow always gets the larger share, which will include the joint dependency of the family as a whole. The children, on the other hand, get all that is truly their share of the dependency, not just 'pocket money' (*Benson v Biggs Wall & Co Ltd* [1982] 3 All ER 300). The greater the number of children, the younger the children are, the larger their share. There is a table showing reported apportionment in *Kemp & Kemp* at 36-195.

Damages for bereavement are not, of course, apportioned.

12.11   Deductions

You might have expected Stage 5 to be 'make any necessary deductions' but it is not, because there are no deductions. This is the effect of FAA 1976, s 4, which provides that any benefits which have accrued, or will accrue, to the dependants as a result of the deceased's death are to be disregarded. No deduction needs to be made, therefore, in respect of sums inherited from the estate, damages recovered under the LR(MP)A 1934, widow's pension, widow's benefit, insurance money, charitable donations, or anything else, even where the result is that the dependants are better off than they would have been but for the death (see, eg, *Pidduck v Eastern Scottish Omnibuses Ltd* [1990] 2 All ER 69 and *McIntyre v Harland & Wolff plc* [2007] 2 All ER 24). Nor can any deduction be made for the value of benefits in money's worth: for example, where a father's second wife is providing a higher standard of motherly services than the children's deceased mother ever did (*Stanley v Saddique* [1992] QB 1). However, s 4 does not prevent the value of a father's services being set off against the value of the deceased mother's services (*Hayden v Hayden* [1992] 4 All ER 681).

Where children were cared for by their mother, who died in the fatal accident, and their care has been taken over by their father, who but for the accident would probably have made no contribution to their welfare, the father's care is a benefit to be disregarded under s 4. However the damages received by the children for the loss of their mother's services are held on trust for the father, who is to be reimbursed for the services he has provided and will provide in the future (*ATH v MS* [2002] NLJ 969).

12.12 No recovery of benefits

A person making a compensation payment under the FAA 1976 is not liable to repay benefits under the Social Security (Recovery of Benefits) Act 1997 (Social Security (Recovery of Benefits) Regulations 1997 (SI 1997/2237), reg 2(2)(a)).

Other equitable remedies

This can only be a brief outline of some of the other important equitable remedies. For further discussion see Goff and Jones, *Law of Restitution* and *Snell on Equity*.

13.1 Personal and proprietary claims

Remedies such as suing for damages for tort or breach of contract are personal remedies, which means that if the person sued is insolvent the client is unlikely to recover any money (subject to any security taken as part of a contractual arrangement).

A few remedies, most notably trust remedies and tracing, give rights *in rem*, which means that the remedy is strictly against the property rather than the wrongdoer, so it is unaffected by the insolvency of the wrongdoer. Provided the claim is made out, and the property can be identified, it belongs to the person seeking the remedy and no other creditor can make claims to it.

13.2 Tracing

Tracing is available where property is taken and dealt with contrary to a person's fiduciary duties. It is mainly used in the context of breaches of trust but it is not confined to these. A tracing order can be made to recover the property itself or the proceeds of sale if they can be sufficiently identified.

13.2.1 Mixed funds

Where proceeds have been paid into a mixed fund, the basic rule is that the first payment in is related to the earliest payment out (*Devaynes v Noble, Clayton's Case* (1816) 1 Mer 572). However, where the money is paid into a bank account, the trustee will be deemed to spend his or her own money before spending a beneficiary's money (*Re Hallett's Estate* (1880) 13 ChD 696).

A beneficiary may be able to claim a charge on property bought from a mixed fund (*Re Hallett's Estate* (above)). It may also be possible for a beneficiary to claim a proportion of any profit made from a mixed fund (*Re Tilley's Will Trusts* [1967] Ch 1179).

13.2.2 Limits to the right to trace

There are limits to the right to trace. A trustee or someone in a fiduciary capacity must admit the claim of a beneficiary, giving priority to it, as must a volunteer. An innocent person will share property equally with a beneficiary who claims a right to trace. Once property has passed to a purchaser for value without notice, a right to trace will be extinguished.

13.3 Constructive trusts

On the facts of a particular case, a constructive trust may arise in equity to provide an additional or alternative remedy. There has been much academic debate as to whether a constructive trust can strictly speaking be regarded as a 'remedy', rather than simply as an operation of substative law. It is clearly so regarded in the United States, but while there is some authority for regarding it as a remedy in the United Kingdom (see especially Lord Denning MR in *Hussey v Palmer* [1972] 1 WLR 1286), there is no agreement on the matter. The technical distinction has little relevance so long as the facts justify the finding of a constructive trust.

In general terms, a constructive trust can arise wherever there is a fiduciary relationship; it does not require the existence of a formal trust (*English v Dedham Vale Properties Ltd* [1978] 1 WLR 93). The broad basis for finding a constructive trust is to prevent unjust enrichment (*Carl Zeiss Stiftung v Herbert Smith & Co (No 2)* [1969] 2 Ch 276; *James v Williams* [2000] Ch 1 (CA)).

A constructive trust has been held to arise in the following circumstances:

(a) Where a person in a fiduciary position gains any unauthorised personal benefit or profit from that position (see *Keech v Sandford* (1726) Sel Cast King 61).

(b) Where particular property is subject to a fiduciary duty (see *Tito v Waddell (No 2)* [1977] Ch 106).

(c) Where property has been acquired as a result of information obtained by someone acting as a fiduciary (see *Boardman v Phipps* [1967] 2 AC 46, but see *Sabnam Investments v Dunlop Heywood* [1999] 3 All ER 652).

(d) Where a stranger to a trust has actual or constructive knowledge of a trust and knowingly receives trust property. There is a very large number of reported cases dealing with the degree of knowledge required and whether there was sufficient proof of knowledge on the facts. If dealing with this issue it is especially important to check recent case-law. An interesting example is *Bank of Credit and Commerce International (Overseas) Ltd (in liquidation) v Akindele* [2000] 4 All ER 221.

(e) A person who dishonestly procures or assists in a breach of trust is liable to make good any resulting loss (see *Belmont Finance Corp Ltd v Williams Furniture Ltd* [1979] Ch 250 and *Royal Brunei Airlines Sdn Bhd v Tan* [1995] 3 WLR 64).

(f) An agent acting for a trust can become a constructive trustee if he or she:

   (i)   becomes chargeable with some part of the trust property; or

   (ii) knowingly assists in a dishonest or fraudulent design on the part of the trustee; or

   (iii) acts without proper instructions.

(See *Blyth v Fladgate* [1892] 1 Ch 337.)

However, an agent such as a solicitor will not become a constructive trustee simply by acting as an agent (see *Barnes v Addy* (1874) LR 9 Ch App 224, *Mara v Browne* [1896] 1 Ch 199 and *Williams-Ashman v Price and Williams* [1942] Ch 219).

13.4 Subrogation

Subrogation involves a person being able to take over the rights or assets of another party to avoid a third party benefiting unjustly from a benefit conferred on them by the first person. The right of subrogation is well established in insurance law. So, for example, where an insurer has paid an employee insurance money in respect of injuries suffered at work, the insurer can take over any rights the insured employee may have had against his or her employer (or third parties). See further Goff and Jones, p 523 *et seq.*

13.5 Quasi-contract

The main quasi-contract remedies are *quantum meruit* and *quantum valebat*. For these remedies there may have been a contract and a dispute over whether there was a breach. Even if the issues are decided in favour of one party, the court may order that party to pay the other a 'reasonable' amount for any benefit conferred or asset transferred if it would be unjust to allow the person to retain that benefit without compensation.

13.6 Benefits conferred in an emergency

Similar principles of avoidance of unjust enrichment underlie the cases where a person has been allowed to claim remuneration for goods provided in an emergency to a person under a legal incapacity or services rendered in an attempt to save life or prevent injury *(Williams v Wentworth* (1842) 5 Beav 325; *Great Northern Railway Co v Swaffield* (1874) LR 9 Ex 132).

13.7 Rights to contribution and recoupment

There are various situations where a person has a common law or statutory right to recover some or all of the money he or she has paid out in satisfying a claim by a third party from someone else whom that third party could have claimed against, or who was somehow involved in the situation which gave rise to the third party's claim. The most important statutory remedy is under the Civil Liability (Contribution) Act 1978. Common law examples arise with joint tenants, partners and joint contractors.

13.8 Benefits conferred through mistake, duress or undue influence

This is a complex and rapidly changing area. Basically, if the claim succeeds, a person may be able to rescind a contract, mortgage, trust or other obligation and recover money or property notwithstanding that there appeared to be, in form at least, a valid contract or gift or other transfer. In dealing with any of these areas it is necessary to establish whether the claim falls within one of the recognised categories which give rise to relief, whether it can be argued it would only involve a small extension of one of those categories or whether you will need to try to rely on a general principle of prevention of unjust enrichment, unconscionable bargains etc. If the latter is the case it is obviously going to be more difficult to convince a court that the remedy is obtainable.

Two recent cases extend and clarify the scope of remedies in cases of payments made under mistakes of law: *Kleinwort Benson Ltd v Lincoln City Council (No 2)* [1998] 3 WLR 1095 (HL), *Nurdin and Peacock plc v D.B. Ramsden & Co Ltd* [1999] 1 All ER 941. Restitutionary remedies in the case of benefits conferred under contracts which later were held to be void have been considered extensively in the 'interest rate swap transaction' cases which followed the decision that local authorities had no power to enter into such transactions. Key decisions in this area include *Hazell v Hammersmith & Fulham London BC* [1991] 1 All ER 545, *Kleinwort Benson Ltd v Sandwell BC* [1994] 4 All ER 890, *Westdeutcshe Landesbank Girozentrale v Islington London BC* [1996] AC 669, *Guinness Mahon & Co Ltd v Kensington & Chelsea Royal London BC* [1998] 2 All ER 272.

13.9 Benefits conferred as a result of fraud or criminal conduct

Irrespective of whether the law recognises general principles of prevention of unjust enrichment, a person has always been able to seek a remedy to prevent someone from benefiting from their fraudulent conduct or other criminal conduct. The remedy could be rescission or return of property.

13.10 Fraudulent preferences and avoidance of voluntary transfers

Where a person becomes insolvent, the creditors may be able to call in property voluntarily transferred by that person to others or used to 'fraudulently' pay off one creditor at the expense of others. Any property called in would form part of the debtor's estate and would be distributed to creditors in accordance with the normal rules of priority of creditors and equal treatment for creditors of equal ranking. See further Insolvency Act 1986, ss 238 to 241.

14

Judicial review

The judicial review of administrative action is a very important area of law which affects a wide range of cases. However, there are clear limits to the scope of judicial review.

14.1 Scope of judicial review

There are a number of restrictions on the availability of judicial review. In summary, those restrictions are:

- Judicial review is only available in 'public law' cases.
- Usually, judicial review may only be used as the remedy of last resort.
- The applicant must have 'sufficient interest'.
- The applicant must act promptly.

Each of these restrictions is considered in the sections which follow.

14.2 Public law cases only

Judicial review procedure is governed by CPR, Part 54. CPR, r 54.1(2)(a) defines a claim for judicial review as meaning a claim to review the lawfulness of (i) an enactment, or (ii) 'a decision, action or failure to act in relation to the exercise of a public function'. It is therefore only 'public law' claims which can be made by way of judicial review. It follows that judicial review is only available against:

- public bodies exercising public functions; and
- 'inferior' courts.

14.2.1 Public bodies

The term 'public body' includes bodies set up by statute, along with government departments and non-statutory bodies which exercise public functions. See *R v Panel on Takeovers and Mergers, ex p Datafin plc* [1987] QB 815 (where a non-statutory body regulating certain business dealings in the City of London was held to be susceptible to judicial review) and *R v Advertising Standards Authority Ltd, ex p Insurance Services plc* (1990) 2 Admin LR 77 (where the Advertising Standards Authority, another non-statutory body, was held to be susceptible to judicial review). Judicial review may thus be claimed against decisions of a diverse range of public bodies and authorities.

Where a body derives its functions and authority from contract, judicial review is not available. See *Law v National Greyhound Racing Club* [1983] 1 WLR 1302 (where the Greyhound Racing Club was held not to be susceptible to judicial review) and *R v Disciplinary Committee of the Jockey Club, ex p Aga Khan* [1993] 1 WLR 909 (where the same decision was reached in the case of the Jockey Club). This is because, in such cases, the applicant can pursue a remedy for breach of contract.

This principle is illustrated by *R v Muntham House School, ex p R* [2000] ELR 287. A pupil at the school was excluded and judicial review of that decision was sought. Most of the fees were in practice paid by a local educational authority, but the school was not a publicly funded school in the sense of receiving grants or other direct funding from the public sector. The local authority entered into a purely contractual relationship with the school to place a child there. Therefore, it was held that the decision by the school to exclude a pupil did not have a sufficient public law character to make it amenable to judicial review.

In *R (Mullins) v Appeal Board of the Jockey Club* [2005] EWHC 2197, the court equated the requirement that the body must be carrying out a public function with the test applied by the House of Lords in *Aston Cantlow and Wilmcote with Billesley Parochial Church Council v Wallbank* [2003] UKHL 37; [2004] 1 AC 546 to determine whether a body is a public authority for the purposes of the Human Rights Act 1998, namely that the essential test is whether the functions of the body are 'governmental' in nature.

Where the public body is a charity, it may be preferable to pursue a remedy under charity legislation. For example, in *Scott v National Trust* [1998] 2 All ER 705, it was held that the National Trust, being a charity of exceptional importance to the nation and being subject to special statutory provisions, constitutes a public body. However, because it is a charity, a challenge should be brought under the special procedure set out in s 33 of the Charities Act 1993; the availability of this alternative remedy meant that judicial review would not normally be granted.

Even if the body is a public body against which judicial review may be sought, judicial review is only available to challenge decisions made by such bodies when they are acting in a public law (rather than private law) capacity. If there is a 'private law' remedy (for example, for breach of contract), the applicant should bring a claim based on that private law claim, rather than seeking judicial review. See *Roy v Kensington and Chelsea and Westminster Family Practitioner Committee* [1992] 1 AC 624, where Lord Bridge of Harwich said (at pp 628–9) that it 'is appropriate that an issue which depends exclusively on the existence of a purely public law right should be determined in judicial review proceedings and not otherwise'. However, 'where a litigant asserts his entitlement to a subsisting right in private law, whether by way of claim or defence, the circumstance that the existence and extent of the private right asserted may incidentally involve the examination of a public law issue cannot prevent the litigant from seeking to establish his right' by means of an ordinary civil claim. So, for example, a person who claims to have been unfairly dismissed from the employment of a public body cannot challenge that decision by way of judicial review.

14.2.2 Inferior courts

Judicial review is also a means by which the decisions of certain courts may be challenged. Decisions of magistrates' courts may be challenged in this way. However, decisions of the Crown Court may only be challenged by judicial review if the decision does not relate to a trial on indictment, since the Supreme Court Act 1981, s 29(3), excludes from the scope of judicial review 'matters relating to trial on indictment'. In *DPP v*

Manchester Crown Court and Huckfield [1993] 1 WLR 1524, Lord Browne-Wilkinson suggested (at p. 1530) that one 'pointer' to the true construction of s 29 would be:

> . . . to ask the question, "Is the decision sought to be reviewed one arising in the issue between the Crown and the defendant formulated by the indictment (including the costs of such issue)?" If the answer is "Yes," then to permit the decision to be challenged by judicial review may lead to delay in the trial: the matter is therefore probably excluded from review by the section. If the answer is "No," the decision of the Crown Court is truly collateral to the indictment of the defendant and judicial review of that decision will not delay his trial: therefore it may well not be excluded by the section.

In *Director of Public Prosecutions v Manchester Crown Court and Ashton* [1994] 1 AC 9, the House of Lords held that s 29(3) applies to matters which affect the conduct of a Crown Court trial (covering orders made before the trial) and matters which are an integral part of the trial process (which covers orders made during, or even at the very end of the trial, together with some pre-trial orders).

Despite the breadth of this definition, the question of what matters relate to trial on indictment has generated a considerable body of case law. For example *R v Harrow Crown Court, ex p Perkins; R v Cardiff Crown Court, ex p M* (1998) 162 JP 527. In the first case, the applicant sought judicial review of the decision of a Crown Court judge not to order the prosecution to pay his costs when they decided to offer no evidence against him. It was held that the exercise of the judge's discretion on the question of costs is an integral part of the trial process (even if the case concludes without the empanelment of a jury) and so judicial review is excluded by s 29(3) of the Supreme Court Act 1981. In the second case, a Crown Court judge refused to make an order to protect the identity of a juvenile defendant under s 39(1) of the Children and Young Persons Act 1933 and it was held that the power to make an order under s 39, which can be exercised in respect of a juvenile defendant, complainant or witness, is collateral to the trial on indictment and so is amenable to judicial review. In *R v Manchester Crown Court, ex p H* [2000] 1 WLR 760, the Divisional Court confirmed that it has jurisdiction to entertain an application for judicial review of an order lifting reporting restrictions under s 39 of the 1933 Act (and declined to follow *R v Winchester Crown Court, ex p B* [1999] 1 WLR 788, where the court had reached the opposite conclusion).

So far as magistrates' courts are concerned, the High Court has jurisdiction to entertain appeals on points of law or jurisdiction both by way of judicial review and through appeals by way of case stated under s 111 of the Magistrates' Courts Act 1980. In *R v Oldbury Justices, exp Smith* (1995) 159 JP 316, it was said that where appeal by way of case stated is available it is generally preferable to challenge a decision of a magistrates' court by that means rather than judicial review (because judicial review is to be regarded as a remedy of last resort and because, on an appeal by way of case stated, the Divisional Court is presented with all the findings of fact made by the magistrates). In *R v North Essex Justices, ex p Lloyd* (2001) 165 JP 117, the Divisional Court said that the most appropriate procedure for challenging a decision of a magistrates' court where the issue is the extent of their jurisdiction is judicial review (since this saves the cumbersome procedure of appealing by way of case stated, and has the advantage that the matter comes before a High Court judge who decides whether or not to give permission to apply for judicial review: see the judgement of Lord Woolf CJ, at para 11). In *Giltinane v Child Support Agency* [2006] EWHC 423 (Fam); [2006] 2 FLR 857, Munby J held that where a would-be appellant is out of time for appealing by way of case stated under s 111 (bearing in mind that the 21-day time limit for commencing the appeal cannot be extended) and would otherwise not receive the justice to which he is entitled, the Administrative Court should give him a remedy by way of judicial review (see paras 11–13).

Judicial review is particularly appropriate where the procedure adopted by the lower court is being questioned. For example, judicial review has been held to be appropriate in the following instances:

(a) The unreasonable refusal of an adjournment to enable a defendant to prepare his case (*R v Thames Magistrates' Court, ex p Polemis* [1974] 1 WLR 1371).

(b) Refusing an adjournment where a defence witness could not attend on the day of the trial without first considering the effect on the defence of having to go ahead without that witness (*R v Bracknell Justices, ex p Hughes* (1990) 154 JP 98).

(c) Failure by the prosecution to notify the defence of the existence of witnesses who could support the defence case (*R v Leyland Justices, ex p Hawthorn* [1979] QB 283).

(d) Failure by the prosecution to inform the defence that the key prosecution witness had a previous conviction for wasting police time, arising out of the making of a false allegation (*R v Knightsbridge Crown Court, ex p Goonatilleke* [1986] QB 1, where the accused was charged with shoplifting).

(e) Ordering a defendant to pay costs without considering his means to pay them (*R v Newham Justices, ex p Samuels* [1991] COD 412).

Decisions of coroners' courts are also susceptible to challenge by way of judicial review (see, for example, *R v Her Majesty's Coroner for Inner West London, ex p Dallaglio* [1994] 4 All ER 139.

Because the scope of judicial review is limited to the review of 'inferior' courts, it does not extend to decisions of the High Court, the Court of Appeal, or the House of Lords.

14.2.3 Judicial review versus private law remedies

In *The Trustees of Dennis Rye Pension Fund v Sheffield City Council* [1998] 1 WLR 840, the Court of Appeal gave guidance for those cases on the borderline between private law and public law. Lord Woolf MR made the following observations (at p 848):

(a) If it is not clear whether judicial review or a private law claim is the most appropriate way to proceed, it is safer to make an application for judicial review.

(b) If a case is brought by way of an ordinary claim (seeking a private law remedy) and the defendant applies to strike the claim out on the ground that it should have been brought by way of judicial review, the court should ask itself whether it is clear that permission would have been granted had the claimant sought to bring judicial review proceedings.

(c) If the claimant brings an ordinary (private law) claim and it is equally, or more, appropriate than an application for judicial review, and the defendant tries to strike the claim out on the basis that it should have been a judicial review claim, the claim should not be struck out.

(d) In cases where the claimant brings an ordinary claim but it is unclear whether proceedings should have been brought by way of judicial review instead, it should be borne in mind that the court can order the case to be heard as a judicial review claim instead of striking the claim out.

(e) The choice made by the claimant as regards the type of claim will not normally be regarded as an abuse of process where that choice has no significant disadvantages for the parties, the public or the court.

In *Clark v University of Lincolnshire & Humberside* [2000] 1 WLR 1988, the Court of Appeal had to consider, in the context of a higher education institution, the competing claims of contract, applications to the Visitor (whose jurisdiction had since been superseded by that of the Office of the Independent Adjudicator), and judicial review. It was held that, although the arrangement between a fee-paying student and a higher education corporation is a contract, disputes suitable for adjudication under the contract's dispute resolution procedures might be unsuitable for adjudication in the courts: where issues of academic or pastoral judgement arise, a university is properly equipped to deal with those issues, whereas a court is not. So, for example, cases where the question is what mark or class of degree ought to be awarded, or whether an aegrotat was justified, are not justiciable in the courts. The court went on to hold that where a university is subject to the supervisory jurisdiction of a Visitor, that procedure should be used rather than litigation in the courts. However, where there is no such provision, and the matter is not one of academic or pastoral judgement, the court can adjudicate on allegations of breach of contractual obligations. The Court held that a contractual claim should not be struck out merely because judicial review would be the more appropriate remedy. If, however, it is clear that the claimant is bringing the case in contract to take improper advantage of the six-year limitation period (as against the three-month time limit for judicial review), the court can strike out the claim if satisfied that the court's processes are being misused or, because of the lapse of time or other circumstances, no worthwhile remedy can be expected.

14.3 Availability of alternative remedies

Judicial review is generally regarded as a remedy of last resort. It follows that other forms of redress must be sought first. In *R v Inland Revenue Commissioners, ex p Preston* [1985] AC 835 at p 852, Lord Scarman said that 'a remedy by way of judicial review is not to be made available where an alternative remedy exists'. Similarly, in *R v Chief Constable of Merseyside Police, ex p Calveley* [1986] QB 424, Lord Donaldson of Lymington MR said (at p 433) that the court, in the exercise of its discretion, will very rarely make judicial review available where there is an alternative remedy by way of appeal, and Glidewell LJ said (at p 440) that 'where application is made for judicial review but an alternative remedy is available, an applicant should normally be left to pursue that remedy. Judicial review in such a case should only be granted in exceptional circumstances'. Thus, if there is a mechanism for appealing against the decision complained of, that mechanism ought to be used; if the result is unfavourable, it may well be possible to challenge the appellate decision by means of judicial review. In *Harley Development Inc v Commissioners of Inland Revenue* [1996] 1 WLR 727, the Privy Council said that where a comprehensive statutory appeals procedure exists but was not used by the applicant, an application for judicial review would only be entertained in exceptional circumstances.

However, this is not a hard-and-fast rule; there are many cases where judicial review has been granted despite the existence of an alternative remedy. In *R v Huntingdon District Council, ex p Cowan* [1984] 1 WLR 501, Glidewell J said (at p 507):

> Where there is an alternative remedy available but judicial review is sought, then in my judgment the court should always ask itself whether the remedy that is sought in the court, or the alternative remedy which is available to the applicant by way of appeal, is the most effective and convenient, in other words, which of them will prove to be the most effective and convenient in all

the circumstances, not merely for the applicant, but in the public interest. In exercising discretion as to whether or not to grant relief, that is a major factor to be taken into account.

See, e.g., *R v Leeds City Council, ex p Hendry* The Times, 20 January 1994, where it was held that where there is a statutory appeal procedure, but it is not apt to deal with the question(s) raised in the particular case, then there is nothing to prevent a claimant from seeking relief by way of judicial review.

In *R v Secretary of State for the Home Department, ex p Capti-Mehmet* [1997] COD 61, Laws J reiterated the principle that an applicant for judicial review will usually be required to exhaust all alternative remedies before the court will grant leave to apply for judicial review and that this rule applies unless there are exceptional circumstances justifying departure from it. His Lordship went on to say that a failure to exhaust alternative remedies brought about by the error or incompetence of the applicant's legal representatives will not of itself constitute an exceptional circumstance; however, such failures do not weigh as heavily against the applicant as a deliberate decision not to exhaust alternative remedies. Exceptional circumstances may arise from a combination of factors which individually would be insufficient. Relevant factors include whether the applicant gave an early intimation of an intention to challenge the decision. Strong legal merits, such that the court is satisfied that the applicant was denied 'substantial justice' before the inferior court, body or tribunal, will weigh powerfully in favour of finding that exceptional circumstances exist.

For example, in *R v Lambeth LBC, ex p Ogunmuyiwa* The Times, 17 April 1997, the applicant had been led to believe that her case would be reviewed by the local authority; however, the local authority failed to carry out that review. Popplewell J held that this case was an exception to the rule that the applicant should have exhausted all other remedies before seeking judicial review. Again, in *R v Wiltshire County Council, ex p Lazard Brothers & Co Ltd* The Times, 31 December 1997, a statutory appeal was available to the applicant. However, the statutory appeal (under the Wildlife and Countryside Act 1981) took the form of a public inquiry. Despite the existence of a statutory remedy which the applicant had not exercised, Dyson J quashed the decision of the council; he held that the council had made a plain error of law and that it would be unfair to require the applicant to go through the costly and time-consuming appeal procedure.

A similar approach was taken in *R v Falmouth & Truro Health Authority, ex p South West Water Ltd* [2001] QB 445. This case was mainly concerned with the abatement of a statutory nuisance. However, Simon Brown LJ (at p 473) made some general comments on cases where there is an alternative to judicial review, such as a statutory appeal: 'If the applicant has a statutory right of appeal, permission [for judicial review] should only exceptionally be given'. The judge considering the application for permission should, however, have regard to all relevant circumstances, including the 'comparative speed, expense and finality of the alternative process, the need and scope for fact-finding, the desirability of an authoritative ruling on any point of law arising, and (perhaps) the apparent strength of the applicant's substantive challenge'.

14.4 Sufficient interest

In order to seek judicial review, the applicant must have 'sufficient interest' in the matter to which the application relates, sometimes known as *locus standi* ('standing'). The applicant must therefore be able to show a legitimate expectation of being heard. This generally requires that the applicant must be directly affected by the decision which is being challenged. In *Council of Civil Service Unions v Minister for the Civil Service* [1985] AC 374, Lord Diplock (at pp 408–9) said that to have a legitimate expectation in respect of a decision, the applicant must be affected by the decision, in that the decision has the effect of:

(a) altering rights or obligations of that person which are enforceable by or against him in private law, or

(b) depriving him of some benefit or advantage which either:

    (i) he has in the past been permitted by the decision-maker to enjoy and which he can legitimately expect to be permitted to continue to do until there has been communicated to him some rational ground for withdrawing it on which he has been given an opportunity to comment, or

    (ii) he has received assurance from the decision-maker that it will not be withdrawn without giving him first an opportunity for advancing reasons for contending that they should not be withdrawn.

Such expectation may be based, for example, on an express promise by the decision-maker (as in *R v Liverpool Corporation, ex p Liverpool Taxi Fleet Operators' Association* [1972] 2 QB 299) or on the practice adopted in the past by the decision-maker (e.g., *R v Secretary of State for the Home Department, ex p Ruddock* [1987] 1 WLR 1482).

It should be noted that even if the applicant is granted permission to seek judicial review (on the basis that he or she has 'sufficient interest') it is open to the court which hears the substantive application for judicial review to decide that the applicant does not in fact have sufficient interest. See *IRC v National Federation of Self-Employed and Small Businesses Ltd* [1982] AC 617 at p 642 per Lord Diplock.

14.5 The need to act promptly

Section 31(6) of the Supreme Court Act 1981 provides:

> . . . where the High Court considers that there has been undue delay in making an application for judicial review, the court may refuse to grant—
>
> (a) leave for the making of the application; or
> (a) any relief sought on the application,
>
> if it considers that the granting of the relief sought would be likely to cause substantial hardship to, or substantially prejudice the rights of, any person or would be detrimental to good administration.

CPR, r 54.5(1), says that the claim form seeking judicial review must be filed 'promptly and in any event not later than three months after the grounds to make the claim first arose'. It follows from the wording of this provision that a claim may fail for delay even if it is brought within the three-month period. PD 54, para 4.1 says that where the claim is for a quashing order in respect of a judgment, order or conviction, the date when the grounds to make the claim first arose is the date of the judgment, order or conviction. If the three-month period has expired, the court may grant an extension of time, but only if there is 'good reason' for doing so. Even if the court considers that there is good reason for extending the period, the court may still refuse permission (or, where permission has been granted, refuse to grant the remedy sought) if it takes the view that the granting of the remedy would cause hardship or prejudice or be detrimental to good administration.

In *Caswell v Dairy Produce Quota Tribunal for England and Wales* [1990] 2 AC 738 at 747, Lord Goff expressed the view that it was appropriate that permission to apply for judicial review out of time should be granted where the judge finds that there is a good reason for extending time; the question of whether the remedy should be withheld on the ground of prejudice or hardship or detriment to good administration should be dealt with at the substantive hearing.

Where there has been delay, any explanation for that delay should be given in the application for permission to seek judicial review.

In *Phillips v Derbyshire County Council* [1997] COD 130 the applicant missed the relevant deadline by four days. Her expert adviser had failed to send papers to her solicitor, and the solicitor had failed to chase the papers. Sedley J held that the series of derelictions of duty by the applicant's advisers did not provide material upon which the court could exercise its discretion to extend time.

In *R v Criminal Injuries Compensation Board, ex p A* [1998] QB 659, the Court of Appeal made the point that 'the better the prospects of success, the readier will the court be to extend time even where the delay is unjustifiable, ie, the merits themselves can contribute to or even supply the "good reason"' (per Simon Brown LJ at p 677). When this case went to the House of Lords (*R v Criminal Injuries Compensation Board, ex p A* [1999] 2 AC 330), it was held that, where permission to apply for judicial review has been given without notice, an application to set permission aside might be made, although such applications are not to be encouraged. Unless permission is set aside, the question of permission cannot be re-opened at the substantive hearing on the basis that there were no grounds for extending time. What the court can do, under s 31(6) of the Supreme Court Act 1981, is to refuse to grant relief on the basis of the applicant's delay (per Lord Slynn of Hadley at p 341).

In *R v Newbury District Council, ex p Chieveley Parish Council* The Times, 10 September 1998, it was noted by the Court of Appeal that important decisions can be taken by public and private bodies, and by individuals, on the strength of some decisions, such as the granting of planning permission. It is therefore in the interests of good administration that any challenge should be made quickly. The court held that this was so even if there is no evidence of actual hardship or prejudice to the rights of third parties.

14.6 Procedure for seeking judicial review

The procedure for seeking judicial review is contained in CPR, Part 54 and PD 54. An application for judicial review has two stages: an application for permission to seek judicial review and then (if permission is granted) the substantive application for judicial review.

14.6.1 Pre-action protocol for judicial review

There is a pre-action protocol for judicial review claims. Paragraph 2 of the pre-action protocol emphasises that judicial review may be used where there is no right of appeal or where all avenues of appeal have been exhausted. Paragraph 3.1 goes on to say that the parties should consider whether some form of alternative dispute resolution procedure would be more suitable than litigation, and if so, endeavour to agree which form to adopt. Both the Claimant and Defendant may be required by the Court to provide evidence that alternative means of resolving their dispute were considered.

Observance of the pre-action protocol is not required in urgent cases, for example, where the claimant is about to be removed from the UK, or where there is an urgent need for an interim order to compel a public body to act where it has unlawfully refused to do so (for example, the failure of a local housing authority to secure interim accommodation for a homeless claimant). In such cases, a claim may be made immediately (para 6).

Paragraph 7 provides that where the use of the protocol is appropriate, the court will normally expect all parties to have complied with it and will take into account compliance or non-compliance when giving directions for case management of proceedings or when making orders for costs. This paragraph goes on to say that, even in emergency cases, it is good practice to fax to the defendant the draft claim form which the claimant intends to issue; also, the claimant is normally required to notify a defendant when an interim mandatory order is being sought.

An integral part of the pre-action protocol is the letter before claim. The purpose of this letter is to identify the issues in dispute and establish whether litigation can be avoided (para 8). Annex A of the pre-action protocol contains a suggested standard format for the letter. Paragraphs 10 and 11 of the protocol go on to summarise the key contents of the letter before claim:

- the date and details of the decision, act or omission being challenged;
- a clear summary of the facts on which the claim is based;
- details of any relevant information that the claimant is seeking and an explanation of why this is considered relevant;
- details of any interested parties known to the claimant (who should also be sent a copy of the letter before claim for information).

Paragraph 12 says that a claim should not normally be made until the proposed reply date given in the letter before claim has passed, unless the circumstances of the case require more immediate action to be taken.

The next part of the pre-action protocol deals with the letter of response from the defendant. Paragraph 13 states that defendants should normally respond within 14 days. Failure to do so will be taken into account by the court and sanctions may be imposed unless there are good reasons. Paragraph 14 goes on to add that where it is not possible to reply within the proposed time limit the defendant should send an interim reply and propose a reasonable extension. Where an extension is sought, reasons should be given and, where required, additional information requested. This will not affect the time limit for making a claim for judicial review, nor will it bind the claimant if he or she considers the extension to be unreasonable. The paragraph does warn that where the court considers that a subsequent claim is made prematurely it may impose sanctions.

Annex B contains a suggested format for the response. Paragraph 16 states that if the claim is wholly denied, or conceded only in part, the reply should say so in clear and unambiguous terms, and should:

- (where appropriate) contain a new decision, clearly identifying what aspects of the claim are being conceded and what are not, or give a clear timescale within which the new decision will be issued;
- (where appropriate) provide a fuller explanation for the decision;
- address any points of dispute, or explain why they cannot be addressed;
- enclose any relevant documentation requested by the claimant, or explain why the documents are not being enclosed; and

- (where appropriate) confirm whether or not any application for an interim remedy will be opposed.

A copy of this response should be sent to all the interested parties identified by the claimant and contain details of any other parties whom the defendant considers also have an interest (para 17).

14.6.2   Seeking permission to apply for judicial review

Part 54 claims for judicial review are dealt with in the Administrative Court. Documents have to be filed at the Administrative Court Office, the Royal Courts of Justice, Strand, London, WC2A 2LL.

Under the *Practice Direction (Administrative Court: Establishment)* [2000] 1 WLR 1654, the parties to an application for judicial review are described in the proceedings as being: 'The Queen on the application of [name of applicant], claimant v [the name of the public body against whom the proceedings are brought], defendant.'

Under CPR, r 54.4, the court's permission to proceed is required in order to bring a claim for judicial review.

14.6.3   The paperwork

The first step in a claim for judicial review is to file a claim form. As well as the matters that normally have to appear in a claim form (see CPR, r 8.2), r 54.6 provides that the claimant has to state:

(a) the name and address of any person he or she considers to be an interested party (defined in r 54.1(2)(f) as any person, other than the claimant and defendant, who is directly affected by the claim);

(b) that he or she is requesting permission to proceed with a claim for judicial review;

(c) any remedy (including any interim remedy) being claimed.

The claim form has to be accompanied by the documents required by PD 54, para 5.6, which provides that the claim form must include or be accompanied by:

- a detailed statement of the claimant's grounds for bringing the claim for judicial review;
- a statement of the facts relied on;
- any application to extend the time limit for filing the claim form;
- any application for directions.

PD 54, para 5.7 provides that the claim form must also be accompanied by:

- any written evidence in support of the claim (or application to extend time);
- a copy of any order that the claimant seeks to have quashed;
- where the claim for judicial review relates to a decision of a court or tribunal, an approved copy of the reasons for reaching that decision;
- copies of any documents on which the claimant proposes to rely;
- copies of any relevant statutory material;
- a list of essential documents for reading in advance by the court (with page references to the passages relied on).

The claim form must be served on the defendant, and (unless the court otherwise directs) on any person the claimant considers to be an interested party, within seven days after the date of issue (CPR, r 54.7).

Where the claim for judicial review relates to proceedings in a court or tribunal, any other parties to those proceedings must be named in the claim form as interested parties (PD 54, para 5.1). It follows that where a defendant in a criminal case seeks judicial review of a decision of a magistrates' court or the Crown Court, the prosecution must always be named as an interested party (para 5.2).

Under CPR, r 54.8, a person served with the claim form who wishes to take part in the judicial review must file an acknowledgement of service not more than 21 days after the service of the claim form. The acknowledgement of service must be served on the claimant, and on any other person named in the claim form, not later than seven days after it is filed. The acknowledgement of service must (if the person filing it intends to contest the claim) set out a summary of the grounds for contesting the claim (and must state the name and address of anyone whom the person filing it considers to be an interested party).

CPR, r 54.9 says that a person who fails to file an acknowledgement of service may not (unless allowed by the court) take part in any hearing to decide whether permission to proceed should be given. However, if that person complies with any direction of the court regarding the filing and service of detailed grounds for contesting the claim (or supporting it on additional grounds), together with any written evidence, he or she may take part in the substantive hearing of the claim for judicial review.

14.6.4   Determining the application for permission

PD 54, para 8.4 provides that the court will generally, in the first instance, consider the question of permission without a hearing. Where there is a hearing, neither the defendant nor any other interested party need attend the hearing unless the court directs otherwise (para 8.5). Where the defendant or any interested party does attend a hearing, the court will not generally make an order for costs against the claimant (para 8.6).

If the applicant has sufficient standing to bring the claim for judicial review and there has not been undue delay, the judge will go on to consider the merits of the application. The test applied by the single judge is whether the claimant's application for judicial review discloses an arguable case.

In *R v Secretary of State for the Home Department, ex p Begum* [1990] Imm AR 1, it was held that, if the judge is satisfied that there is no arguable case, the application for permission should be refused. If the judge is satisfied that there is an arguable case, permission should be given. If the judge is uncertain whether or not there is an arguable case, the application for permission should be adjourned to enable a hearing to take place so that oral arguments from both the claimant and the defendant (and other interested parties) may be heard.

14.6.5   Refusal of permission

CPR, r 54.12 provides that if the court, without a hearing, refuses permission to proceed or gives permission that is subject to conditions or on certain grounds only, the court will serve its reasons for making the decision along with the order itself.

Under CPR. r 54.12(3), 'the claimant may not appeal but may request the decision to be reconsidered at a hearing' and (under r 54.12(4)) must file a request for such a hearing within seven days of the service of the court's reasons for the decision).

CPR, r 54.13 states that neither the defendant, nor anyone else served with the claim form, may apply to set aside an order giving the claimant permission to proceed.

In *R v Secretary of State for Trade & Industry, ex p Eastaway* [2000] 1 WLR 2222, the House of Lords held that, under CPR, Part 52, permission (from the lower court or the Court of Appeal) is required to appeal to the Court of Appeal against refusal by a judge to grant permission to apply for judicial review. No further appeal lies to the House of Lords.

Where the claimant seeks to rely on grounds other than those for which the court gave permission to proceed, the court's permission is required (CPR, r 54.15). In *R (Smith) v Parole Board* [2003] EWCA Civ 1014; [2003] 1 WLR 2548, the Court of Appeal held that a judge hearing a substantive judicial review application should require substantial justification before allowing a claimant to advance an argument in relation to which permission was refused at a contested oral permission hearing. However, if the judge comes to the conclusion that there is good reason to allow argument on that ground, bearing in mind the interests of the defendant, he can give permission for that to happen, even if no new legal or factual situation had arisen (per Lord Woolf CJ at para 16).

14.6.6   Procedure if permission is given

Under CPR, r 54.14, once the claimant has been given permission to proceed, the defendant (and anyone else served with the claim form who wishes to contest the claim or to support it on additional grounds) must, within 35 days after service of the order giving permission, serve:

- detailed grounds for contesting the claim (or supporting it on additional grounds); and
- any written evidence.

Where the party filing the detailed grounds intends to rely on documents not already filed, he or she must file a paginated bundle of those documents when filing the detailed grounds (PD 54, para 10.1).

Any person may apply for permission to file evidence or to make representations at the judicial review hearing (CPR, r 54.17).

Where all the parties agree, the court may decide the claim for judicial review without a hearing (CPR, r 54.18).

Otherwise the claimant must file and serve a skeleton argument not less than 21 working days before the date of the hearing of the judicial review claim (PD 54, para 15.1). The defendant (and any other party wishing to make representations at the hearing) must file and serve a skeleton argument not less than 14 working days before the date of the hearing (para 15.2). The skeleton arguments must contain:

- a list of issues;
- a list of the legal points to be taken (together with any relevant authorities, with page references to the passages relied on);
- a chronology of events (with page references to the bundle of documents);
- a list of essential documents for advance reading by the court;
- a list of persons referred to.

In *Tweed v Parades Commission for Northern Ireland* [2006] UKHL 53; [2007] 1 AC 650, the House of Lords gave guidance on discovery in the context of judicial review. Since a challenge to an administrative decision by way of judicial review raises predominately legal issues, disclosure will not ordinarily be necessary for fairly disposing of the matters in issue. However, it is no longer the rule that disclosure will be ordered only where the decision-maker's affidavit can be shown to be materially inaccurate or misleading. The courts should adopt a more flexible and less prescriptive approach, and should judge the need for disclosure on the facts of the individual case. Where the claim raises the issue of the proportionality of a decision restricting a protected Convention right, this will, on the substantive application, call for careful factual assessment in the context of the relevant margin of appreciation; it follows that the court, on an application for disclosure, should take account of those factors when considering whether to make the order sought. Even in cases involving issues of proportionality, disclosure should be carefully limited to the issues which require it in the interests of justice.

14.6.7   Expedited hearing

The sheer weight of cases where judicial review is sought means that claims can take a long time to be dealt with. In urgent cases, an expedited hearing may be sought. In such a case, the claim form must contain a request for an expedited hearing and must set out the reasons why such a hearing is sought.

14.6.8   Hearing an application for judicial review

Criminal cases are heard by a Divisional Court (normally two High Court judges, although in complex cases there may be three); civil cases are heard by a single judge (unless the judge who gives permission for the application to proceed directs that the case be heard by a Divisional Court).

The hearing takes the form of legal argument based on the contents of the claim form and the written evidence. Since the evidence is in written form, no witnesses are usually called. In rare cases, however, witnesses can be cross-examined on their evidence. This will only be so where there is a genuine dispute of fact which has to be resolved and which cannot properly be resolved simply on the basis of the written evidence or where the court considers that a party's evidence might be misleading or, in a material respect, incomplete (*R v Arts Council of England, ex p Women's Playhouse Trust* The Times, 20 August 1997).

In *R (G) v Ealing LBC* [2002] EWHC 250 (Admin) it was held that although there is no specific provision in CPR, Part 54 for the court, in judicial review proceedings, to receive oral evidence and to order the cross-examination of witnesses on their witness statements/affidavits, the court has the power (under CPR, r 32.1 or through its inherent jurisdiction) to do so. This power will, however, only be exercised in exceptional cases.

At the hearing counsel for the claimant speaks first, followed by counsel for the defendant; counsel for the claimant has the right to reply.

14.6.9   Costs

Practice statement (QBD (Admin Ct): Judicial Review: Costs) [2004] 1 WLR 1760 stipulates that a grant of permission to pursue an application for judicial review (whether made on the papers or after oral argument) will be deemed to contain an order that costs will be 'costs in the case'. Should the judge granting permission wish to make a different order, that fact should be reflected in the order granting permission.

In *Davey v Aylesbury District Council* [2007] EWCA Civ 1166, the Court of Appeal gave guidance on recovery of costs incurred prior to the grant of permission to seek judicial review. Sedley LJ (at para 21) said that, on the conclusion of full judicial review proceedings in a defendant's favour, the nature and purpose of the particular claim is relevant to the exercise of the judge's discretion as to costs. In contrast to a judicial review claim brought wholly or mainly for commercial or proprietary reasons, a claim brought partly or wholly in the public interest, albeit unsuccessful, may properly result in a restricted order (or no order) for costs. If awarding costs against the claimant, the judge should consider whether they are to include preparation costs. It will be for the defendant to justify these. If the judge makes an order for costs in a defendant's favour but does not distinguish between pre-permission and post-permission costs, the order has to be regarded as including any reasonably incurred preparation costs. However, a defendant who chooses to attend and oppose an oral application for permission cannot ordinarily expect to recover the costs of doing so even if permission is refused, although such costs may be allowed in exceptional circumstances (see *R (Mount Cook Land Ltd) v Westminster City Council* [2003] EWCA Civ 1346).

14.7 Grounds for seeking judicial review

In *Council of Civil Service Unions v Minister for the Civil Service* [1985] AC 374, Lord Diplock (at p 410) identified three broad heads under which judicial review might be sought: illegality, irrationality and procedural impropriety.

14.7.1 Illegality

Lord Diplock defined illegality in this context by saying that 'the decision-maker must understand correctly the law that regulates his decision-making power and must give effect to it' (ibid p 410). In other words, the decision must be within the decision-maker's jurisdiction. An act is outside jurisdiction (*ultra vires*) where the decision-maker purports to exercise a power which he or she does not possess, or else uses a power for a purpose other than the purpose for which the power was granted.

Where a discretionary power is being exercised, the decision-maker must not adhere to a fixed policy without having regard to the circumstances of the particular case under consideration. See *R v Secretary of State for the Home Department, ex p Findlay* [1985] AC 318 (a challenge to the Home Secretary's parole policy). The point is that there is no objection to a decision-maker having a policy, provided consideration is given to each individual case to see if there is any reason why the policy should not apply to that case (see *R v Port of London Authority, ex p Kynoch Ltd* [1919] 1 KB 176).

14.7.2 Irrationality

Another word for irrationality is 'unreasonableness'. The classic definition of unreasonableness was set out by Lord Greene MR in *Associated Provincial Picture Houses Ltd v Wednesbury Corporation* [1948] 1 KB 223 at p 234: a decision may only be quashed if it is 'so unreasonable that no reasonable [decision-maker] could ever have come to it'.

In many cases, the basis for claiming that the decision is an unreasonable one will be that the decision is flawed by irrelevance. In *Wednesbury* (at pp 233–4), Lord Greene MR said that the court is entitled to investigate whether a decision-making body 'has taken into account matters which it ought not to take into account, or conversely, has refused to take into account matters or neglected to take into account matters which it ought to take into account'.

For example, in *R v Lewisham London Borough Council, ex p Shell (UK) Ltd* [1988] 1 All ER 938, a local authority boycotted Shell's products because that company had connections in South Africa (which was then subject to a system of racial apartheid); this boycott was declared unlawful, because the decision was motivated by irrelevant considerations.

Although the courts remain reluctant to usurp the function of the original decision-maker, there is a discernible (albeit tentative) shift away from the traditional *Wednesbury* approach in cases involving human rights. For example, in *R v Secretary of State for the Home Department, ex p Javed* [2001] EWHC Admin 7, Turner J was considering an asylum case. His Lordship said that, although the courts have historically been reluctant to evaluate evidence when reviewing decisions of the executive, under the Human Rights Act 1998 the court has a 'positive duty' to give effect to the European Convention on Human Rights and to ensure that there is an effective remedy in cases of suspected breach of the Convention rights. It follows that where an executive decision needs to be reviewed on the facts, the court is competent to carry out that exercise once the relevant material has been placed before it. An appeal to the Court of Appeal ([2002] QB 129) was dismissed.

However, in *R (Isiko) v Secretary of State for the Home Department* [2001] 1 FLR 930 (another immigration case) the Court of Appeal said that, in reviewing a decision of the executive to see if it complies with the Human Rights Act 1998, the court will not substitute its decision for that of the executive, but will decide whether the decision-maker has exceeded the discretion given to him. The executive's discretion has to be exceeded before a decision can be categorised as unlawful. In the area of immigration and deportation, for example, difficult choices have to be made between the rights of the individual and the needs of society and it is appropriate for the courts to recognise that there is an area of judgment within which the judiciary will defer, on democratic grounds, to the considered opinion of the elected body or person whose decision was said to be incompatible with an individual's Convention rights. Nonetheless, where a fundamental right is engaged, the court will insist that that fact is recognised by the decision-maker, who is therefore required to demonstrate that his proposed action does not interfere with the individual's right, or if it does, that there exist considerations which amount to substantial objective justification for the interference. The graver the impact of the decision in question upon the individuals affected by it, the more substantial the justification that is required. Within that framework, the court would give due deference to the primary decision-maker (per Schiemann LJ at para 31).

In *R v Secretary of State for the Home Department, ex p Daly* [2001] 2 AC 532, Lord Steyn (at para 28) pointed out that differences in approach between the traditional *Wednesbury* ground of review and the approach of proportionality (the approach adopted by the European Court of Human Rights) may sometimes yield different results. At para 27, Lord Steyn points out that the doctrine of proportionality 'may require the reviewing court to assess the balance which the decision-maker has struck, not merely whether it was within the range of rational or reasonable decisions'. The proportionality test may therefore 'go further than the traditional grounds of review in as much as it might require attention to be directed to the relative weight accorded to interests and considerations'. This does not, said Lord Steyn (at para 28), mean that there has been a shift to 'merits review': the respective roles of judges and administrators are fundamentally different and will remain so. Even in cases involving Convention rights, the intensity of review in a public law case will depend on the subject matter in hand.

In *R (Samaroo) v Secretary of State for the Home Department* [2001] EWCA Civ 1139, the applicants were challenging deportation decisions. The Court of Appeal held that in deciding what proportionality requires in any particular case, the issue will usually have to be considered in two distinct stages. Dyson LJ (at para 19) said that, at the first stage, the question is: 'Can the objective of the measure be achieved by means which are less interfering with an individual's rights?' The 'essential purpose of this stage of the inquiry is to see whether the legitimate aim can be achieved by means that do not interfere, or interfere so much, with a person's rights under the Convention'. That inquiry must be undertaken by the decision-maker in the first place. His Lordship (at para 20) said that, at the second stage, 'it is assumed that the means employed to achieve the legitimate aim are necessary in the sense that they are the least intrusive of Convention rights that can be devised in order to achieve the aim'. The question at this stage is: 'Does the measure have an excessive or disproportionate effect on the interests of affected persons?' At para 25, his Lordship goes on to say that, 'Where the legitimate aim cannot be achieved by alternative means less interfering with a Convention right, the task for the decision-maker, when deciding whether to interfere with the right, is to strike a fair balance between the legitimate aim on the one hand, and the affected person's Convention rights on the other'. Moreover, achieving a 'fair balance involves comparing the weight to be given to the wider interests of the community with the weight to be given to an individual's Convention rights. Some rights are regarded as of especial importance and should for that reason be accorded particular weight . . . the more serious the interference with a fundamental right and the graver its effects, the greater the justification that will be required for the interference' (para 28). How much weight the decision-maker gives to each factor will be the subject of 'careful scrutiny by the court. The court will interfere with the weight accorded by the decision-maker if, despite an allowance for the appropriate margin of discretion, it concludes that the weight accorded was unfair and unreasonable. In this respect, the level of scrutiny is undoubtedly more intense than it is when a decision is subject to review on traditional *Wednesbury* grounds, where the court usually refuses to examine the weight accorded by the decision-maker to the various relevant factors' (para 39).

In *South Bucks District Council v Coates* [2004] EWCA Civ 1378, the Court of Appeal gave guidance on the manner in which a judge should explain, in his reasons, a decision that turns essentially on a test of proportionality. Lord Phillips MR said, at para 7, 'there is one cardinal rule. The judge's reasons should make clear to the parties why he has reached his decision. Where he has had to balance competing factors it will usually be possible to explain why he has concluded that some have outweighed others. Even where the competition is so unequal that the factors speak for themselves it is desirable to say so.'

Judicial review may also be granted to prevent a public authority from acting in a way that defeats the claimant's legitimate expectations. For example, in *R (Nadarajah) v Secretary of State for the Home Department* [2005] EWCA Civ 1363, it was said that 'where a public authority has issued a promise or adopted a practice which represents how it proposes to act in a given area, the law will require the promise or practice to be honoured unless there is good reason not to do so' (per Laws LJ at para 68). A public body's promise or practice as to future conduct may only be departed from in circumstances where to do so is the public body's legal duty, or is otherwise a proportionate response, having regard to a legitimate aim pursued by the public body in the public interest (ibid). This principle applies both to procedural and substantive expectations.

14.7.3 Procedural impropriety

Most claims of procedural impropriety involve alleged breaches of the rules of natural justice. There are two fundamental rules of natural justice:

(a) The rule against bias (sometimes described by the Latin phrase *nemo judex in re sua* or *nemo judex in causa sua,* which mean that no one should be a judge in his or her own cause). The point is that the decision-maker should not have an interest in the outcome of the case under consideration. There must be a 'real danger of bias on the part of the relevant member of the tribunal in question, in the sense that he might unfairly regard (or have unfairly regarded) with favour, or disfavour, the case of a party to the issue under consideration by him' (*R v Gough* [1993] AC 646 at p 670 per Lord Goff of Chieveley).

In the case of *Re Medicaments and Related Classes of Goods (No 2)* [2001] 1 WLR 700, the Court of Appeal reconsidered the *Gough* test for bias in the light of the case law of the European Court of Human Rights. Lord Phillips of Worth Matravers MR (at para 85) said that a 'modest adjustment' had to be made to the *Gough* test:

> . . . the court must first ascertain all the circumstances which have a bearing on the suggestion that the judge was biased. It must then ask whether those circumstances would lead a fair-minded and informed observer to conclude that there was a real possibility, or a real danger, the two being the same, that the tribunal was biased.

In *Porter v Magill* [2002] 2 AC 357 (at para 103), Lord Hope of Craighead said that:

> . . . the question is whether the fair-minded and informed observer, having considered the facts, would conclude that there was a real possibility that the tribunal was biased.

(b) The right to a fair hearing (sometimes described by the Latin phrase *audi alteram partem* which means 'hear the other side'). In *Ridge v Baldwin* [1964] AC 40 a chief constable was dismissed from office without receiving any notice of his proposed dismissal and without being given any opportunity to argue against his dismissal. The House of Lords held it to be essential to a fair decision-making process that the person who is the subject of the decision should:

    (i) have notice of the allegations which he or she has to meet (e.g., in *R v Huntingdon District Council, ex p Cowan* [1984] 1 WLR 501 the refusal of an entertainment licence was quashed on the ground that the applicant had not been informed of the objections which the police had made to the grant of the licence); and

    (ii) have an adequate opportunity to meet those allegations by making representations (whether orally or in writing) and, in appropriate cases, by calling evidence in support of those representations (eg, in *R v Secretary of State for the Home Department, ex p Harry* [1998] 1 WLR 1737, it was held that where the Home Secretary decides not to accept the recommendation of a Mental Health Review Tribunal that a patient should be transferred to a less secure hospital, the Home Secretary is entitled to seek advice from other sources, such as the Advisory Board on Restricted Patients. However, the patient should be furnished with the report or at least be informed of the gist of it, and should be given the opportunity to make written representations).

In *R (Beeson) v Dorset CC* [2002] EWCA Civ 1812; [2003] HRLR 11, the Court of Appeal said that, if there is no reason of substance to question the objective integrity of the first instance process (whatever may be said about its appearance), the added safeguard of judicial review 'will very likely satisfy the Art 6 standard unless there is some special feature of the case to show the contrary' (per Laws LJ at para 30).

14.7.4 The giving of reasons

In *R v Secretary of State for the Home Department, ex p Doody* [1994] 1 AC 531, the House of Lords held that even though there is no general duty to give reasons for a decision, in many cases the reasons for the decision will have to be revealed 'as an effective means of detecting the kind of error which would entitle the court to intervene' (per Lord Mustill at p 565). In *R v Harrow Crown Court, ex p Dave* [1994] 1 WLR 98, for example, it was held that when it dismisses an appeal under s 108 of the Magistrates' Courts Act 1980 against summary conviction by a magistrates' court, the Crown Court should give sufficient reasons to demonstrate that it had identified the main contentious issues in the case and how it had resolved them (per Pill J at p 107).

In *R v Ministry of Defence, ex p Murray* [1998] COD 134, it was held that where a statute confers the power to make decisions affecting individuals but does not contain an express requirement that the decision-maker must give reasons for the decision, the court will imply such a requirement if, but only if, the interests of fairness so require.

In *Adami v Ethical Standards Officer of the Standards Board for English* [2005] EWCA Civ 1754, it was held that a judge hearing a statutory appeal from a specialist tribunal which has given inadequate reasons for its decision has a discretion to remit the matter to the tribunal so that it can supply adequate reasons.

14.7.5 The effect of the Human Rights Act 1998

We have already seen (particularly in the context of the immigration/deportation cases referred to in **14.7.2** above) that the courts have displayed some willingness to extend the bounds of judicial review. It is important that the courts continue to do so. In *Smith and Grady v United Kingdom* (2000) 29 EHRR 493, the European Court of Human Rights noted that the effect of Article 13 is to require the provision of a domestic remedy allowing the competent national authority both to deal with the substance of the relevant Convention complaint and to grant appropriate relief. However, Article 13 does not go so far as to prescribe a particular form of remedy, Contracting States being afforded a margin of appreciation in conforming with their obligations under this provision. However, when the present case (which concerned the outlawing of homosexuality in the armed forces) came before the Court of Appeal, that court made it clear that, since the Convention did not (at that time) form part of English law, questions as to whether the application of that policy violated the applicants' rights under Article 8 and, in particular, as to whether the policy had been shown by the authorities to respond to a pressing social need or to be proportionate to any legitimate aim served, were not questions to which answers could properly be offered. The sole issue before the domestic court was whether the policy could be said to be 'irrational'. Lord Bingham MR had held that a court was not entitled to interfere with the exercise of an administrative discretion on substantive grounds save where the court was satisfied that the decision was unreasonable in the sense that it was beyond the range of responses open to a reasonable decision-maker. In judging whether the decision-maker had exceeded this margin of appreciation, the human rights context was important, so that the more substantial the interference with human rights, the more the court would require by way of justification before it was satisfied that the decision was reasonable. It was, however, further emphasised that, notwithstanding any human rights context, the threshold of irrationality which an applicant was required to surmount was a high one. The Court of Appeal had gone on to hold that the policy in question could not be said to be beyond the range of responses open to a reasonable decision-maker and, accordingly, could not be said to be 'irrational'. However, the European Court concluded that, in such circumstances, it was clear that the threshold at which the domestic courts could find a policy irrational was placed so high that it effectively excluded any consideration by the domestic courts of the question whether the interference with the applicants' rights answered a pressing social need or was proportionate to the national security and public order aims pursued, principles which lie at the heart of the European Court's analysis of complaints under Article 8 of the Convention. The court accordingly found that there had been a violation of Article 13 of the Convention.

Similarly, in *Hatton v United Kingdom* (2003) 37 EHRR 28 (a case concerning excessive noise from aircraft), the Grand Chamber of the European Court of Human Rights noted that the applicants had no remedy in private law. Judicial review proceedings were capable of establishing that the arrangements governing night flights were unlawful because the gap between Government policy and practice was too wide. However, the court observed that the scope of review by the domestic courts was limited to the classic English public law concepts (such as irrationality, unlawfulness and patent unreasonableness) and did not, at the relevant time (prior to the entry into force of the Human Rights Act 1998), allow consideration of whether the claimed increase in night flights under those arrangements represented a justifiable limitation on the right to respect for the private and family lives or the homes of those living in the vicinity of Heathrow airport. In these circumstances, the scope of review by the domestic courts was not sufficient to comply with Article 13 and so there had been a violation of Article 13 of the Convention.

In *Tsfayo v UK* [2007] HLR 19, the European Court of Human Rights had to consider the adequacy of judicial review as a remedy in a case concerning the refusal of housing benefit. The Court held that, where a decision is reviewed by a body that is not independent of the parties to the dispute (in this case, a review board staffed by councillors from the local authority whose decision was being challenged), the existence of judicial review is not a sufficient safeguard for the purposes of Article 6 of the ECHR (the right to a fair trial), since the High Court does not have jurisdiction to re-hear evidence or to substitute its own views as to the credibility of the parties. It follows that, in such a case, there exists no possibility for the central factual issue at dispute to be determined by an independent and impartial tribunal. The European Court therefore held that there had been a breach of Article 6.

These cases may be contrasted with the case of *Vilvarajah v United Kingdom* (1992) 14 EHRR 248 where the European Court found that the test applied by the domestic courts in applications for judicial review of decisions by the Secretary of State in asylum matters coincided with the court's own approach under Article 3 of the Convention.

It is submitted that the position may be summarised as follows. For the judicial review process to comply with Article 13 in a case where Convention rights are engaged, the court must take full account of those Convention rights and must be prepared to look at the merits of the decision being reviewed, not just the procedure by which that decision was reached. This requires the court to consider whether the decision is a proportionate way of achieving a legitimate aim. In those cases where Convention rights are not engaged, it is of course open to the court to adopt the traditional approach, that the sole issue is whether the decision was a lawful decision reached by the correct procedure.

14.8 Remedies

The remedies which may be granted following an application for judicial review are set out in CPR, r 54.2 and include:

(a) A 'quashing order' (formerly known as *'certiorari'*): this has the effect of quashing the decision being challenged.

(b) A 'mandatory order' (formerly known as *'mandamus'*): this has the effect of requiring the defendant to do something, most commonly to compel a decision-maker to reconsider the original decision.

(c) A 'prohibiting order' (formerly known as 'prohibition'): the effect of this remedy is similar to that of an injunction, in that it prevents a public body from acting or continuing to act in a way which is unlawful.

CPR, r 54.19, provides that where the court makes a quashing order, it may remit the matter to the decision-maker and direct the decision-maker to reconsider the matter and reach a decision in accordance with the judgment of the court. On the other hand, where the court considers that there is no purpose to be served in remitting the matter to the decision-maker, the court may (subject to any statutory provision) take the decision itself.

Additionally, under r 54.3, the court has the power to grant what would normally be regarded as 'private law' remedies, namely:

(a) *Declaration*. The effect of a declaration is to state the law on a particular point. So, if a decision is quashed because the decision-maker misunderstood the law, the court can grant a declaration setting out the correct interpretation of the law (e.g., *R v West London Coroner's Court, ex p Gray* [1988] QB 467).

(b) *Injunction*. This has the same effect as a prohibiting order but with one difference, which is that an injunction may be an interim remedy (i.e., pending the full hearing) whereas a prohibiting order may not be granted as an interim remedy.

A claim for judicial review may include a claim for damages but cannot be used to claim damages only (r 54.3(2)).

More than one remedy may be sought in the same application.

The grant of any judicial review remedy is discretionary. Reasons for refusing to grant the remedy sought include such matters as:

(a) The conduct of the applicant, so that the applicant does not deserve assistance (e.g., *Dorot Properties Ltd v Brent London Borough Council* [1990] COD 378).

(b) Adverse consequences to the public as a whole, or the impact on third parties (e.g., *R v Panel on Take-Overs and Mergers, ex p Guinness plc* [1990] 1 QB 146).

(c) If no harm has been done, in that the following of the proper procedure by the decision-maker would have made no difference (e.g., *R v Secretary of State for the Environment, ex p Walters* (1998) 30 HLR 328, where the Court of Appeal held that even if a decision-maker fails to comply with a statutory consultation process, the court is entitled to refuse to grant relief in judicial review proceedings).

14.9 Interim remedy

There is a power to grant an interim remedy in judicial review proceedings. In *R v Ministry of Agriculture, Fisheries & Food, ex p Monsanto* [1999] QB 1161, it was held that the court should apply the principles which govern the grant of an interim injunction (see *American Cyanamid v Ethicon* [1975] AC 396) to the question of whether to grant an interim remedy in judicial review proceedings.

14.10 Further reading

There are a number of textbooks on judicial review, including:

De Smith, Woolf and Jowell, *Judicial Review of Administrative Action,* 6th edn (revised), Sweet & Maxwell, 2007.
Fordham, *Judicial Review Handbook,* 5th edn, Hart Publishing, 2008.
Manning, *Judicial Review Proceedings: a Practitioners' Guide,* 2nd edn (revised), Legal Action Group, 2004.
Southey and Fulford, *Judicial Review: A Practical Guide,* Jordan Publishing, 2004.
Supperstone et al, *Judicial Review,* 3rd edn (revised), Butterworths, 2005.

Real property law

15.1 Repossession

15.1.1 The primary remedy

The primary remedy available as of right to the owner of land is repossession by means of an action for recovery of land.

The applicant must prove title as the owner of the land in question and establish an intention to repossess. The onus is then on the occupier to show that he or she has a right either under a licence, tenancy or otherwise to remain in possession. The procedure is governed by Part 55 of the Civil Procedure Rules 1998.

15.1.2 Possession claims against trespassers

CPR, Part 55, provides the landowner with a rapid remedy against anyone who occupies the land without her or his consent. The landowner need only issue a claim form claiming possession. Five clear days, or two clear days in case of non-residential premises, after service of the claim form the court may make an order for possession. Where the occupier entered as a trespasser the court has no power to suspend the order. The order will be effective even though the landowner cannot discover the names of the occupiers. This procedure is used most commonly against squatters although it is also available against ex-licensees. The court has power under the Housing Act 1980, s 89, to suspend an order against certain ex-licensees (eg, an occupier under a restricted contract or secure tenancy) for 14 days or up to 6 weeks in case of exceptional hardship.

15.1.3 Interim possession orders

Section III of CPR, Part 55, contains rules that enable a landowner to obtain a possession order against occupiers who entered the land as trespassers. The landowner applies by a claim form, supported by affidavit and various undertakings, eg, as to paying damages, for an interim possession order, which the court may make not less than three days after the date of issue of the application. The order commands the occupier to vacate the premises within 24 hours of service and informs the occupier of the date for a hearing in the presence of both parties not less than seven days later. Under the Criminal Justice and Public Order Act 1994, s 76, it is a criminal offence for such an occupier to remain in the premises after this 24-hour period has elapsed and the occupier may be arrested by a uniformed constable without warrant. The Act also imposes criminal liability on a landowner who obtains an interim possession order by knowingly or recklessly making false or misleading statements (s 75). Guidance is given to local authorities in the use of such proceedings against unauthorised campers by Department of Environment circular (for its effect on proceedings see *R v Brighton & Hove Council, ex p Marmont* [1998] 2 PLR 48). For the use of s 113 by a licensee, see *Manchester Airport plc v Duttan* The Times, 5 March 1999, CA.

15.1.4 Damages for trespass

A landowner may claim damages against a trespasser for trespass. Such a claim will include compensation for the use and occupation of the land which is normally awarded on the basis of the current letting value of the property. Where the occupier is a former tenant and holds over as a tenant at will/on sufferance this part of the claim is generally known as a claim for 'mesne profits' becoming damages for trespass when the owner terminates the tenancy at will/on sufferance, eg, by demanding possession.

15.1.5 Landlord and tenant—additional remedies

As between landlord and tenant various additional remedies are available.

15.1.5.1 Damages for breach of covenant

This is an ordinary contractual remedy.

15.1.5.2 Forfeiture

This is only available where the lease expressly provides for forfeiture for breach of covenant or where there is a breach of a condition. Procedures vary according to the type of covenant breached:

(a) *Rent.* The landlord must make a formal demand for rent unless either the lease per mitting forfeiture contains a provision dispensing with this requirement—every well-drafted lease will contain such a provision—or, in some circumstances, when there is more than six months' rent in arrear.

(b) *Other covenants.* In most cases the Law of Property Act 1925 (LPA 1925), s 146 requires a notice to be served which:

   (i) specifies the breach complained of;

   (ii) if the breach is remediable, requires the tenant to remedy it;

   (iii) where the landlord wants financial compensation, calls on the tenant to pay it.

See also Leasehold Property (Repairs) Act 1938, s 1 and Housing Act 1996, ss 81 and 82, for additional requirements of a valid s 146 notice imposed in the case of forfeiture for breach of repairing covenant and for failure to pay service charges, respectively.

Forfeiture will not be available if the breach has been waived, eg, by the landlord accepting rent with knowledge of the breach unless the breach is a continuing one, eg, of a repairing covenant.

Even if the landlord takes steps to forfeit the lease, a tenant may still apply to the court for relief from forfeiture. This will be granted more readily in the case of forfeiture for non-payment of rent than where the forfeiture is for breach of some other covenant.

15.1.5.3 Action to enforce payment and distress

A landlord may enforce payment of rent either by an action for the money or by distress (seizing the tenants' goods). A landlord should beware. Distress is an intricate remedy.

If the distress is illegal, excessive or irregular, the landlord may be liable for damages for wrongful distress.

15.1.5.4   Statutory protection of residential occupiers

Generally when a landlord is dealing with a tenant or a licensee of a dwelling house, regard should be had to the provisions of the Protection from Eviction Act 1977 (as amended by the Housing Act 1988) which:

(a) impose criminal penalties for the unlawful eviction and harassment of residential occupiers;

(b) require a notice to quit served in respect of a tenancy to be of at least four weeks' duration and to contain prescribed information;

(c) require the service of a four-week notice containing prescribed information to terminate most periodic licences;

(d) require a landlord to effect forfeiture through court proceedings rather than by a physical re-entry onto the land;

(e) in the case of residential tenants and licensees not entitled to the statutory protection given by the Acts mentioned in the next paragraph, restrict the owner to recovering possession through court proceedings;

(f) provide a civil claim for damages against a landlord who unlawfully evicts a residential occupier in breach of these requirements.

Further, in the case of tenants entitled to statutory protection under the Rent Act 1977 (protected tenants), the Housing Act 1985 (secure tenants), or the Housing Act 1988 (assured tenants), the landlord is restricted in the exercise of his or her common law rights to possession, eg, on service of a notice to quit and will normally have to prove the existence of statutory grounds for possession. Note, however, that most assured tenancies granted after 28 February 1997 will take effect as assured shorthold tenancies and as such will be subject to an easily satisfied mandatory ground for possession (Housing Act 1988, s 19A added by Housing Act 1996, s 96).

15.2   Mortgagee's remedies

There are a number of options open to a mortgagee when mortgagors fail to keep up with instalment payments under a mortgage.

15.2.1   Action for money due

The mortgagee can sue for the money due once the date for repayment has arrived. This is unlikely to be the best remedy for the mortgagee unless perhaps the mortgagor has substantial other assets and the value of the property mortgaged has fallen below the amount owed. More often the mortgagee will use other powers to enforce a sale and then, if there is a shortfall, sue the mortgagor for the difference.

15.2.2   Foreclosure

A mortgagee can apply for an order for foreclosure when the mortgagor is in breach of obligations under the mortgage which provide that the principal sum secured under the mortgage becomes due. If a foreclosure order is granted and made absolute, the legal title to the mortgaged property is automatically transferred to the mortgagee and the mortgagor loses all rights in the property. So in a subsequent sale of the property any proceeds above the amount owed under the mortgage can be retained by the mortgagee.

Because of the potential unfairness to the mortgagor, foreclosure is a procedurally cumbersome remedy and there is uncertainty for the mortgagee. An order can be set aside even after it has been made absolute (*Campbell v Holyland* (1877) 7 ChD 166). Also the mortgagor can apply for, and the court readily grants, an order substituting an order for sale for the foreclosure (LPA 1925, s 91(2)). This means that the mortgagor receives any proceeds of sale left after discharging the debt, costs and expenses of sale in the same way as if the mortgagee had exercised its powers of possession and sale in the first place. For these reasons foreclosure is rarely used by institutional lenders.

15.2.3 Possession

Most institutional lenders' standard mortgage conditions give the mortgagee a right to possession of the property without there being any breaches of the mortgagor's obligations. It is very rare that a mortgagee will enforce the right to possession without there being arrears of repayment instalments and without having obtained an order for possession. The right to possession is usually exercised only as a preliminary step to exercising the power of sale. However, in a potentially far-reaching decision, *Ropaigealach v Barclays Bank plc* [1999] 3 WLR 17, the Court of Appeal reasserted the view that as mortgagees were entitled to possession, they could use their common law right to re-enter the property peacefully and take possession, and that s 36 of the Administration of Justice Act 1970 had not extinguished this right nor did s 6 of the Criminal Law Act 1977 apply.

If there are arrears outstanding, the mortgagee will usually be granted an order for possession unless (rarely) the mortgagor successfully applies to have the mortgage set aside for, for example, undue influence, or (much more commonly) the mortgagor can claim the benefit of one of the statutory regimes which provide some protection (Administration of Justice Act 1970, s 36, for residential occupiers of 'dwelling houses' or alternatively Consumer Credit Act 1974, s 129, for commercial or residential 'regulated agreements'). Under s 36, possession will be suspended if the mortgagor can satisfy the court that the arrears on the instalments due (not the principal sum secured) are likely to be paid within a 'reasonable time'.

15.2.4 Sale

A power to sell is implied into every mortgage made by deed (see LPA 1925, s 101).

The exercise of that power is conditional upon any one of the following requirements being satisfied:

(a) that a notice requiring payment of the mortgage money has been served on the mortgagor and there has been a default for three or more months in the payment of part of it or all of it; or

(b) the interest payments must be two or more months in arrears; or

(c) there must be a breach of some provision of the mortgage deed other than the covenant for payment of the mortgage money or interest.

One advantage of a sale over foreclosure is that the power to sell is generally exercisable without a court order.

Once possession is obtained, it is usually not necessary to obtain a court order to sell the mortgaged property.

The mortgagee in possession owes the mortgagor a duty of care in relation to the property while in possession and in relation to carrying out the sale (as does an estate agent who has conduct of the negotiations for sale) although the extent of the duties is not entirely clear (*Parker-Tweedale v Dunbar Bank plc* [1991] Ch 12; *Cuckmere Brick Co Ltd v Mutual Finance Ltd* [1971] Ch 949; *Garland v Ralph Pay & Ransom* (1984) 271 EG 106; *Morgan v Lloyds Bank plc* [1998] 3 Lloyd's Rep 73).

Conduct of the sale can be given to the mortgagor (*Cheltenham and Gloucester plc v Booker* (1997) 29 HLR 634).

15.2.5 Appointment of a receiver

There is a power to appoint a receiver in the case of all mortgages made by deed (see LPA 1925, s 101). In the absence of a deed a mortgagee may still apply, in appropriate cases, for a receiver to be appointed. Obviously one disadvantage here is that extra costs will be incurred by such an application.

15.3 Order for sale under the Trusts of Land and Appointment of Trustees Act 1996

If the trustees under a trust of land refuse to sell or exercise powers of management or if any requisite consent cannot be obtained, any person interested may apply to the court for a vesting or other order for giving effect to the proposed transaction under the Trusts of Land and Appointment of Trustees Act 1996.

Unlike under trusts for sale, the new trusts of land make no distinction between the powers of sale and postponement of sale—they are of equal weight. The factors that the 1996 Act require the court to take into account in deciding whether to order a sale are based on the case law which developed interpreting the old s 30 of the LPA 1925. It is unlikely that there will be a great difference in the way the courts deal with those applications. The main concerns will still be what was the purpose of the trust and whether that purpose still subsists. It is also likely that the courts will remain reluctant to refuse an order for sale where the application is brought by the trustee in bankruptcy of one co-owner (*TSB Bank plc v Marshall* [1998] 3 EGLR 100).

15.4 Easement

Where there is an infringement of an easement, a claim for an injunction and/or damages may be brought. The claimant may also ask for a declaration as to the extent or scope of an easement (*Lomax v Wood* [2001] 1 All ER 80). In extreme cases the remedy of abatement may be used (see *Lagan Navigation Co v Lambeg Bleaching, Dyeing & Finishing Co* [1927] AC 226). This is a self-help remedy usually consisting of removing the obstacle complained of.

15.5 Registered land

The usual remedy for people who claim they have suffered loss as a result of an omission of their interests in the records at the Land Registry is to apply for financial compensation from the Land Registry itself (Land Registration Act 1925). However, on 13 October 2003 the 1925 Act will be repealed and the Land Registration Act 2002 will replace it. The new Act provides for the appointment of an independent adjudicator.

If the loss is as a result of failure to register, rather than a mistake at the Registry, there may be a professional negligence claim against those who handled any dealings with the interest.

An application can be made to rectify the register to ensure that for the future it includes the interest claimed (LPA 1925, s 82). This remedy is at the discretion of the Chief Registrar. Claims for rectification can be made by consent as a result of negotiations to avoid litigation or after a court decision. It can also be used where a person is claiming to be the new legal owner of a piece of land by virtue of adverse possession. It is rare for rectification to be granted where the result would adversely affect the title of the proprietor unless the proprietor has caused or contributed to the error by fraud or negligence or there are other special circumstances which make it unjust not to rectify (see *Emmet on Title*, para 20.022 et seq.). For an example, see *N. Allee & Co v David Hodson & Co* [2001] All ER (D) 141.

Note that the Land Registration Act 2002 changed the position on adverse possession. After 13 October 2003 the Limitation Act 1980 applies to unregistered land only. The Land Registration Act 2002 applies to registered land—a squatter who has been in adverse possession for 10 years may apply for registration in place of the registered proprietor.

15.6 Exercise

PROBLEM

Mr and Mrs Bowler had a joint mortgage with the Great and Good Building Society. They were two months in arrears in their instalment payments after they both had lost their jobs. At a hearing at the Kingswood County Court they argued that they would be able to pay off the arrears within four years. The district judge rejected their defence and granted possession. The Bowlers moved in with relatives. The building society did not get an order for sale but put the property for sale straightaway. It has been on the market for about six months. The building society has just informed the Bowlers it has had an offer of £45,000 for the property which it is likely to accept. The Bowlers paid £47,000 for the property in 1992. The mortgage was for £44,000. The Bowlers have just sought legal advice. They say they have been told by a friend who is an estate agent that the firm the building society is using have done very little to market the property and that if the property had been well marketed and looked after over the last six months it should fetch over £48,000.

SOLUTION

The Bowlers are out of time to lodge an appeal against the granting of the order for possession (14 days from the order being made) and it does not appear in any case that they would be able to show that no reasonable judge would have granted the order.

The building society did not need to get an order to allow it to sell as it could rely on its statutory power or a power granted in the mortgage.

The building society as mortgagee in possession does owe the Bowlers a duty of care. It is clear that it will be in breach if it does not take reasonable steps to protect the property from, for example, vandalism, but it does not have to repair, redecorate etc to make the property more attractive to potential buyers. The Bowlers may be able to argue that the building society should have rented the property out for the six months and so the property would have been better kept and rental income would have been received (*Brandon v Brandon* (1862) 10 WR 287). However, the building society might well be able to defend such a claim by saying that it was not 'wilful default' not to rent out the property because it might have made it more difficult to sell.

There is a common law duty, and, in the case of a building society, a statutory duty to take 'reasonable care' to obtain the best price for the property (Building Societies Act 1986, Sch 4, para 1(1)(a), *Cuckmere Brick Co Ltd v Mutual Finance Ltd* [1971] Ch 949). On the facts known at present it is unlikely that the Bowlers could obtain an injunction to prevent sale as there is no clear breach of these duties. They could sue the building society for damages but they would have difficulty both in establishing a breach and showing the measure of loss. The sale was put in the hands of an estate agent. Provided some efforts were made to market the property which were within the broad range of acceptable marketing strategies, it would be hard to show a breach of the duty of care by either the building society or the estate agent. The cases tend to support the view that the lender is not obliged to wait for the market to improve or take special steps to sell the property (*Predeth v Castle Philips Finance Co Ltd* [1986] 2 EGLR 144).

If, which appears unlikely on present information, a claim succeeded, the damages the Bowlers would receive would be based on what they should have received from the sale if there had been no breach. As this is speculative, the court is traditionally conservative in estimating what price would have been achieved. They would have received the price less the costs of sale (which might have been higher) and the sums owed to the lender as well as the lender's costs. It is likely that if the proposed sale goes ahead the Bowlers will still owe the building society some money. This shortfall would be taken into account in calculating damages.

If the sale goes ahead and there is a shortfall, the building society can sue the Bowlers for that amount notwithstanding the sale. If they have no means, the building society may not think it worth pursuing the claim, at least in the short term.

16

Remedies in the law of trusts

16.1 Introduction

Students should note that the following outline is purely for general guidance, not least in that many academic courses emphasise basic principle rather than trust remedies. Such brief notes involve generalisations, and any remedy that appears appropriate must be fully researched for application to a particular case. This section is intended to provide a guide to approach and thought processes rather than a comprehensive answer.

16.2 Identifying precisely what issues require to be resolved

In trying to decide which remedy is appropriate in a particular case, certain issues require to be resolved.

16.2.1 What is the problem?

- There is some doubt about whether a trust has arisen or the terms of a trust (see **16.3**).
- There is a trust and the terms are clear, but there is doubt as to whether a particular action can be carried out (see **16.4**).
- There is a trust with clear terms, but something has been done which does not appear to be within the terms of the trust (see **16.5**).

16.2.2 Be clear as to the viewpoint from which you approach the problem

- From the position of the settlor.
- From the position of a trustee.
- From the position of a beneficiary.

Do note that for any of these you might be making or defending a claim.

16.2.3 Which court has jurisdiction?

- Trust matters are assigned to the Chancery Division.
- County courts have jurisdiction in certain trust matters.

16.3   Doubts about the validity of the trust

Any difficulty as to whether a trust has arisen and, if so, what its terms are, is primarily a matter of substantive law. Consider the relevant substantive law to see if, on the facts of the case, a valid trust has or has not arisen and, if so, what its terms are.

If advising the settlor, your aim will be to avoid the need for recourse to any remedies by clarifying or altering any doubtful provisions. If the trust has been set up and is operating, the settlor may be able to make alterations if the trust instrument provides for this; otherwise it is no longer the settlor's concern.

The trustees are at risk from future claims by beneficiaries, or potential beneficiaries, if they apply the trust funds in ways which, when challenged later, prove to be incorrect because a provision was invalid. In advising the trustees you need to balance the benefit of protection for the trustees from such possible claims against the need not to waste trust funds on unnecessary applications to court.

If, after careful consideration of the substantive law, you consider that there is no real doubt, then an application should not be made to court and the trustees will be able to resist a charge that they acted in 'wilful default' by showing that they relied on legal advice. If there is any serious doubt about the meaning but, under whatever interpretation is proved correct, the beneficiaries and all potential beneficiaries are *sui juris,* then they can give their consent to the trustees' interpretation. Otherwise it is necessary for the trustees to apply to the court to construe the trust document or testamentary disposition by means of a Part 8 claim. All those whose interests may be affected by the outcome should be made defendants. The remedy sought is directions as to the answers to particular questions relating to the meaning of provisions in the document. Other consequential remedies can be sought such as drawing up accounts and directions for application of property *cy près* where there is a failed charitable disposition (see also the *Drafting* manual).

It is rare, although not impossible, for a beneficiary or someone claiming to be a beneficiary to bring a construction claim. Usually they are defendants and can argue their point of view in that capacity. If the trustees do not apply for a construction claim, a disappointed potential beneficiary would have to consider bringing a claim for breach of trust (see below).

16.4   Doubts about powers

Although a trust may be clearly valid, there may be doubts about whether a particular transaction can or cannot properly be carried out within its terms. Answers here are again largely a matter of specific legal principle, and the following notes merely make some general suggestions. The starting point must always be to identify precisely what the terms of the trust are and to seek to interpret them.

The settlor can alter the settlement to give the trustees new powers only if the trust deed permits. If it does not, the problem is for the trustees alone.

The trustees have to consider whether they consider it is necessary or advisable to have a particular power. The beneficiaries can give their views but the trustees must make the decisions and they are under no obligation to consult or follow the wishes of the beneficiaries (unless the trust deed says they must consult).

If it is considered by the trustees that the power is necessary, and the beneficiaries are *sui juris,* their consent can be obtained to waive their rights to sue in the future in relation to what would amount to a breach of trust. In the case of a charitable trust, the Charity Commissioners can authorise certain transactions which are not expressly permitted in the trust deed.

In all other circumstances it will be necessary for the trustees to apply to court.

The general power to help in such a case is provided by the Trustee Act 1925 (TA 1925), s 57, which provides that where some transaction is required in the management or administration of any property vested in trustees which is in the opinion of the court expedient, but which cannot be carried out because no power to carry it out has been given to the trustees, then the court may confer the necessary power on the trustees, subject to such conditions as the court thinks fit. This power is wide and flexible (see, eg, *Mason v Fairbrother* [1983] 2 All ER 1078).

An alternative, which may be of assistance in appropriate circumstances where the terms of the existing trust are causing difficulty, is an application under the Variation of Trusts Act 1958.

16.5 Possible breach of trust

If the existence and terms of a trust are clear, but some action has been performed or not performed and a beneficiary objects to its performance or non-performance, there may have been a breach of trust. What actions and omissions amount to a breach are beyond the scope of these notes, which only outline how to approach a case, but where there is a breach, a range of remedies may be available (see **16.6**).

16.5.1 Identifying a potential breach

Beneficiaries (whether with a fixed or future interest or just a right to be considered under a discretionary trust) can bring a claim for breach of trust if it appears that the trustees have failed in their duties in any way. This could be by positive actions or by failing to control other trustees or agents.

The main difficulty in advising beneficiaries is that they often have very little information on the administration of the trust and so it is difficult to decide what sort of breaches may have occurred. The beneficiaries have a right to see the trust documents and accounts, and, if they do not have these, the first step is to demand them (*Re Londonderry's Settlement* [1965] Ch 918).

16.5.2 Analysing the potential breach

First it is necessary to identify specifically:

- What exactly is alleged to be a breach.
- Whether there is more than one potential breach.
- When each possible breach was committed.

Then the person(s) who may have committed the breach must be identified. For example:

- One or more of the trustees.
- Anyone else, eg, an agent acting for the trustees.
- Any beneficiary who might be liable for instigating a breach.

Next it must be decided which of the potential defendants should actually be sued:

- Who is likely to have sufficient assets to indemnify the beneficiary?
- Is the case against a possible defendant legally or factually weak?
- Are there any reasons for not suing a potential beneficiary, such as family reasons?

Lastly, what has been lost from the trust as a result of the alleged breach must be identified as precisely as possible:

- In terms of capital.
- In terms of income.
- In terms of specific assets.

It is only in the light of a proper and accurate analysis of the above areas that the lawyer can review the range of possible and/or appropriate remedies.

16.5.3   Liability

While a trustee is prima facie liable only for his or her own acts, he or she will also be liable for the acts of a co-trustee where he or she:

- has stood by while a breach of trust was committed;
- leaves trust administration in the hands of a co-trustee without inquiry;
- leaves the trust funds in the sole control of a co-trustee;
- fails to take appropriate steps on becoming aware of a breach of trust.

Where on the facts more than one trustee is responsible for a breach, liability will be joint and several (see *Bahin v Hughes* (1886) 31 ChD 390). Execution can be levied by a successful claimant beneficiary against any trustee held liable. As between trustees, however, liability is shared equally, so if one trustee pays more than his or her appropriate share for a breach, he or she can claim a contribution from any other trustees found liable.

The court has a power to exempt a person from liability to make a contribution, and therefore potentially to make another trustee solely liable. This can be done where:

- One trustee alone received or misappropriated trust funds, or otherwise benefited from the breach.
- One trustee was a solicitor who advised on the breach.
- One trustee is also a beneficiary, making that trustee liable to the extent of his or her beneficial interest (*Chillingworth v Chambers* [1896] 1 Ch 685).

A solicitor trustee's partners cannot be held vicariously liable for a fraudulent breach of trust (*Walker v Stones* [2000] 4 All ER 412). For a consideration of when it is appropriate to relieve a trustee of a small estate of liability to account, see *Re Evans (deceased)* [1999] 2 All ER 777.

For guidance on a drafting Particulars of Claim in a breach of trust action, see the *Drafting* manual, **Chapter 28**.

16.6   The range of remedies

16.6.1   Financial compensation

The measure of compensation varies with the type of breach committed, but basically it is always based on a liability to make good the loss caused to the trust.

Note that normally capital loss will be compensated from the date of loss with interest. So long as the interest on capital represents the loss of capital growth, a claim for lost income will also lie; but take care to avoid double recovery where interest represents lost income.

It should be appreciated that in most cases money claimed will be repaid to the trust for proper administration, rather than paid directly to a claimant beneficiary.

The following categories give some guide to the measure applied in particular circumstances.

16.6.1.1   Payment of trust funds to wrong person

Liability is to make good to the trust the amount wrongly paid out with interest.

16.6.1.2   Improper sale of authorised investments

Liability, at the option of the beneficiary, is:

- To make good the value at which the authorised investment was sold, less any proceeds of sale of any improper investment purchased with the proceeds.

- Or to repurchase the authorised investment with credit for the proceeds of sale of any improper investment purchased.

- Or to place the beneficiaries in the position they would have been in if the authorised investment had not been sold (*Re Massingberd* (1890) 63 LT 296).

In any event, the trustee can claim no credit if the authorised investment has also fallen in value.

16.6.1.3   Unauthorised investment

If the unauthorised investment results in a loss, liability is to sell it and make good any loss with interest. If the unauthorised investment results in a loss of interest, liability is to make up the difference between the interest that was received and the interest that might have been received from an authorised investment.

If the unauthorised investment results in a profit, liability is that the profit can be claimed for the trust. Alternatively, if all beneficiaries are of age and *sui juris,* they can adopt the unauthorised investment (*Re Lake* [1903] 1 KB 439).

If unauthorised activity results in no loss to the trust, and the resulting assets are held for the beneficiaries, there is no loss to be compensated, eg, a building is built on trust land without authority (*Vyse v Foster* (1872) LR 8 Ch App 309).

16.6.1.4   Improper retention of unauthorised investment

Liability is the difference between the price for which the investment is finally sold, and what it would have fetched if sold at the correct time.

16.6.1.5   Non-investment

Money can be held in a bank account while an investment is being sought (TA 1925, s 11), but should not be left uninvested for an unreasonable time.

Liability for non-investment is to make good any interest lost due to failure to invest. If there is a failure to invest in a specified investment, liability is to purchase as much of that investment as could have been purchased at the time the duty to purchase arose (*Nestlé v National Westminster Bank plc* [1993] 1 WLR 1260).

16.6.1.6   Use of trust funds for private purposes

If the trustee makes private use of the trust funds, liability is:

(a) To make good any capital loss, with interest (at a higher rate and compound if the money has been used in the trustee's business; see *Attorney-General v Alford* (1855) 4 De G M & G 843).

(b) Alternatively, to pay over to the trust any actual profit received (or, if funds have been mixed, an appropriate part of any profit).

In an interesting recent example the House of Lords held that beneficiaries had a right to choose between a lien and a proportionate share of an asset irrespective of whether there had been a mixing of funds (*Foskett v McKeown* [2000] 3 All ER 97).

16.6.1.7   Fraud

If a trustee acts fraudulently, liability is not only to make up any capital loss, but to pay compound interest.

16.6.1.8   Interest on financial compensation

Interest will normally be awarded on capital ordered to be repaid to the trust. Interest is normally at a basic flat rate (formerly 4%, but now based on the Special Investment Account rate), but a higher rate may be granted in cases of fraud, where a higher rate of interest ought to have been received by the trust, or where the trustee has personally benefited from a higher rate of return. Simple interest will normally be awarded, compound interest in limited cases.

16.6.1.9   Taxation of financial compensation

No deduction will be made to take account of tax that might have had to be paid on the assets but for the breach (*Re Bell's Indenture* [1980] 1 WLR 1217; *Bartlett v Barclays Bank Trust Co Ltd (No 2)* [1980] 2 All ER 92).

16.6.2   Taking an account

The claim for an account has a long history, first in common law, and then as a remedy available in a Chancery Court to support a legal or equitable right. An account can usefully be claimed by a beneficiary against a trustee or an executor, as well as in partnership, agency, and real property cases. For rules regarding the taking of an account see CPR, Part 40, and for a summary order for an account, CPR, Part 25. Note that it is normally appropriate in a breach of trust action to seek the taking of an account and the payment of sums found due rather than seeking damages.

16.6.2.1 Nature of an account

An account consists of a schedule of all sums due from one side to the other, setting off sums due the other way, to reach a figure due to compensate the applicant. It can take into consideration any relevant payments, eg, rent received.

An application for an account should be accompanied by an application for an order that any sum found due be paid over to the trust.

An account can be ordered only where a breach has been proved, not merely to see if there has been a breach (*Re Wrightson* [1908] 1 Ch 789).

16.6.2.2 Obligation to replace assets

An account is appropriate to a trust claim rather than a claim for damages as the obligation is to replace assets. Rules of assessment of damages such as remoteness have no place in assessing trust loss.

An account can be ordered with regard to the whole of the trust property, or to the part with regard to which a breach has been proved (*Re Tebbs* [1976] 1 WLR 924).

16.6.2.3 Accounts and wilful default

Where there is an omission to act rather than an active breach, an account is taken on the basis of wilful default, ie, on the basis of what would have been received but for the wilful default (this does not necessarily imply a conscious failure to act so long as the failure involves a breach of trust). At least one act of wilful default must be referred to in the statement of case and proved to get an account on this basis.

16.6.2.4 Defence to the claim

It is a defence to a claim for an account that the parties have already stated in writing sums due between them, arriving at a balance figure. This will not succeed, however, if there has been any mistake or fraud to vitiate the account.

16.6.3 Following and tracing and constructive trusts

Following and tracing are rights *in rem* against a particular item of property or an item that has been substituted for it, rather than against a trustee. Such remedies will be particularly useful where a beneficiary has a good reason for wishing to recover a particular item of property, either because of what the item is, or because the trustee is unlikely to have sufficient assets to satisfy a claim personally (see *Re Diplock* [1948] Ch 465 and *Foskett v McKeown* [2000] 3 All ER 97).

Although tracing was available at common law, it is now subject to equitable principles, and will therefore not be granted if it would be inequitable to do so.

Where a trustee has obtained other property which was not the subject of the trust but as a result of his or her position as a trustee, it is likely to be imposed with a constructive trust and the trustee is obliged to bring it into the trust.

These remedies are considered further in **Chapter 13**.

16.7 Exercise

PROBLEM

Juliet, who is 16 years old, is a beneficiary under a trust set up by her grandfather, Colin Lewis. She has not seen the terms of the trust but knows that her three cousins are also beneficiaries. She has received varying amounts of money and, since she was 11, her school fees have been paid from the trust.

At the beginning of term Juliet's father, Steve, was informed by her school that the fees had not been paid by the trustees despite a number of reminders. Steve was unable to contact the trustees, who are his uncle Joe and an accountant friend of his father, Fred Treece. Steve eventually spoke to Joe's wife. She was very evasive but said that Joe was having a bit of trouble with Fred and that he had discovered a few problems with Joe's handling of the finances. She said Joe had gone to Fred's house in Cumbria to try to sort things out. Steve paid the school fees himself to avoid Juliet having any disruption to her schooling.

Steve is now very concerned about the trust. He has seen some accounts, although they are not very recent. He showed them to an accountant friend who said that the bulk of the trust fund seemed to be in investments which are very safe but produce very low income and that there were a number of odd-looking withdrawals from the fund.

SOLUTION

There appears to be enough evidence to commence a breach of trust claim. The claim can be brought by Juliet (acting through her father as next friend). The other beneficiaries do not have to be involved as the remedy sought is not damages for loss but reconstitution of the trust fund. She does not have to show she has personally lost financially, only that the trustees have breached their duties. The trustees would have to make up the loss to the fund and account for any profits they had made in breach of their duties.

Steve does not have a direct claim against the trustees for the school fees as he is not a beneficiary and (presumably) there is no contract between him and the trustees.

Up-to-date accounts and a copy of the trust deed should be formally requested from the trustees as Juliet has a right to copies (*Re Londonderry's Settlement* [1965] Ch 918).

Juliet can choose whether to proceed against Fred and Joe or just one of them at this stage and wait to commence proceedings against the other. If it is discovered that the trustees, in breach of their duties, have transferred trust assets to other people then tracing remedies against that property can be considered.

Juliet will have personal claims against the trustees as well as being able to trace any trust property in their hands and any profits they have made.

Joe will be liable for any fraudulent losses caused by Fred if Joe has not supervised and checked up on him properly.

Depending on the precise wording of the trust document, there is no obvious breach of trust in leaving the fund in safe investments. There is no duty to speculate! However, there may well be a breach if they have not diversified the funds, kept a balance between investment production and capital growth and kept the investments under review. If it was found that the trustees breached these duties, there would have to be an inquiry into what the funds would have been worth if properly invested. The courts are likely to go for a very conservative estimate (*Nestlé v National Westminster Bank plc* [1993] 1 WLR 1260).

The situation needs to be kept under careful watch. If more evidence comes to light, injunc-tive relief to protect the funds may be expedient. Juliet could also consider applying to have the trustees replaced or an additional trustee appointed. This can be done in the breach of trust application or, if urgent, by an interim application.

17

Remedies for unlawful discrimination

17.1 Introduction

The law of discrimination has developed considerably since the first effective legislation in the mid-1970s. Introduced to address discrimination on grounds of sex, marital status and race, it has now been extended to other areas, notably disability, sexual orientation, religion or belief and age. Article 14 of the European Convention on Human Rights makes discrimination unlawful in respect of Convention rights. Most cases have arisen in the context of employment and some categories of discrimination only apply to the employment context. However, the principles apply to other areas and major case law developments have arisen from these.

This chapter will introduce the basic concepts required to understand the law of discrimination, but will then focus on the remedies available. If you wish to explore the basic concepts further you will find a fuller exposition in the ***Employment Law in Practice*** manual. To apply the law to real situations, however, you are advised to refer to the main practitioner texts, eg (in the employment field) *Harvey on Industrial Relations and Employment Law,* which is available as a loose-leaf encyclopaedia or within LexisNexis Butterworths.

17.2 Legal framework

Both international and domestic provisions provide for unlawful discrimination:

- Equal Pay Act 1970 (EqPA 1970) (as amended);
- Treaty of Rome (Article 141);
- Sex Discrimination Act 1975 (SDA 1975);
- Equal Pay Directive 75/117;
- Race Relations Act 1976 (RRA 1976);
- Equal Treatment Directive 76/207;
- Sex Discrimination Act 1986;
- Disability Discrimination Act 1995 (DDA 1995);
- Human Rights Act 1998 (incorporating Article 14 of the European Convention);
- Disability Rights Commission Act 1999;

- Sex Discrimination (Gender Reassignment) Regulations 1999 (SI 1999/1102);

- Race Relations (Amendment) Act 2000;

- Race Directive 2000/43;

- Framework Directive on Equal Treatment in Employment 2000/78;

- Special Educational Needs and Disability Act 2001;

- Employment Equality (Religion or Belief) Regulations 2003 (SI 2003/1660) (EE(RB) Regs);

- Employment Equality (Sexual Orientation) Regulations 2003 (SI 2003/1661) (EE(SO) Regs);

- Disability Discrimination Act 1995 (Amendment) Regulations 2003 (SI 2003/1673) (DDAA Regs);

- Equality Act 2006 (EA 2006);

- Exployment Equality (Age) Regulations 2006 (SI 2006/1031) (EE(A) Regs).

17.2.1   What types of discrimination are made unlawful?

17.2.1.1   The nature of the discrimination

Three types of discrimination are recognised by the law: direct discrimination, indirect discrimination and victimisation. These three are not necessarily available in all circumstances.

17.2.1.2   The grounds for discrimination

The 1970s legislation made discrimination unlawful on grounds of race (RRA 1976); sex (SDA 1975, EqPA 1970); and marital status (SDA 1975). To these were later added disability (DDA1995); gender reassignment (Sex Discrimination (Gender Reassignment) Regulations 1999) and, in the employment field, sexual orientation (EE (SO) Regs), religion or belief (EE (RB) Regs) and age (EE(A) Regs).

The Human Rights Act 1998 prohibits discrimination on much wider grounds: 'sex, race, colour, language, religion, political or other opinion, national or social origin, association with a national minority, property, birth or other status', but only in relation to Convention rights brought into UK law.

The Framework Directive 2000/78 requires Member States to prohibit discrimination in employment in respect of religion or belief, disability, age or sexual orientation. The EE(RB) and EE(SO) Regs 2003 provide for this in respect of religion and belief and sexual orientation. The DDAA Regs 2003 introduce a number of changes to the DDA 1995. The EE(A) Regs came into force on 1 December 2006.

How does the law approach sexual orientation and gender reassignment?

Until the implementation of the EE(SO) Regs 2003 neither common law nor the existing statutory provisions protected against discrimination on grounds of sexual orientation. Although Article 8 of the European Convention protects against discrimination on grounds of homosexuality (*Smith and Grady v United Kingdom* [1999] IRLR 734) neither the domestic courts nor the European Court of Justice felt able to interpret the existing legislation in such a way. The 2003 Regulations now provide an appropriate remedy.

By contrast the ECJ has held gender reassignment to fall within the Equal Treatment Directive (*P v S and Cornwall County Council* (C-13/94) [1996] IRLR 347). As a result the Sex Discrimination (Gender Reassignment) Regulations 1999 SI amend SDA 1975, adding a new s 2A.

17.2.1.3   The circumstances of discrimination

SDA 1975, RRA 1976 and DDA 1995 provide for discriminatory actions to be unlawful in the fields of employment (Part II of each Act), education and the supply of goods, facilities, services and premises (Part III of SDA 1975 and RRA 1976, Parts III and IV of DDA 1995) and in respect of discriminatory practices, advertisements, instructions and pressure to discriminate (Part IV of SDA 1975 and RRA 1976). The EqPA 1970, EE(RB) Regs 2003, EE(SO) Regs 2003, EE(A) Regs 2006 and the Framework Directive apply only to employment and related situations. Article 14 of the European Convention is a 'parasitic' right, and may only be relied upon by those claiming under one of the other Articles of the Convention.

17.3   Basic concepts explained

17.3.1   Direct discrimination

This is 'less favourable treatment' on unlawful grounds. Thus denial of a job to a person without the requisite qualifications is 'less favourable treatment' but is not unlawful because there is no provision to make these grounds unlawful. Denial of the same job on grounds of sex, race or disability would be unlawful direct discrimination. The claimant will typically compare herself with the successful candidate who was not of the same sex or racial group, although a hypothetical comparator may be used where no real comparator exists.

Segregation on grounds of race is unlawful, but not segregation on grounds of sex.

The concept of 'grounds of race' has proved complex. The grounds are defined as those relating to colour, race, nationality or ethnic or national origins (RRA 1976, s 3(1)). 'Ethnic origins' has been further explained by the House of Lords in *Mandla v Dowell Lee* [1983] 2 AC 548, recognising that the concept of ethnicity encompasses cultural identity as well as racial identity.

Direct discrimination, if established, may never be justified.

The claimant has the burden of establishing a prima facie case against the respondent. A finding of unlawful discrimination should follow unless the respondent can prove that there was no unlawful discrimination (SDA 1975, s 63A; RRA 1976, s 54A). Guidance is available from *Barton v Investec Henderson Crosthwaite Securities Ltd* [2003] IRLR 332.

17.3.1.1   How is pregnancy dealt with?

Dismissal on grounds of pregnancy where an employee has been recruited for an unlimited term is direct discrimination (*Webb v EMO Air Cargo (UK) Ltd* (C-32/93) [1994] QB 718). In the same case the ECJ established that it is improper to attempt to compare a pregnant woman with a man similarly incapacitated for medical or other reasons. Pregnancy is also an inadmissible reason for dismissal, entitling the dismissed employee to make an unfair dismissal claim without serving the normal one-year qualifying period and making it unnecessary to prove that the dismissal was unreasonable in all the circumstances (Employment Rights Act 1996, s 99).

Outside the employment field (and in employment cases not involving dismissal) a remedy is available on a similar analysis (see the decision of the House of Lords in *Webb v EMO Air Cargo (UK) Ltd* [1995] IRLR 645).

17.3.2 Indirect discrimination

The concept of indirect discrimination is currently only available in respect of claims under SDA 1975, RRA 1976, EE(RB) Regs 2003, EE(SO) Regs 2003 and EE(A) Regs 2006.

It is intended to deal with situations of unintended or covert discrimination. For example, in the situation above (**17.3.1**), denial of a job because of a lack of qualifications was not unlawful direct discrimination. However, if the qualification was one which relatively few people of a particular racial group had, the requirement could have a discriminatory effect (whether intended or not) on members of that racial group. It will only be actionable if the claimant has suffered a detriment because of inability to meet the requirement. The burden of establishing all this rests on the claimant.

It could, of course, be that the qualification concerned is a legitimate requirement for that job. The legislation has recognised this fact by allowing a defence of justification of indirectly discriminatory provisions. The concept of justification still applies to non-employment cases, but in employment cases, since October 2005, it has been replaced with the concept of 'proportionality'. This is the concept also used in the more recent legislation which has flowed from the Framework Directive 2000/78. The burden of establishing justification or proportionality falls on the respondent.

The requirements for establishing indirect discrimination have recently been changed. The original version required the claimant to establish that she had been faced with a 'condition or requirement' which, although applied to everyone, was such that a 'considerably smaller proportion' of her sex or racial group could comply with it. If, as a result of not being able to comply with it, she suffered a detriment, she had established a prima facie case of indirect discrimination. This 'traditional' version of the concept is exemplified by s 1(1)(b) SDA 1975:

> *1.—(1) In any circumstances relevant for the purposes of any provision of this Act, other than a provision to which subsection (2) applies, a person discriminates against a woman if—*
>
>   *. . .*
>
>   *(b) he applies to her a requirement or condition which he applies or would apply equally to a man but—*
>
>   *(i) which is such that the proportion of women who can comply with it is considerably smaller than the proportion of men who can comply with it, and*
>   *(ii) which he cannot show to be justifiable irrespective of the sex of the person to whom it is applied, and*
>   *(iii) which is to her detriment because she cannot comply with it.*

This terminology continues to apply to non-employment race and sex discrimination cases. However, in sexual orientation and religion and belief and in employment race and sex discrimination cases 'condition or requirement' is replaced by 'provision, requirement or practice'. This is a much easier test to meet, especially as 'requirement or condition' has been construed strictly (*Perera v Civil Service Commission* [1983] IRLR 166).

The second concept to be relaxed in certain cases is the requirement to show a 'considerably smaller proportion' of the claimant's group unable to comply. This test, which may require detailed statistical evidence to satisfy, continues to apply to non-employment RRA 1976 and SDA 1975 cases. However, employment RRA 1976 and SDA 1975 cases and claims under the EE(RB) Regs 2003, EE(SO) Regs 2003 and EE(A) Regs 2006 are subject to a new test: 'which puts or would put persons of the same [sexual orientation] as that other at a particular disadvantage when compared with other persons'.

This more modern wording, which reflects the influence of the Framework Directive 2000/78 is exemplified by s. 1(2)(b) SDA 1975:

> *1 . . . .*
>
> *(2) In any circumstances relevant for the purposes of a provision to which this subsection applies, a person discriminates against a woman if—*
>
> *. . .*
>
> *(b) he applies to her a provision, criterion or practice which he applies or would apply equally to a man, but—*
>> *(i)   which puts or would put women at a particular disadvantage when compared with men,*
>> *(ii) which puts her at that disadvantage, and*
>> *(iii) which he cannot show to be a proportionate means of achieving a legitimate aim.*

This requirement will be simpler to establish than that requiring establishment of 'considerably smaller proportions' of people in different categories. It is therefore important to check precisely which of the various provisions apply to the circumstances in which you are representing a client.

17.3.2.1   How is disproportionate impact proven?

Where the 'considerably smaller proportion' test applies, statistical evidence may well be necessary. The courts recognise that this should not be over-elaborate (*Perera v Civil Service Commission* [1983] IRLR 166), and the Court of Appeal has expressed support for a common-sense approach (*London Underground Ltd v Edwards (No 2)* [1998] IRLR 364). This is a technical area. For more discussion, see paragraphs **8.1.2** and **8.2.1** of the **Employment Law in Practice** manual.

17.3.2.2   How can a claim of indirect discrimination be defended?

Where the legislation requires the defendant to show justification (eg, SDA 1975 s 1(1)(b)(ii) above) this must be objectively justified on economic grounds (*Bilka-Kaufhaus v Weber von Hartz* (Case 170/84) [1987] ICR 110, where the ECJ indicated that the indirectly discriminatory provisions must respond to a real need, be appropriate in achieving that aim and be necessary in order to achieve it). The justification must be irrespective of race or sex (*Mandla v Dowell Lee* [1983] 2 AC 548).

Where the legislation uses the concept of proportionality to establish a defence (eg, reg 3(1)(b)(iii) above) a balancing exercise is expected between the needs of the alleged discriminator and those of the alleged victim. In fact, the Directive uses the term 'appropriate and necessary'. The explanatory memorandum to the new Regulations explains that this term was not used because of its very strict interpretation in English jurisprudence and that 'proportionality' incorporates the concept of necessity.

17.3.3   Victimisation

This is provided for by SDA 1975, s 4; RRA 1976, s 2; DDA 1995, s 55; EE(RB) Regs 2003, reg 4; EE(SO) Regs 2003, reg 4; and EE(A) Regs 2006, reg 4. People who suffer less favourable treatment because they carry out a protected act are victimised and are entitled to a remedy. Protected acts include bringing claims, giving evidence, making allegations or doing other things by reference to the discrimination legislation (or intending to do so).

17.3.4   May affirmative action programmes be lawful?

Although the results of past discrimination continue to disadvantage many individuals the law makes all discrimination (including 'positive discrimination') in the specified fields unlawful. Limited exceptions, however, exist where properly approved affirmative action programmes may be lawful (see SDA 1975, ss 47–48 and RRA 1976, ss 35–38).

17.4   Disability discrimination

DDA 1995 prohibits direct discrimination on grounds of disability in the fields of employment, education and the supply of goods, facilities, services and premises. Indirect discrimination is not covered and a claim of direct discrimination may be met by a defence of justifiability. The Act is framed somewhat differently from the SDA 1975 and RRA 1976 and is thus better considered separately. Basic concepts are defined separately in the different Parts of the Act. References in this section will generally be to Part II.

17.4.1   Who is able to make a claim?

A remedy is available for people who have a disability, defined as a physical or mental impairment causing a substantial long-term adverse effect on the ability to carry out normal day-to-day activities (see DDA 1995, Sch 1, and the Meaning of Disability Regulations 1996 (SI 1996/1455)). Progressive conditions such as multiple sclerosis are included.

In deciding whether this test is met, tribunals should consider what the applicant cannot do rather than what they can do (*Goodwin v The Patent Office* [1999] IRLR 4). The activities to be considered include:

- mobility;
- manual dexterity;
- physical co-ordination;
- continence;
- the ability to lift and carry;
- speech, hearing and eyesight;
- memory or ability to concentrate, learn or understand; and
- perception of the risk of danger.

17.4.2   Discrimination on grounds of disability

DDA 1995 (as amended) establishes different headings of discrimination from those in the earlier legislation. The case law on the other discrimination legislation is therefore not a safe guide to interpretations of DDA 1995 concepts.

17.4.2.1   Disability-related discrimination

Section 3A(1) provides:

> . . . a person discriminates against a disabled person if—
>> (a) for a reason which relates to the disabled person's disability, he treats him less favourably than he treats or would treat others to whom that reason does not or would not apply, and
>> (b) he cannot show that the treatment in question is justified.

It is not necessary for the claimant to find a comparator in the same position (apart from the disability). This is because the effects of the disability normally place the disabled person in a different position from others. The focus in DDA 1995 claims is on the employer's justification, which must be both 'material' and 'substantial' (s 3A(3)).

This is the only form of disability discrimination which may be justified. Guidance may be found in *Williams vJ Walter Thompson Group Ltd* [2005] IRLR 376 (CA).

17.4.2.2 Failure to comply with a duty to make reasonable adjustments

Section 3A(2) provides:

> . . . *a person also discriminates against a disabled person if he fails to comply with a duty to make reasonable adjustments imposed on him in relation to the disabled person.*

Where arrangements (such as the rules governing disciplinary hearings) or physical features of premises (such as entry steps which could be supplemented by a ramp) cause a substantial disadvantage to a disabled person, the employer or service provider must make reasonable adjustments. What is reasonable depends on the perspectives of both the disabled person and the person considering making the adjustment. The Code of Practice relating to disability in employment (see the Disability Discrimination (Guidance and Code of Practice) (Appointed Day) Order 1996 (SI 1996/1996)) indicates that the following should be considered:

- The effectiveness of the adjustment in removing the disadvantage.
- The practicability of making the adjustment.
- The cost of making the adjustment.
- The disruptive effect of making the adjustment.

Guidance on how this analysis should be approached is provided by *Morse v Wiltshire CC* [1998] IRLR 352, although the same case's references to justification no longer apply, as this defence has been abolished since 1 October 2004.

17.4.2.3 Direct discrimination

Section 3A(5) provides for direct discrimination (less favourable treatment on the grounds of disability). As in the SDA 1975 and RRA 1976, such direct discrimination is not justifiable. The claimant is required to show a comparator whose circumstances are the same or not materially different.

Two examples may help to distinguish s 3A(5) and s 3A(1) claims.

(a) Where an employer is faced with two similarly qualified applicants one of whom is disabled, and rejects the disabled candidate on the grounds of disability, s 3A(5) will apply. No justification may be argued.

(b) Where a disabled candidate performs less well than a non-disabled comparator, less favourable treatment may involve breach of s 3A(1) subject to possible employer justification and the duty to make reasonable adjustments.

17.4.2.4 Discrimination by way of victimisation

Those victimised for taking action under DDA 1995 may bring a claim under s 55(3) (see **17.3.3**).

17.5   Discrimination in employment

This is the field most widely affected by the discrimination legislation. All the provisions identified in **17.2** affect the employment relationship.

Note that where the claimant complains of sex discrimination in pay or other terms of the contract of employment the claim should be under the Equal Pay Act 1970, and special procedural rules apply to such claims (see **17.9** below).

Specific provisions can be found in SDA 1975, ss 6–21; RRA 1976, ss 4–15; DDA 1995, ss 4–18; EE(RB) Regs 2003; the EE(SO) Regs 2003; and the EE(A) Regs 2006.

There is a defence peculiar to the employment field. Discrimination which would otherwise be unlawful may be lawful if it relates to a genuine occupational requirement (SDA 1975, s 7; RRA 1976, s 5; EE(RB) Regs 2003, reg 7; EE (SO) Regs 2003, reg 7; and the EE(A) Regs 2006, reg 8). Examples would include employing only women to supervise a female changing room or only those of Japanese origin as waiters in a Japanese restaurant.

There are particular provisions relating to the employment of partners by partnerships, the operation of employment agencies, membership of trade unions, gaining qualifications and the provision of vocational training.

17.5.1   Individual remedies for discrimination in employment cases

17.5.1.1   Jurisdiction and limitation period

Employment tribunals have jurisdiction to hear these claims (SDA 1975, s 63; RRA 1976, s 54; DDA 1995, s 8; EE(RB) Regs 2003, reg 28; EE(SO) Regs 2003, reg 28; EE(A) Regs 2006, reg 36).

The limitation period is three months from the last discriminatory act complained of, although the tribunal may extend the period if it is 'just and equitable' to do so (a relatively broad provision). Note also that where a claimant claims a right provided for by a Directive, time only begins to run when the Directive is fully brought into effect in the UK.

17.5.1.2   What orders can the tribunal make?

A tribunal can make the following orders:

(a) An order declaring the rights of each party (SDA 1975, s 65(1)(a); RRA 1976, s 56(1)(a); EE(RB) Regs 2003, reg 30(1)(a); EE(SO) Regs 2003, reg 30(1)(a); EE(A) Regs 2006, reg 38(1)(a)) or a declaration to the same effect (DDA 1995, s 8(2)(a)).

(b) An award of compensation including compensation for injury to feelings (SDA 1975, s 65(1)(b); RRA 1976, s 56(1)(b); Race Relations (Remedies) Act 1994; DDA 1995, s 8(2)(b); EE(RB) Regs 2003, reg 30(1)(b); EE(SO) Regs 2003, reg 30(1)(b); EE(A) Regs 2006, reg 38(1)(b)).

(c) A recommendation of action to be taken within a specified time, in default of which additional compensation can be ordered (SDA 1975, s 65(1)(c); RRA 1976, s 56(1)(c); DDA 1995, s 8(2)(c); EE(RB) Regs 2003, reg 30(1)(c); EE(SO) Regs 2003, reg 30(1)(c); EE(A) Regs 2006, reg 38(1)(c)).

DDA 1995 also provides for criminal penalties (a fine of up to £5,000) in respect of those who knowingly or recklessly give false assurances that, because of some provision in the legislation, an unlawful act is not, in fact, unlawful.

17.5.2   Tribunal procedure

This is provided for in SDA 1975, s 63, RRA 1976, s 54 , DDA 1995, s 8, EE(RB) Regs 2003, reg 28, EE(SO) Regs 2003, reg 28 and EE(A) Regs 2006, reg 36. Tribunal procedures are regulated by the Employment Tribunal (Constitution and Rules of Procedure) Regulations 2004 (SI 2004/1861). For a more detailed exposition see the ***Employment Law in Practice*** manual. There are a number of features peculiar to these proceedings.

17.5.2.1   The questionnaire procedure

SDA 1975, s 74, RRA 1976, s 65, DDA 1995, s 56, EE(RB) Regs 2003, Sch 2, EE(SO) Regs 2003, Sch 2 and EE(A) Regs 2006, Sch 3, respectively, provide for the claimant to submit a questionnaire to the employer, the answers to which are admissible in evidence. A failure to respond timeously, or answers which are evasive or equivocal, entitle the tribunal to draw such inferences as it thinks fit, including an inference that there has been unlawful discrimination.

Precedents showing how a questionnaire might be prepared and how a respondent might reply may be found in the ***Employment Law in Practice*** manual.

17.5.2.2   The role of ACAS

The Advisory, Conciliation and Arbitration Service has a duty to promote settlement in employment tribunal cases. Either party may approach ACAS at will. Alternatively an ACAS Conciliation Officer may approach the parties if there appears to be a reasonable prospect of settlement.

17.5.2.3   Pre-hearing review

This procedure is designed to weed out hopeless cases. Either party may request a pre-hearing review, or the tribunal itself may decide to hold one. Evidence is not heard. Where the tribunal concludes that either claim or defence has no reasonable prospect of success it may require that party to pay a deposit of up to £500 before continuing to bring or defend the claim.

17.5.2.4   Appeals

An appeal against an employment tribunal decision lies to the Employment Appeal Tribunal and must be made within 42 days of the extended written reasons being sent to the parties.

17.6   Discrimination in other fields

17.6.1   Education

Discrimination in education is addressed by SDA 1975, ss 22–28, RRA 1976, ss 17–19 and DDA 1995, ss 28A–31C. Much of the provision in relation to disability has been provided for by the Special Educational Needs and Disability Act 2001.

Discrimination is actionable in the following situations:

- in terms of admission;
- by not accepting an application;
- in access to benefits, etc;
- by excluding, or causing other detriment.

There are statutory exemptions which apply to single-sex establishments and further education courses in physical training.

17.6.1.1 Who is responsible for discriminatory acts?

SDA 1975, s 22, RRA 1976, s 17 and DDA 1995, Sch 4A, para 1 provide tables specifying who is deemed responsible for acts of discrimination in respect of different types of school or other institution.

17.6.1.2 Remedies for discrimination in education

In sex and race cases no application may be made unless notice has been given to the Secretary of State and until either the Secretary has not responded within two months of that notice, or does not wish to consider the matter (SDA 1975, s 66; RRA 1976, s 7). An application may then be made to a County Court for any remedy available for breach of statutory duty.

Where such notice has been given, the limitation period is eight months from the last act complained of.

The Special Educational Needs and Disability Act 2001 provides for a Special Educational Needs and Disability Tribunal (DDA 1995, ss 28H–28I) to hear such claims.

17.6.2 Goods, facilities, services and premises

Discrimination in the field of goods, facilities, services and premises is covered by SDA 1975, ss 29–36; RRA 1976, ss 20–27; and DDA 1995, ss 19–28. Discrimination in this field will be actionable on denial of the goods, facilities or services concerned or on denial of equal quality or terms.

17.6.2.1 What facilities and services are covered?

SDA 1975, s 29(2), RRA 1976, s 21(2) and DDA 1995, s 19(3) provide an illustrative but non-exhaustive list of examples:

- access to and use of any place which members of the public or a section of the public are permitted to enter;
- accommodation in a hotel, boarding house or other similar establishment;
- facilities by way of banking or insurance or for grants, loans, credit or finance;
- facilities for education;
- facilities for entertainment, recreation or refreshment;
- facilities for transport or travel;
- the services of any profession or trade or any local or other public authority.

Non-profit-making voluntary bodies are excepted from these provisions of the sex discrimination legislation, as are certain other situations (for example, single-sex toilets (SDA 1975, ss 34, 35)).

17.6.2.2 When will discrimination in the provision of housing or in the disposal of premises be actionable?

A claim will lie if discrimination is shown in the following instances:

- in offering or refusing housing, etc;
- in the operation of any waiting list;
- in access to any benefits;

- by denying access to any benefits, etc;
- by eviction or causing other detriment.

17.6.3 Individual remedies for discrimination in the provision of goods, facilities, etc

The remedy lies in an application to the County Court. In cases brought under RRA 1976, application is made to a designated County Court; in cases brought under SDA 1975 or DDA 1995, application is made to a County Court.

For procedure, see CCR Ord 49, r 17 (preserved in CPR, Sch 2). Notice must be given to the Commission for Racial Equality, Equal Opportunities Commission or Disability Services Commission (as appropriate), who may support the claim by giving advice or assistance and can recoup their costs from any damages ordered to be paid to the applicant by the court.

Note that the questionnaire procedure (see **17.5.2.1** above) applies in these cases.

17.6.3.1 Limitation period

A claim must be brought within six months of the act complained of.

17.6.3.2 Who hears the case?

In SDA 1975 cases, either party or the judge can summon an assessor, whose costs will be met out of public funds.

In RRA 1976 cases the case will be heard by a judge and two assessors, unless the parties agree to dispense with them.

17.6.3.3 What are the powers of the court?

The court may make orders which it could make on a successful claim in the law of tort, ie:

- a declaration of rights;
- an order for damages (at large), including an order for damages for injury to feelings;
- an injunction to prohibit or mandate certain acts.

17.6.4 Preparing a case

Whether acting for a claimant or a respondent in individual discrimination claims it is important to approach the case preparation in a systematic way which reflects the conceptual basis of the legislation and the procedural provisions that exist. These are presented in Table 17.1.

17.7 Harassment and discrimination

Although the discrimination legislation makes no direct mention of harassment, case law has brought it firmly within the concept of direct discrimination where it is motivated by grounds of race, sex or disability (*Porcelli v Strathclyde Regional Council* [1986] ICR 564). The European Commission Recommendation and Code of Practice 'Protecting the Dignity of Women and Men at Work' 92/131/EEC OJ L49 reinforces this principle in the employment context. Outside that context the provisions of the Protection from Harassment Act 1997 create civil and criminal liability, whether or not there is a discriminatory motive.

Most discrimination cases are of sexual harassment.

17.7.1   What is sexual harassment?

The EC Code of Practice describes sexual harassment as 'unwanted conduct of a sexual nature, or other conduct based on sex, affecting the dignity of women and men at work'. It can include unwelcome physical, verbal or non-verbal conduct. Guidance has been provided by the Employment Appeal Tribunal in *Reed & Bull Information Systems Ltd v Stedman* [1999] IRLR 299.

17.7.2   Who is liable for harassment?

The individual harasser is clearly liable. However, where an employer fails to take proper steps to prevent harassment the employer may be vicariously liable. A broad view of the 'course of employment' has been adopted (*Tower Boot Co Ltd v Jones* [1997] IRLR 168 (CA) and *Chief Constable of the Lincolnshire Police v Stubbs* [1999] IRLR 81 (EAT)).

17.7.3   What remedies are available?

The remedies for those suffering from harassment that constitutes direct discrimination are the same as in other direct discrimination cases.

Where the Protection from Harassment Act 1997 applies, damages and an injunction may be available, and criminal proceedings may be brought in appropriate cases. An employer may be held vicariously liable for harassment under the 1997 Act (*Majrowski v Guy's and St Thomas's NHS Trust* [2005] EWCA Civ 251; [2005] IRLR 340).

17.8   Compensation in cases of individual discrimination

17.8.1   Compensation in direct and indirect discrimination cases

Compensation is available in cases of direct discrimination and in indirect discrimination on grounds of sex (SDA 1975, s 65(1B)). In cases of indirect discrimination on grounds of race, compensation is not available if the respondent can prove that the action complained of was unintentionally discriminatory (RRA 1976, s 57). This provision has been interpreted restrictively in *J.H. Walker v Hussain* [1996] IRLR 11.

The main element of most compensation claims will be the conventional measure: the actual loss caused by the discrimination. However, where injury to feelings can be shown, compensation will be made for that and in appropriate circumstances (for example, where an employer has behaved particularly badly) aggravated damages may also be awarded. Exemplary damages may be available on the standard grounds in *Rookes v Barnard* [1964] AC 1129 since the House of Lords held that the remedy was not restricted to causes of action in existence in 1964 (*Kuddus v Chief Constable of Leicester Constabulary* [2002] 2 AC 122).

Table 17.1 Disrimination checklist—how to prepare a case

Checklist applicant	Checklist respondent

1. *Is there an actionable claim?*
  (a) Does the discriminatory act relate to a field covered by the legislation?
  (b) Is it an act that gives an individual a right of claim?
  (c) When did the act occur?
  (d) When do time limits run out?
2. *Is this a case of direct or indirect discrimination?*
See respondent's checklist for matters to be considered in each type of claim.
3. *How is the discrimination to be proved?*
  (a) What evidence is provided in the papers?
  (b) What does the lay client say happened?
  (c) Is a conference necessary to establish lay client's side of the case?
  (d) What further evidence is required (including statistical evidence in indirect discrimination cases)?
  (e) Where can the evidence be obtained?
    (i) If a questionnaire has been sent:
    Have replies been received? Are they clear and unequivocal?
    If they are not what inferences should the court/tribunal draw?
    (ii) If a questionnaire has not been sent, consider sending one. Should it be in standard form or are there specific questions to ask if discrimination is to be proven?
    (iii) Is a Code applicable and has it been broken?
  (f) What has happened to the applicant since the discriminatory act?
    (i) What financial loss has the applicant suffered?
    (ii) To what extent have the applicant's feelings been injured?
    (iii) What evidence is required to establish financial loss and/or injury to feelings?
	1. *What allegations of discrimination have been made?*
	2. *Is the application within time limits?*
	3. *In direct discrimination cases, does the respondent admit allegations?*
	  (a) If not, with what facts does the respondent disagree? What evidence supports the respondent's view of the facts? How is that evidence to be proven? What interpretation of the law might avoid a finding of discrimination?
	    (i) What the respondent is willing to do for the applicant.
	    (ii) What would be the result of action?
	    (iii) Negotiate a settlement—consider a calculation agreement.
	4. *If the allegation is of indirect discrimination*
	  (a) Was a requirement or condition (or in employment cases a provision, criterion or practice) applied?
	  (b) Does it have a disproportionately adverse impact on the claimant's racial group or gender?
	  (c) What statistical evidence might undermine the allegation of disproportionate impact?
	  (d) Did the applicant suffer any detriment as a result? What evidence is there of detriment?
	  (e) Was the requirement or condition (or provision, criterion or practice) justified or proportionate? If so why, and how is justification to be proved?
	5. *Is the whole application one in which the principle: de minimis non curat lex could apply?*
	6. *What submissions could be made to reduce damages?*
	7. *What might be done to avoid or agree recommended action for the future?*

17.8.2   What may be awarded for injury to feelings?

A significant element of many awards is given to cover injury to feelings. Guidance is available from the Court of Appeal in *Vento v Chief Constable of West Yorkshire Police* [2003] IRLR 102, where three bands were identified:

(a) The top band should normally be between £15,000 and £25,000, eg, where there has been a sustained campaign of harassment; awards above £25,000 should only be made in exceptional cases.

(b) The middle band of £5,000 to £15,000 should be used in serious cases falling short of the top band.

(c) The lower band of £500 to £5,000 is appropriate for less serious cases, eg, one-off events. In general, awards of less than £500 are to be avoided altogether, because they risk being so low as to be derisory.

In the instant case the court awarded £18,000 for injury to feelings and a further £5,000 in aggravated damages.

17.9   Equal pay

Where discrimination on grounds of sex is alleged to arise within the contract of employment, claims should be made under the Equal Pay Act 1970, or, where no remedy is available under that Act, under Article 141 of the EC Treaty. The Act provides that there is an 'equality clause' in all contracts of employment, breach of which entitles the applicant to a remedy. Both men and women may make use of these provisions, although claims by women are far more common.

17.9.1   The remedy

The remedy is a claim to an employment tribunal which, if the claim is established, may import the more favourable term into the claimant's contract. The tribunal may make a declaration of rights and may award compensation as appropriate, including compensation for arrears of unequal pay.

17.9.1.1   How is a claim established?

The claimant must cite a comparator of the other gender within the same employment, whose job involves:

- like work;
- work rated as equivalent (eg by a job evaluation study); or
- work of equal value.

If this is established the claimant will be entitled to the same contractual terms as the chosen comparator.

17.9.1.2   Is there a defence available to the employer?

An employer may successfully defend an equal pay claim by establishing that the contractual difference is genuinely due to a material factor other than sex. Examples would include employees working on incremental salary scales where a newly appointed woman sought equal pay with a man who did the same job, but earned more, having moved up the salary scale over a period of years. The pay difference there is not due to sex.

The test for whether such a material factor defence is valid is closely related to that for justification of indirect discrimination (*Bilka-Kaufhaus GmbH v Weber von Hartz* (Case 170/84) [1987] ICR 110). See **17.3.2.2** above.

17.9.2   Procedure

Where a claim is based on the comparator doing like work, or work rated as equivalent, the tribunal procedure is similar to other tribunal proceedings (see Employment Tribunal (Constitution and Rules of Procedure) Regulations 2004 (SI 2004/1861), Sch 1. Equal value claims, however, are treated differently (see Sch 4). The tribunal may make an initial evaluation on the evidence and, where it is sufficiently clear, rule that the jobs are, or are not, of equal value. Where it is not sufficiently clear the tribunal will commission a report from an independent expert. That report will then be subject to argument from the parties and the tribunal will take the final decision of fact (see the Sex Discrimination and Equal Pay (Miscellaneous Amendments) Regulations 1996 (SI 1996/438)).

17.10   Enforcing the law

As well as enforcement in the courts and tribunals by individuals suffering from discrimination, the legislation has established Commissions, which may not only support selected individual cases, but may also conduct formal investigations. These are intended to deal with more widespread discrimination, for example, practices throughout a particular industry, employer or authority which are considered to have a discriminatory effect.

The original three Commissions were the Equal Opportunities Commission (EOC), the Commission for Racial Equality (CRE) and the Disability Rights Commission (DRC). The Equality Act 2006 s 1 established a new Commission for Equality and Human Rights (CEHR) which came into existence on 18 April 2006. On 1 October 2007 it took over the work of the existing Commissions. Details of the work of the CEHR is available from its website: <http://www.equalityhumanrights.com/en/Pages/default.aspx>

Codes of Practice have been prepared which are admissible in evidence before courts and tribunals as to the standards to be expected in a variety of fields and circumstances. They are now provided for by EA 2006, s 14.

17.10.1   Formal investigations

The Commission may institute an investigation on its own initiative provided that it believes that there has been an unlawful discriminatory act (EA 2006, s 20). The Secretary of State may require it to conduct an investigation. Where a number of individuals have suffered from discriminatory practices such an informal investigation may provide them with an effective remedy. These enforcement powers and procedural stages are presented in **Figure 17.1** below.

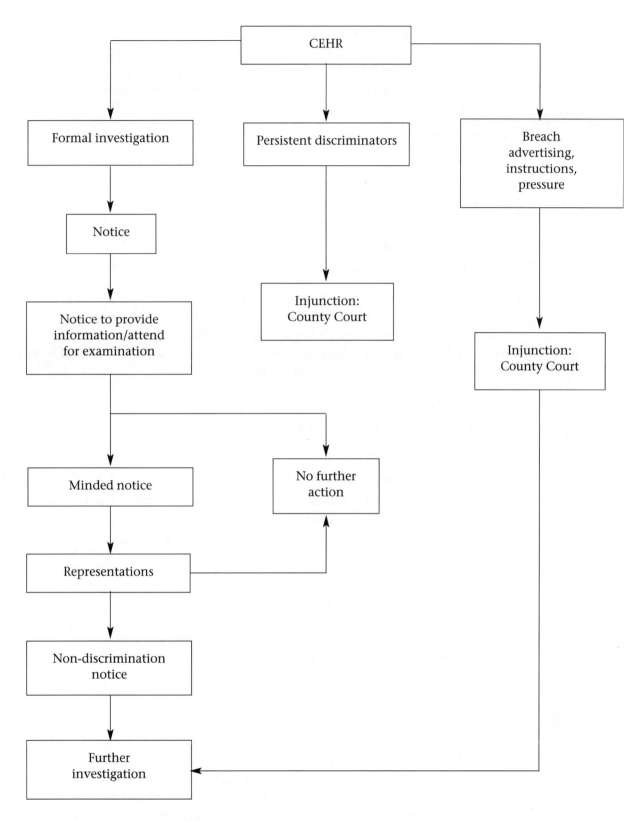

Figure 17.1 Powers of the CEHR to enforce the law. Details of these powers may be found in **17.10.1–17.10.3**.

17.10.1.1   What are the procedures for a formal investigation?

The Commission must draw up terms of reference stating that the persons named are believed to have done or be doing specified unlawful acts. If required to investigate by the Secretary of State, all parties named must be given notice of the investigation.

The CEHR may, by notice, require a person who:

- is believed to be committing unlawful discriminatory acts; or
- applies a requirement or condition which results in an unlawful act of indirect discrimination or victimisation, whether or not there is a specific victim; or
- advertises in a discriminatory way; or
- gives instructions to others to discriminate; or
- induces others to discriminate; or
- is subject to such a notice being ordered by the Secretary of State

to provide specific written information or to attend for oral examination and produce such documents as may be required which are in that person's possession or control, subject to the rules of evidence governing the production of documents in the High Court. If a failure to comply with such a notice occurs or is reasonably believed to be likely an order can be obtained from the County Court.

17.10.1.2   What are the possible results of a formal investigation?

Following a formal investigation the CEHR may:

(a) recommend future action;

(b) recommend a change in the law;

(c) deliver the report to the Secretary of State (when that investigation was requested by the Secretary of State), who must publish it;

(d) publish the report or make it available for inspection (subject to a fee if required);

(e) serve a notice stating that the Commission is minded to serve a non-discrimination notice (NDN) on the person formally investigated. This minded notice must specify the grounds on which the NDN is contemplated, and give an opportunity for representations to be made either orally or in writing within 28 days. The Commission must take account of any such representations before issuing an NDN.

17.10.1.3   What is a non-discrimination notice?

This is a notice that requires the person served to commit no further such acts of discrimination. Where the notice requires a change of practice, then the Commission must be informed that the change in practice has been made. It may also require the person served to provide the Commission with further information and specify the time and manner in which that information is to be provided, which must be no later than five years from the date of the notice.

An appeal against an NDN must be made within six weeks of the NDN being served. Appeals in relation to employment matters will be heard in the employment tribunal, and those in relation to other fields of discrimination will be heard in the County Court for the district in which the acts to which the requirements relate were done. In RRA 1976 cases this must be a designated County Court.

The NDN should be accompanied by a statement of the findings of fact. The notice of appeal should specify each finding of fact that is challenged, each allegation of fact which it is intended to prove, and any other grounds on which it is alleged that the requirements contained in the NDN are unreasonable.

Appeals are governed by CPR, Part 52.

17.10.1.4 What are the powers of the court or tribunal on appeal?

If the requirement contained in the NDN is considered unreasonable because it is based on an incorrect finding of fact or for any other reason, the court or tribunal must quash the requirement. The court or tribunal may direct that a requirement be substituted for the quashed requirement. It is possible to challenge all or any of the findings of fact on which the requirements contained in the notice were based.

17.10.2 Claim against the persistent discriminator

The Commission may apply to a County Court for an injunction restraining a person who, within five years of a finding of discrimination made in an employment tribunal or County Court, or within five years of the issue of an NDN, discriminates or who continues to apply a condition or requirement which is discriminatory but which has no specific victim, from continuing to act unlawfully.

17.10.3 Discriminatory advertisements, instructions and pressure to discriminate

Only the Commission has the power to enforce compliance with these aspects of the legislation (SDA 1975, s 38(6); RRA 1976, s 29(6). Application may be made to an employment tribunal (employment matters) or to a County Court (other fields) for a decision as to whether the allegation of discrimination can be made out, or to a County Court for an injunction where the Commission believes that a breach of this part of the legislation has occurred and that further breaches are likely unless restrained by order (EA 2006, s 25).

17.11 Exercises

17.11.1 Exercise 1

PROBLEM

The ABC Building Society is unwilling to advance money for the improvement of terraced houses without front gardens in an area where many members of ethnic minority groups live. Your instructing solicitors have presented you with a copy of a report which states that 86% of ethnic minority families living in that area live in terraced houses without front gardens, and that 46% of white families living there live in terraced houses without front gardens.

Please advise in the following situations on appropriate procedure and remedies, treating each as independent of the other:

(a) A, who owns a terraced house without a front garden in this area, and is a member of an ethnic minority group, believes she has been indirectly discriminated against. The ABC Building Society has refused to advance money on a mortgage for improvements to her home as a result of this policy.

(b) The local Community Relations Council has received a number of complaints from residents in the same situation as A, but who are unwilling to take action themselves as they fear that they will be seen as troublemakers and be denied any chance of a mortgage if they were to do so.

SOLUTION

(a) This concerns facilities by way of banking or loans for finance which is a field in which racial discrimination is illegal. See RRA 1976, s 21(2). As 14% of ethnic minority families can comply with the condition (86% cannot), and 54% of white families can comply (46% cannot), the pro portions suggest that this meets the requirement that a considerably smaller proportion of A's racial group can comply with the condition compared with the proportion of people not in A's racial group who can comply.

A's remedy is to file a claim under the RRA 1976 in the County Court where the ABC Building Society carries on business or in the district where the act took place (perhaps the relevant branch of the society). ABC will have a defence if it can justify the condition irrespective of race; a financial motive for the condition will not be sufficient reason to constitute justification.

There is no need for A to prove that ABC had an intention to discriminate. However, if ABC can show that the effect of the condition was unintentional, then no damages will be awarded to A. Generally A will be able to recover injury to feelings plus other losses subject to proof of causation. It is unlikely that A would obtain an injunction against ABC and the likely remedy would be a declaratory order and a recommendation as to action to avoid further discrimination.

(b) The Community Relations Council should make a complaint to the Commission for Equality and Human Rights. EA 2006, s 20 gives the CEHR power to investigate allegations of discriminatory behaviour. The CEHR may issue a recommendation to the ABC and investigate whether this has been com plied with. If not, it may issue an NDN, which ABC may appeal in the County Court. Failure to comply with an NDN entitles the CEHR to file an action in the County Court. A possible action exists in the European Court of Human Rights, although both routes require a long period of time and A and others needing immediate protection may not see the benefit.

17.11.2   Exercise 2

PROBLEM

Mrs Smith has been sexually harassed at work by her section supervisor, Mr James. Her complaints consisted of: Mr James asking her out, touching her and pressing against her whenever he had cause to come into her office, and telling others in the company that she was free with sexual favours and that when he had finished with her he would pass her on.

When Mrs Smith first complained to Mr James's line manager, she was told that she should be flattered. It was only a week later, when she spoke to the Human Resources Manager, that her complaint was taken seriously.

Mr James has now been dismissed, and Mrs Smith has decided to continue to work for her employers. You are asked to advise her as to her remedies (if any), the best forum in which to pursue them, and the amount of damages she is likely to recover.

European Community law remedies

18.1 Introduction

European Community law (Community law) enables private individuals and legal persons to obtain remedies in the national courts of Member States, the European Court of Justice (ECJ) and the Court of First Instance (CFI).

The ability of parties to use Community law in national courts is not covered here. However, questions may arise in national courts as to the interpretation or validity of EC laws and such questions may be referred to the ECJ. See **18.2.** This chapter considers preliminary references (Article 234 (ex 177) EC), judicial review (Articles 230 and 232 (ex 173 and 175)), claims for damages (Article 288 (ex 215)), the plea of illegality (Article 241 (ex 184)) and infringement proceedings under Article 226 (ex 169).

18.2 Preliminary rulings

18.2.1 What is a preliminary ruling?

A preliminary ruling is given by the ECJ on a Community law point, either on interpretation or validity of Community law. Such a ruling will have been requested by a national court during proceedings before that court in which the Community point has arisen. Provision for this is made in Article 234 (ex 177) of the EC Treaty. It is an indirect action before the ECJ, with the ECJ intervening in national litigation. The CFI cannot hear preliminary references; see Article 225 (ex 168a).

English rules for preliminary references are in the Civil Procedure Rules, Part 68 and Practice Direction 68 and the Criminal Procedure Rules 2005 (SI 2005/384), r 75. The procedure has three stages:

- The national court makes the reference.
- The national proceedings are suspended.
- The national court applies the ECJ ruling to the case and continues to judgment.

18.2.2 In what areas of Community law does the ECJ have jurisdiction to give rulings?

The ECJ can give rulings on the interpretation of Community law (Article 234(1)(a), (b), (c) EC). This includes, for example, the EC Treaty, treaties amending or supplementing it, acts of the Community institutions and international treaties entered into by the Community. These rulings may include decisions as to whether a particular provision has direct effect.

The ECJ also gives rulings on the validity and interpretation of acts of the Community institutions (ie, Community secondary legislation) (Article 234(1)(b) EC) and on the interpretation of the statutes of any body established by an act of the Council if the statutes so provide.

The ECJ cannot rule on the facts of the case before the national court, nor on the validity of national law and its incompatibility with Community law. The national court alone has jurisdiction in these matters, although the effect of a preliminary reference is often to determine the outcome of a case in a particular way. The national court should not ask questions on these matters. If it does, the ECJ may reformulate the question so that it can be answered in a more abstract manner or may refuse to answer the question. However, the questions are likely to be closely related to the facts of the particular case.

The ECJ cannot tell the national court what to refer or how to exercise its discretion to refer. These are matters for the national court.

The national court may not interpret Community law if there is doubt about its meaning. It should refer any questions to the ECJ for interpretation. Equally it cannot rule on the validity of a Community provision (Foto-Frost v Hauptzollamt Lübeck-Ost (314/85) [1987] ECR 4199). The ECJ has stated that if, in the course of litigation in a national court, an argument appears to be well founded that a particular Community act is invalid, the national court has no choice but to make a preliminary reference on the matter. Only where such an argument is manifestly ill-founded may the national court determine the matter for itself, by dismissing the argument. See *R (International Air Transport Association and European Low Fares Association) v UK Department of Transport* (C-344/04), judgment of 10 January 2006 (The Times, 16 January 2006).

18.2.3   Who can refer a question to the ECJ?

Questions can be referred only by national courts or tribunals. An individual cannot ask the ECJ directly for a preliminary ruling, but a party to a claim before the national court may apply to the national court for a reference to be made. The national court alone has the discretion to decide to refer.

18.2.3.1   Courts which must refer

A national court against which there is no judicial remedy in national law is obliged to refer to the ECJ when a Community question arises (Article 234(3)). There are two views about which court that might be: it can be the highest court in the particular case (predominant view) or the highest court in the land (ie, House of Lords in the United Kingdom).

A court against which there is no judicial remedy is not obliged to refer if:

(a) The question has already been decided by the ECJ (although a further reference can be made).

(b) The meaning of the Community provision in question is clear, obvious and the court is free from doubt as to meaning. In this case, however, the national court must also be convinced that the meaning is equally clear to the courts of other Member States and to the ECJ (*CILFIT v Ministry of Health* (283/81) [1982] ECR 3415). This criterion should not be easy to satisfy. However, see the Queen's Bench Divisional Court ruling in *R v Manchester Crown Court, ex p DPP* (cited below at **18.2.4**).

A court against which there is no judicial remedy *must* refer a question if it involves a topic within a field under Title IV of the EC Treaty. This covers issues concerning visas, asylum, immigration, and judicial co-operation in judicial matters. In such situations, *only* this court has jurisdiction to make the reference. See Article 68(1) EC.

18.2.3.2 Courts that may refer

Any court or tribunal may refer a question to the ECJ if a preliminary ruling is *necessary to enable the court to give judgment* (Article 234(2)). This applies to all courts which are not the court of last resort.

Regardless of the nomenclature given to a court or tribunal in a Member State, the court must first be considered a genuine court by the ECJ in order to be able to use Article 234. The ECJ will not accept a reference from a body that it does not consider to be a court. The ECJ has a broad view of what constitutes a court—see *Pretore di Salo* (14/86) [1987] ECR 2545, where a public prosecutor/examining magistrate was held to be a 'court'. The ECJ will consider, for example: Is the referring body established by law? Is it permanent, with a compulsory jurisdiction? Is it independent—does it have any link to the organ which created the act under challenge? Is its procedure *inter partes*—who has a right to be heard there? Was there a debate? Is the decision one of a judicial nature? Does the body apply rules of law? See *Dorsch Consult v Bundesbangesellschaft Berlin* (C-54/96) [1997] ECR I-4961. For a very interesting review of this concept and Article 234 generally, including a call for a new definition of 'court or tribunal' (ignored by the ECJ), see the opinion of Advocate General Ruiz-Jarabo Colomer in *De Coster v Collège des Bourgmestre et Échevins de Watermael-Boitsfort* (Case C-17/00) [2001] ECR I-9445. As the enforcement of European competition law was decentralised, following the significant changes made in 2003–04, it became increasingly likely that national competition authorities (such as the Office of Fair Trading in the UK) would wish to use preliminary references. Indeed, this process began quite quickly; see, in particular, the reference by the Greek Competition Commission (*Sylfait v GlaxoSmithKline AEVE* (C-53/03). In his Opinion, Advocate General Jacobs used a broad, purposive, interpretation of what constituted a 'court or tribunal', and said the reference should be admissible; see also the article by Komninos in [2004] ECLR 106. However, more recently, concerns have been expressed about the workload of the ECJ on preliminary references and consequent delays in the resolution of domestic litigation. It has been suggested (see Komárek, [2007] 32 European Law Review 467) that the ability to make a preliminary reference should generally be limited to the final appeal court in each Member State. So far, that suggestion has not been adopted; the ECJ has shown more enthusiasm for speeding matters up by (i) resolving references without taking an Opinion from an Advocate General and (ii) proposing the introduction of an 'urgent preliminary reference procedure' (taking weeks to turn a reference around instead of nearly two years).

The ECJ has historically taken a broad view of what constitutes a court or tribunal *of a Member State*: a court in French Polynesia was stated to be such a court and entitled to make use of Article 234 in *Leplat v French Polynesia* (C-260/90) [1992] 2 CMLR 512.

18.2.4 At what stage in litigation can a national court make a reference?

A national court has power to refer:

(a) if a Community question is raised in the case before it; and

(b) a preliminary ruling on the question is necessary to enable the national court to give judgment.

The national court alone can decide how to exercise its discretion to refer. The following are considerations which the national court may take into account in exercising this discretion:

(a) Are the facts of the case decided? The stage in the case when the reference should be made is for the national court to decide *(Pretore di Salo v Persons Unknown (14/86) [1987] ECR 2545)*. In theory a reference can be made at any stage, but it is preferable if the facts have been decided and legal issues clarified first. Although a magistrates' court may refer a question, it is preferable that a reference is made at a later stage after all the evidence has been adduced and there is no question of the respondent being acquitted on the facts *(R v Plymouth Justices, ex p Rogers* [1982] QB 863)*. However, magistrates' courts have referred questions—eg, about Sunday trading *(Torfaen Borough Council v B & Q plc (145/88) [1990] 2 QB 19)*.

(b) Are the relevant issues clarified?

(c) Are questions of national law settled?

(d) Is the Community point potentially decisive of the case?

(e) Is there a consistent line of ECJ case law on the Community point, and should it be followed?

(f) Is the Community point unclear?

Other considerations *might* include:

(a) The difficulty of the Community point.

(b) Delay. This could take up to two years, with national proceedings suspended until the ECJ remits the reference. Delay played a large part in the refusal of the Divisional Court to refer an issue to the ECJ in *R v Manchester Crown Court, ex p DPP* [1992] 3 CMLR 329.

(c) Costs.

(d) Views of the parties. A reference is more likely if both parties agree it is necessary.

(e) Workload of the ECJ.

See the judgment of Lord Denning MR in *H.P. Bulmer Ltd v J. Bollinger SA* [1974] Ch 401 and the many later cases that have considered *Bulmer.*

National courts may make references in interlocutory proceedings. There is no obligation on courts from which there is no judicial remedy to make a reference in interlocutory proceedings, provided the decision is subject to review in subsequent proceedings, which may be started or requested by either party *(Hoffman-La Roche AG v Centrafarm Vertriebsgesellschaft Pharmazeutischer Erzeugnisse mbH (107/76) [1977] ECR 957)*.

For the procedure on making an application for a preliminary reference, see the *Advocacy* manual, **Chapter 34.** See also CPR PD 68.

18.2.5   What is the effect of a preliminary ruling on the case?

A preliminary ruling on interpretation or validity is binding on the national court in the case in which the ruling is sought. If the Community provision thus ruled upon is decisive to the judgment, the court has to decide the case according to the ruling. For an interesting attempt to circumvent the binding nature of a preliminary ruling, see the article by Jukka Snell examining a judgment of Laddie J: *European Courts and Intellectual Property: A Tale of Hercules, Zeus and Cyclops* [2004] ECLR 178. This article analyses the litigation surrounding use of the Arsenal FC trade mark. It notes the conclusion of Laddie

J that he could ignore parts of the ECJ ruling where the ECJ appeared to engage in fresh fact-finding, as this would exceed the ECJ's jurisdiction under Article 234. His analysis was set aside in the Court of Appeal, but his manoeuvre suggests an interesting means to sidestep preliminary rulings that individual national judges are unhappy with.

18.2.5.1   Does a preliminary ruling have retrospective application?

A preliminary ruling on interpretation and validity is deemed to declare what the law has always been. It usually has retrospective effect. However, the ECJ may impose temporal restrictions on the effect of a ruling in exceptional cases if retroactivity of the ruling would cause serious repercussions (usually economic) or uncertainty in the law. The limitations apply only to the actual case in which the ruling is sought. See, eg, *Defrenne v Sabena (No 2)* (43/75) [1976] ECR 455.

The ECJ may also limit the effect of the ruling in other ways, eg, only vertical (not horizontal) direct effect for directives; direct effect only for overt (not covert) sex discrimination. These limitations are not restricted to the actual case in which the ruling is sought.

18.2.5.2   What happens if the English courts do not comply with previous preliminary rulings?

If the English courts fail to follow previous preliminary rulings on validity or interpretation, the Commission may be able to bring an enforcement claim against the UK (see Article 226 EC at **18.7**).

18.3   Claims for annulment using Article 230 EC

18.3.1   Introduction

Article 230 (ex 173) provides a direct claim in the ECJ, to annul the acts of Community institutions. To bring a successful claim under Article 230, there are three jurisdictional barriers to overcome.

18.3.1.1   Nature of the act

The following acts may be reviewed:

- acts adopted jointly by the European Parliament and the Council;
- acts of the Council;
- acts of the Commission;
- acts of the European Central Bank;
- acts of the European Parliament, if intended to produce legal effects *vis-à-vis* third parties.

If the act is not within the items listed above, one cannot use Article 230 to seek its annulment. Does the act have legal effect? Only such acts may be challenged under Article 230. So, an act which is merely advisory and thus produces no legal changes is immune from attack. An example would be an opinion from the Commission. In order to minimise those acts which may not be challenged, the ECJ has traditionally used a broad interpretation of acts which produce legal effects—see, eg, the *ERTA* case, *Commission v Council* (22/70) [1971] ECR 263. However, there are limits to the category. In *Nederlandse Associatie van de Farmaceutische Industrie v Commission* (T-1 13/89) [1990] ECR II-797, the applicants sought to annul letters sent to themselves and the appropriate Dutch govern-ment ministry. The letters stated that certain agreements concerning the Dutch pharma-ceuticals market fell within Article 85 (now 81) EC but should be exempted if two specific conditions were met. The CFI upheld a Commission objection to the admissibility of the action—the letters were purely factual in nature and could not have any influence over the applicants' legal position. A more worrying illustration of this tendency to restrict the acts which are susceptible of review came in the case of *R J Reynolds Tobacco Holdings Inc v Commission* (C-131/03 P) [2006] ECR I-7795. Here, the ECJ ruled that a company against whom the Commission had begun civil proceedings in the USA could not use Article 230 to seek review of the decision to commence such proceedings, as this did not 'per se determine definitively the obligations of the parties . . . That determination can result only from the judgment of the [US] court' (see para 93 of the judgment of the CFI, approved in para 58 of the ECJ judgment). The ECJ stated that the company had not been denied effective judicial protection as a result of the ruling by the CFI that the complaint was inadmissible. See also Arnull, *When is an act not an act?* [2007] 32 Eu L Rev 1.

18.3.1.2   Parties

Does the applicant have *locus standi?* This divides into two categories, the privileged and the non-privileged applicants.

(a) The privileged applicants are the Council, the Commission and the Member States (Article 230(2)). These parties have an absolute right to seek annulment of any act, so long as it was intended to have legal effect. Under the original Treaty provision, the European Parliament had no standing to apply. In 1990, the ECJ discovered a 'common law right of action' allowing the Parliament to seek annulment. Subse-quently, the Treaty was amended so that it expressly permitted such applications by the Parliament, also by the Court of Auditors and the European Central Bank. (The two latter institutions have now been removed by the Treaty of Nice 2001.) Applications by privileged applicants are heard by the Court of Justice.

(b) The non-privileged applicants are natural or legal persons (Article 230(4)). Appli-cations by non-privileged applicants are heard by the CFI. In order to use Article 230, parties in this category must demonstrate an interest in the (challenged) act. This can be done in any one of three ways:

   (i)   The act is a decision, addressed to the applicant.
   (ii) The act is a decision addressed to another but is of direct and individual con-cern to the applicant.
   (iii) The act is in substance a decision, although in the form of a regulation, and is of direct and individual concern to the applicant.

Decisions are individual measures, eg, 'Bloggs Plc has broken the Community competi-tion laws'. Regulations are normative measures, intended to affect everyone, eg, 'all cars produced in the Community from 1990 onwards must be capable of using lead-free pet-rol'. 'A natural or legal person is individually concerned by a [regulation] that concerns him directly if [that regulation] affects his legal position, in a manner which is both definite and immediate, by restricting his rights or by imposing obligations on him'—see the CFI in *Jégo-Quéré et Cie SA v Commission* (T-177/01) [2002] ECR II-2365. It has been sug-gested that the difficulty of fulfilling the requirements of direct and individual concern can, in some cases, result in the absence of effective legal protection for private parties. See, for example, the powerful Opinion of Advocate General Jacobs in *Unión de Pequeños Agricultores v Council of the European Union* (Case C-50/00 P) [2002] ECR I-6677. However, the ECJ there reiterated that this is a matter for the Member States to address, either through Treaty amendment or through changes to their own legal systems to ensure effective access to the ECJ through use of Article 234.

If (and only if) the act and the applicant fall within the preceding criteria can that applicant challenge that act.

18.3.1.3   Limitation period

The claim must be started within a limitation period of two months. The period starts from the date the act was published, or when it was communicated to the applicant by the institution or when the applicant found out about the act. There are also grace periods set out in the rules of procedure of the Court of Justice. The safest, and simplest, course is to start proceedings as soon as is practicable after learning of the act.

18.3.2   Grounds on which an act may be annulled

(a) Once the jurisdictional barriers are overcome, one of the four grounds of illegality must be established. These are:

  (i) Lack of competence. This is similar to ultra vires. This ground will be satisfied if either an EC institution acts in a field not covered by the Treaty, or if one institution acts in a field expressly reserved for another.

  (ii) Infringement of an essential procedural requirement. This is a difficult category to define since many of the judgments of the Court interpreting it seem to have been made on an ad hoc basis. Not every procedural requirement will be regarded as 'essential'; not all of the 'essential procedural requirements' are laid down in the rules of procedure. An example of an essential procedural requirement is the obligation to give reasons for promulgating all legally binding acts (Article 253 (ex 190) EC). The institution must make it clear, usually within the act itself, why and how the act has been created.

  (iii) Infringement of the EC Treaty or of a rule of law relating to its application. Since the powers of the institutions derive from the Treaty, almost any error by an EC institution could be regarded as an infringement of the Treaty. This ground of illegality is frequently used by applicants and the European Court. The 'rules of law' are those which the European Court regards as underpinning the Treaty. Examples include international treaties and general principles of law (equality, legitimate expectations, proportionality).

  (iv) Misuse of power. This is rarely used, probably because it is difficult to establish. The motives of the institution or official responsible for the act must be examined.

(b) If the applicant can prove that at least one of the grounds of illegality applies, the act will be annulled. The European Court seems not to be too concerned with maintaining rigid divisions between the four grounds of illegality—it is sufficient if at least one is clearly applicable; the Court may not even refer to it specifically in its judgment. In practice, ground (iii) covers most successful applications for annulment.

For detailed analysis of the interpretation and application of Article 230, reference should be made to standard textbooks on EC law (eg, Hartley, *Foundations of EC Law;* Lenaerts, Arts and Maselis, *Procedural Law of the European Union*). As an aid to following your way through the Article, a flowchart is included (see **Figure 18.1**).

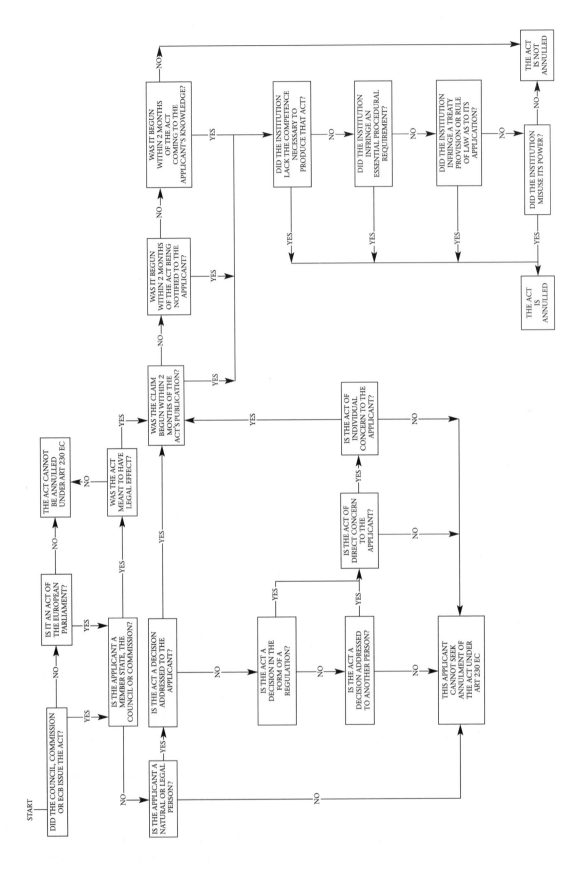

Figure 18.1   An action for annulment under Article 230

18.3.3 The effect of a successful claim under Article 230

The challenged act is annulled and void. No further action based on the act is permitted; all acts done pursuant to the annulled act must usually be undone (see Article 231 (ex 174) EC). The Court cannot amend the act nor substitute a new act. It is possible, though, to preserve some of the challenged act if the parts which require annulment can be severed from the whole.

For reasons of legal certainty and continuity, acts which are possibly invalid (voidable) are presumed to have legal effect unless and until they are successfully challenged in court. There is only one exception to this presumption that these defective acts continue to have legal effect until either annulled or withdrawn—this occurs when the act is regarded as legally non-existent. For the act to be legally non-existent, it must be tainted by an irregularity whose gravity is so obvious that it cannot be tolerated by the Community legal order—such a finding is reserved for quite extreme situations (see, for example, *Commission v BASF AG* (C-137/92 P) [1994] ECR I-2555). In most situations, therefore, one must challenge acts pursuant to Article 230 (ex 173) EC and do so within the limitation period. Once that period has elapsed, the only way to attack the legality of such acts is to raise a plea of illegality under Article 241 (ex 184) EC (see **18.6**).

18.4 Claim under Article 232 EC for a failure to act

18.4.1 Introduction

Article 232 (ex 175) is, to a large extent, the mirror image of Article 230 (ex 173). Whereas Article 230 is used to annul existing acts of the EC institutions, Article 232 is used to complain about the absence of an act.

18.4.2 The basis of a claim using Article 232

The legal basis is that there has been inaction on the part of a Community institution (the Council, Commission or European Parliament). This inactivity must constitute an infringement of the EC Treaty; for it to do so, the institution must be under a duty to act. This duty can be imposed either by the EC Treaty itself or by secondary legislation, enacted pursuant to the Treaty.

The Court of Justice has indicated that if the Treaty requires an institution to enact a measure by a certain date and that institution fails to do so, there may be a potential claim under Article 232. Whether or not a claim can be pursued will depend upon the discretion, if any, which is given to the institution. If it has a choice as to the aims of the enactment, then a failure to legislate will only give rise to an Article 232 claim; if it has a choice only as to the means to be employed to get a specific result, then there is an obligation to act and an omission will justify a claim under Article 232.

18.4.3 Who can use Article 232?

(a) Privileged applicants. These are the Member States and the institutions of the Community. They may complain to the Court of Justice about any failure to act in breach of an obligation; there is no need to prove a special interest in the case.

(b) Non-privileged applicants. Any natural or legal person can complain that a Community institution has failed to address an act to it (ie, take a measure of individual application). This applies to any act except recommendations and opinions (ie, acts which are not legally binding). In practice, this means that people or businesses can complain about a failure to pass a decision which will affect their legal position, either as the putative addressee of such a decision or because it will be of individual and direct concern to them (see *T Port v Bundesanstalt fur Landwirtschaft und Ernährung* (C-68/95) [1996] ECR I-6065).

18.4.4   The procedure for a claim using Article 232

Before one begins proceedings alleging a failure to act, the institution concerned must be given an opportunity to act. A written communication is sent to the institution, setting out specifically what measures it is suggested that the institution should take. The document must also warn that a failure to take these measures will be followed by a claim under Article 232. The institution then has two months in which to act.

Such action by the institution need only be a 'definition of its position'. It seems that almost any communication from the institution within the two months will suffice to define its position, even if it is a simple refusal to act. If this communication is susceptible of review under Article 230, its annulment may be sought, thus putting the onus back on the institution to act. But the communication is not always reviewable, and the other party may then be left without a remedy—unable to force the institution to act and with no act of which complaint can be made. It is possible that this situation may be regarded as incompatible with Articles 6 and 13 of the ECHR; see *Jégo-Quéré et Cie SA v Commission* (see **18.3.1.2**).

18.4.5   Going to court

If the institution does not define its position within the two-month period, it is then possible to bring a claim in the CFI (or Court of Justice, for privileged applicants). The applicant has a further two months within which the claim must be brought. If the institution is found guilty of failure to act, it will be required to take all the measures necessary to comply with the judgment of the Court (see Article 233 (ex 176) EC) although no specific steps will be ordered by the Court of Justice.

18.4.6   Using Articles 230 and 232 together

It is not always clear (to an applicant who wants to use the Article 232 procedure) whether the EC institution has failed to define its position within the two months or not. This is likely to be the case where the institution does not take the desired steps but does send a letter, refusing to act as required. In such circumstances, the applicant may be unsure whether the letter is a definition of position.

One way to deal with this is to start proceedings under both Articles 230 and 232, alleging that the letter is not a definition of position (and thus Article 232 is the basis of the claim) but that, if the Court finds it is a proper definition, then it should be annulled (thus proceeding under Article 230 EC).

18.5   Non-contractual liability of the EC under Article 288(2)

18.5.1   Introduction

Article 288(2) (ex 215(2)) states that ' . . . the Community shall, in accordance with the general principles common to the laws of the member States, make good any damage caused by its institutions or by its servants in the performance of their duties'.

Article 235 (ex 178) EC gives exclusive jurisdiction to the European Court to deal with claims under Article 288(2).

18.5.2   What must be shown in a claim under Article 288(2)?

From the express terms of the Article, a number of elements can be seen:

- Damage must have been suffered (usually by the applicant, although it seems that the right to sue can be assigned).

- A Community institution or its servants must have acted or omitted to act in the performance of its duties.

- Both the damage and the act (or omission) are causally linked.

A fourth element has been read into Article 288(2) by the European Court. This is the notion that the act or omission must be wrongful, sometimes referred to as 'fault'. This has been justified by reference to the general principles of law common to the Member States. This fourfold test was reaffirmed by the court in *Campagnia Italiana Alcool SAS Di Mario Mariano & Cov Commission* (C-358/90) [1992] 2 CMLR 876.

18.5.2.1   Damage

The applicant must allege clearly those injuries which have actually been sustained and on what basis he or she says that the Community should make good. The European Court will demand proof of the damage, although when determining liability it may not look at the exact amount involved. Sometimes, if satisfied that some damage has occurred, the Court will give a ruling on liability only and postpone its assessment of damages to a later date. Under Article 288(2) the Court may declare the Community liable for imminent damage (so long as it is foreseeable with sufficient certainty). It does not matter that the damage cannot be precisely quantified yet. When one establishes the cause of damage, one may have to act swiftly in order to forestall even greater damage.

Interest can be claimed by an applicant. It is usually awarded from the date of judgment.

The Court sometimes awards compensation for non-pecuniary loss (see *Adams v EC Commission* (145/83) [1985] ECR 3539). The Commission was found to be liable to Mr Adams for a breach of confidentiality. It was ordered to pay him £100,000 for his mental anguish. More usually, an applicant seeks compensation for pecuniary loss. Such pecuniary loss should not be based on speculation, eg, the profit that was expected on a contract which in fact was never made because of the Community's wrongful act.

18.5.2.2   An act or omission of an institution or its servant

The acts or omissions of the servants of the EC have rarely been the express basis of an action under Article 288(2). On an occasion when the issue of Community liability for its servants arose, the Court held that the Community is only liable for those acts of its servants which are 'the necessary extension of the tasks entrusted to the institution'. The Court seems to regard this as a difficult test to satisfy.

18.5.2.3 Causation

This is required by Article 288(2) and is always acknowledged by the Court as a necessary condition for liability. Nevertheless, the Court gives little overt consideration to it in the reported cases. A quite relaxed interpretation seems to be applied.

18.5.2.4 Fault

The Court has not gone so far as to declare the Community liable under Article 288(2) in the absence of fault, even though the idea of strict liability for the acts of public bodies exists in some Member States. The court requires proof of a wrongful act or omission. An act may be wrong either in its purpose or its procedure; a wrongful omission occurs when there is a duty to act which has not been performed.

18.5.3 Relationship between Article 288(2) and Articles 230 and 232

An overlap can be seen between these three Articles. The limitation period for claims under Article 288(2) is five years from the date of injury. Hence, if a party wanted to sue on the basis of an act or omission which could have been challenged under Articles 230 or 232 but was not, the limitation period for claims for review could be greatly extended.

The Court has stated that a claim for compensation under Article 288(2) is an independent form of claim. The fact that to award damages under this Article might have the same effect as a claim for review should not render it inadmissible. The practical result is that the time limits within which one may challenge acts which could have been reviewed under Articles 230 or 232 are extended by Article 288(2).

18.5.4 Legislative acts of the Community

The Court has ruled very restrictively on the admissibility of claims under Article 288(2) for damage caused by *legislative acts* (ie, those acts which a non-privileged applicant could not challenge under Article 230—usually Regulations).

Where a party sues because of damage caused by a legislative act *and* that act involved choices of economic policy, then there is no liability under Article 288(2) unless:

- A superior rule of law has been broken.
- The breach is sufficiently serious.
- The rule of law is one designed to protect the individual.
- The basic elements of Article 288(2) are satisfied.

Superior rules of law are the same as those rules which are applied by the Court in claims under Article 230 EC. A sufficiently serious breach has been interpreted as demanding proof of a manifest and grave disregard of the limits on the exercise of the Community's powers. 'A rule of law intended to protect the individual' requires the rule to protect clearly the interests of a class or classes, and if it does so, then an individual within such class may sue.

The leading case is *Aktien-Zuckerfabrik Schöppenstedt v Council* (5/71) [1971] ECR 975. The ECJ has noted that a finding that a legislative measure is invalid does not, of itself, mean that the Community has incurred non-contractual liability for damage caused to individuals. For such liability to exist, an applicant must go on to prove that a sufficiently serious breach of a superior rule of law for the protection of the individual had occurred: *Industrie-en Handelsonderneming Vreugdenhil BV v Commission* (C-282/90) [1992] ECR I-1937.

18.5.5 Shared responsibility

Sometimes a Community measure empowers a Member State to act on its behalf. An example is a Community act which imposes a levy on specific imported goods. The act may put the tasks of ascertaining the amount due in each case and its collection into the hands of the Member State. If following the annulment of the Community act, reimbursement of such a levy is sought, from whom should it be claimed? From the Community or the Member State?

The Court has held that where a legislative act of the Community has been implemented by national authorities, then an individual who alleges that he or she has suffered a loss by virtue of such implementation may challenge the validity of the act in national courts, suing the national authorities. The national court will be able to refer the question of the validity of the Community act to the ECJ under Article 234 (ex 177). But the existence of this method of redress will effectively protect the individual only if it can result in the alleged damage being made good. It follows that a claim by an individual for damages under Article 288(2) in the European Court will be admissible, notwithstanding that the individual has not used legal remedies available in national law, so long as it is not disputed that those remedies were incapable of guaranteeing him or her effective protection.

18.6 Plea of illegality under Article 241 EC

18.6.1 Introduction

Article 241 (ex 184) applies only to regulations. It provides protection for those against whom it is sought to apply an illegal regulation.

18.6.2 The grounds for making the plea

The grounds for making the plea of illegality are precisely the same as those used in a claim under Article 230. The claim is that, although the measure has not been annulled under Article 230, nevertheless it is invalid and should not be relied on in the current proceedings.

18.6.3 When may this protection be claimed?

Article 241 provides only for an indirect challenge to the validity of an EC regulation, ie, one made in the course of other proceedings in the European Court. It gives no direct right of claim in the European Court, nor does it allow an indirect attack to be made in the course of litigation in a national court (this is the function of Article 234(b) EC).

Article 241 can be relied on in the following situations:

(a) In a claim under Article 230. If the legality of a measure which is apparently legal is challenged, an earlier measure, which is the legal foundation of the later one, might be attacked.

(b) In a claim under Article 232. If the refusal of the EC institution to act is apparently valid, being based on an existing law, that law might be challenged using Article 241.

(c) In a claim under Article 226. If a Member State is accused of acting in violation of Community law and the Commission brings a claim under Article 226, it seems that the Member State could rely on the plea of illegality as a defence. It would argue that the law it has violated is illegal.

(*Note*: This would not be possible if the Member State was the 'person' to whom the original law was addressed.)

18.6.4   Who can use Article 241?

Article 241 may be invoked by 'any party' to proceedings, in which a regulation is in issue.

(a) A Member State may be able to challenge any legislative act, regardless of the fact that it could have used Article 230 (see *Italy v Council* (32/65) [1966] ECR 389; *Commission v Belgium* (156/77) [1978] ECR 1881).

(b) A natural or legal person may use Article 241 to challenge any legislative measure (it cannot use Article 230 because it has insufficient interest or 'standing').

(c) A natural or legal person may use Article 241 to challenge an individual measure if it was not the addressee of the measure. Although an Article 230 claim may have been possible in such circumstances, this may not have been realised within the three-month time limit for an Article 230 claim. The European Court has taken a generous attitude here.

(d) The addressee of an individual measure cannot use Article 241—the measure should have been challenged under Article 230.

18.6.5   Effect of the plea of illegality

If the illegality of the measure can be established in what is, essentially, a collateral argument, then the legal basis for the main legislation will usually have been lost. Article 241 provides a parasitic line of attack on validity of EC measures, it does not create a separate claim.

18.7   Enforcement claims against Member States under Article 226 EC

18.7.1   Introduction

Article 226 (ex 169) is used (and only used) by the European Commission in order to ensure that Member States comply with their obligations under the EC Treaty. The Commission will give the Member State concerned an opportunity to discharge its obligations before proceeding further, but if this opportunity is not taken, the Commission can then bring the matter before the European Court. Only the Commission brings claims under Article 226. Private or legal persons cannot initiate such a claim, although they can complain to the Commission about an infringement. The Commission has no duty to pursue the complaint, although it often does.

The Commission will not start an enforcement claim in every instance of non-compliance that comes to its attention. It may not be expedient to publicise an incident of non-compliance. The Commission will be in contact with the Member State in-formally to see whether or not it is in breach of Community law and, if so, to persuade the State to rectify its position. The Commission has a discretion whether or not to bring proceedings under Article 226.

18.7.2   What sort of omissions lead to an enforcement claim?

The non-compliance of the Member State may exist because of either action or inaction on its part. To act in contravention of an EC law may result in an enforcement claim; similarly, a failure to act when required to do so by EC law exposes the State to the same risk. Examples include the failure of a Member State to implement a directive within the allotted time, either properly or at all, and passing national laws which infringe Treaty Articles.

The mere existence of a national law which is inconsistent with an EC law can expose a State to an enforcement claim. This is so even if the Member State disavows any intention to use the national law. The continued existence of such a law creates uncertainty for those who might wish to rely on Community law.

Failure to implement a directive into national law, within the allotted time, may also expose a Member State to a claim in its own courts. Such claims may be brought by individuals or companies who allege that they have suffered loss as a result of the Member State's failure. See, eg, *Francovich v Italy* (C6/90, 9/90) [1991] ECRI-5357. For a recent review of the use of this principle of State liability in the courts of the Member States, see Granger, *National applications of Francovich and the construction of a European administrative ius commune* [2007] 32 European Law Review 157.

18.7.3   Procedure under Article 226

18.7.3.1   The invitation to submit counter arguments

If the Commission considers that a Member State has failed to fulfil a Treaty obligtion, it will invite the Member State to submit its arguments about the issue. The invitation will be written, indicating what specific allegations the Commission is interested in and why. If no reply is received, the Commission may renew its invitation. The Commission must take care when issuing the invitation since the contents of the letter will form the basis of any subsequent enforcement claim in the Court of Justice.

If the Commission concludes that the Member State has not discharged an obligation which Community law has imposed on the State (and the situation has not been rectified by the Member State following the Commission's formal invitation to submit observations), then the Commission will deliver a reasoned opinion.

18.7.3.2   The reasoned opinion

The reasoned opinion serves two purposes. First, it is a statement of the facts and law which establish a violation of the Treaty. The detail of the opinion must be adhered to by the Commission: if it subsequently takes the matter to the Court it may not raise any new violations. Secondly, it should indicate what steps must be taken by the State to end the violation, and set a time limit for those steps to be taken.

18.7.3.3   Still no compliance? Go to court

Once the Commission has issued its reasoned opinion and the time limit has expired without remedial steps being taken by the defaulting State, the Commission may take the matter to the European Court. No time limit is imposed on the Commission within which an enforcement claim must be brought before the Court. The Commission has freedom as to when (as well as if) an enforcement matter should be raised with the Court.

The Court will consider the issue of non-compliance, together with any defence which the Member State may raise, and then deliver judgment. An example of such a defence is that the Commission itself has violated the Treaty in its investigation or reasoned opinion. Whilst these procedural arguments have succeeded in the Court on occasion, generally States are unsuccessful in defending enforcement claims.

18.7.4   Consequence of continued default

If the Court finds against the Member State, the State must take the necessary measures to comply with the judgment.

If the defaulting State fails to take the 'necessary measures', under Article 228, the Commission may pursue it for a second time to the European Court, seeking a financial penalty for non-compliance.

18.7.5   Interim relief in urgent cases

In cases of urgency, the Commission can apply to the European Court for interim measures to be taken, pursuant to Article 243 EC. For example, see *Commission v United Kingdom* (31/77 R and 53/77 R) [1977] ECR 921, where the UK was ordered to terminate certain financial aid to pig producers forthwith.

European Convention on Human Rights and Fundamental Freedoms

19.1 Introduction

The European Convention on Human Rights is an international treaty of the Council of Europe which was adopted in 1950, ratified by the UK in 1951 and entered into force in 1953. It provides a mechanism for individuals to enforce their Convention rights against State parties. It is administered by the Council of Europe and the European Court of Human Rights.

19.1.1 The Council of Europe

After the horrendous atrocities of the Second World War, the Council of Europe, an intergovernmental organisation, comprising 47 Member States currently, was established in 1949. Its aims are:

(a) to protect human rights, pluralist democracy and the rule of law;

(b) to promote awareness and encourage the development of Europe's cultural identity and diversity;

(c) to seek solutions to problems facing European society (discrimination against minorities, xenophobia, intolerance, environmental protection, human cloning, Aids, drugs, organised crime, etc);

(d) to help consolidate democratic stability in Europe by backing political, legislative and constitutional reform.

19.1.2 The European Court of Human Rights

The European Commission of Human Rights was set up in 1954 and the European Court of Human Rights was established in 1959. A single permanent Court was established in 1998 to replace the Commission and the original Court and the current Court consists of a number of judges equal to the number of contracting States.

The Court sits in three-judge committees to sift out unfounded cases, and in the large majority of cases sits as a seven-judge Chamber. In cases where there is a serious issue concerning the interpretation or application of the Convention, a case may be referred to a Grand Chamber of 17 judges, either by a Chamber before judgment, or by one of the parties within three months of a Chamber judgment. Chamber judgments become final after three months and Grand Chamber judgments are final. The Court's final judgments are binding on the State concerned (ie on the government, not the courts).

19.1.3   Classification of Convention rights

Convention rights are classified as being either absolute, qualified or limited.

Absolute rights are those which cannot be restricted in any circumstances, not even in times of war or other public emergency. These are Articles 2 (right to life), 3 (the prohibition of torture, inhuman or degrading treatment), 4(1) (the prohibition of slavery) and 7 (the prohibition of retrospective criminal penalties).

Qualified rights are those which are subject to restriction clauses which enable the general public interest to be taken into account. They are Articles 8 (right to respect for private and family life), 9 (freedom to manifest religion or belief), 10 (freedom of expression), 11 (freedom of assembly), 14 (discrimination) and Protocol 1, Article 1 (the right to property).

Limited rights are those in relation to which the Government can enter a derogation. These are Articles 4(2) and 4(3) (the prohibition of forced or compulsory labour), 5 (liberty), 6 (fair trial), 9(1) (freedom of thought), 12 (right to marry), Protocol 1, Article 2 (the right to education), Protocol 1, Article 3 (the right to free elections) and Protocol 6, Article 1 (abolition of the death penalty).

The operation of the restrictions was considered by the Privy Council in *Brown v Stott (Procurator Fiscal, Dunfermline)* [2001] 2 WLR 817, where the Privy Council held that there was no breach of the privilege against self-incrimination under Article 6 for a prosecutor to rely on an obligation of a registered keeper of a motor vehicle to supply information as to the identity of the driver under s 172 of the Road Traffic Act 1988. The section did not represent a disproportionate response to the high incidence of death and injury on the roads by reason of the misuse of cars and the Convention had to be read as balancing Community rights with individual rights.

19.1.4   Convention concepts

Popular Convention concepts include the 'margin of appreciation', the Convention being considered to be a 'living instrument' and the 'hierarchy of authority'.

19.1.4.1   Margin of appreciation

In some cases, the European Court of Human Rights will allow States a margin of appreciation in their assessment of necessity and proportionality—thus States will be allowed some latitude or discretion in evaluating their public policy decisions. Lord Hope stated in *R v DPP, ex p Kebilene* [1999] 3 WLR 972:

> By conceding a margin of appreciation to each national system, the court has recognised that the Convention, as a living system, does not need to be applied uniformly by all States but may vary in its application according to local needs and conditions. This technique is not available to the national courts when they are considering Convention issues arising within their own countries. But in the hands of the national courts also the Convention should be seen as an expression of fundamental principles rather than as a set of mere rules. The question which the courts will have to decide in the application of these principles will involve questions of balance between competing interests and issues of proportionality . . .

19.1.4.2   Living instrument

Attitudes and cultures change over time. The Convention is regarded as a 'living instrument' which evolves and develops and 'must be interpreted in the light of present-day conditions' (*Tyrer v United Kingdom* (1978) 2 EHRR 1). The Strasbourg case law provides a floor, not a ceiling, and old Convention case law must be approached with caution.

19.1.4.3   Hierarchy of authority

The decisions of the Commission (previously) and the Court are not binding on domestic courts. The governments do, however, regard themselves to be bound and will generally take steps to give effect to the Court's decisions, eg by amending legislation.

19.2   The Human Rights Act 1998

The Human Rights Act 1998 was enacted to enable certain rights contained in the European Convention on Human Rights to be directly enforceable in domestic courts. The Act was brought into force on 2 October 2000. The right of application to the European Court of Human Rights in Strasbourg, France, is, however, maintained.

The Human Rights Act 1998 has revolutionised the courts' interpretation and application of legislation. Section 1 and Sch 1 define the 'Convention rights' which have been incorporated, subject to any designated derogations or reservations. Article 13 (the right to an effective remedy) was not specifically included as a 'Convention right' within this definition.

19.2.1   Convention rights

19.2.1.1   The vertical effect

The rights operate vertically, ie they affect relations between private individuals and public authorities. Individuals have an additional cause of action against public authorities.

Section 6 of the Act created a new public law wrong in relation to the acts or proposed acts of public authorities. Under s 7, a victim who alleges a breach of Convention rights against a public authority can make a claim under s 7(1)(a) based on the breach alone, or under s 7(1)(b) based on other pre-existing rights of action in domestic law. This has become widely known as the 'vertical effect' of the Act.

19.2.1.2   The horizontal effect

The horizontal effect of the Act suggests that the Convention will affect relations between individuals, ie because the courts are defined by s 6 of the Act as public authorities. Relations between individuals will be affected indirectly, as the courts need to act compatibly with the Convention when adjudicating in an action between individuals.

19.2.1.3   Limitation period

Section 7(5) provides that the general limitation period for action under s 7(1)(a) is one year from the date on which the act took place or 'such longer period as the court or tribunal considers equitable having regard to all the circumstances'. There is no limitation for those seeking to rely on breaches in other proceedings under s 7(1)(b).

19.2.2   The main provisions

19.2.2.1   Section 1—the Convention rights

This section sets out the Convention rights as the rights and fundamental freedoms set out in Articles 2 to 12 and 14 of the Convention, Articles 1 to 3 of the First Protocol, and Articles 1 and 2 of the Sixth Protocol, as read with Articles 16 to 18 of the Convention. These rights are declared to have effect for the purposes of the Act.

19.2.2.2 Section 2—interpretation of Convention rights

This section provides that any court or tribunal determining a question which has arisen in connection with a Convention right must take into account the jurisprudence of the Strasbourg bodies—the European Court, Commission of Human Rights and the Committee of Ministers, whether before or after the coming into force of the Act, so far as, in the opinion of the court or tribunal, it is relevant to the proceedings.

19.2.2.3 Section 3—interpretation of legislation

This section provides that primary and subordinate legislation is to be read and given effect in a way which is compatible with Convention rights, so far as it is possible to do so, and applies to all legislation, whenever enacted. It is also provided that if it is not possible to read legislation so as to give effect to the Convention, the validity, continuing operation or enforcement of the legislation will not be affected. In such circumstances, the higher courts may make a declaration of incompatibility under s 4. Recent examples of cases in which this provision was applied are as follows:

(a) In *R v A* [2001] 2 WLR 1546, the House of Lords held that s 41(3)(c) of the Youth Justice and Criminal Evidence Act 1999 was to be interpreted in accordance with the obligation under s 3 that the test of admissibility of any evidence of previous sexual relations between an alleged rapist and the complainant was whether it was so relevant to the issue of consent that to exclude that evidence would endanger the fairness of the trial under Article 6.

(b) In *R v Lambert* [2001] 3 WLR 206, the House of Lords held that s 28(2) of the Misuse of Drugs Act 1971 could be interpreted in accordance with the obligation under s 3 as only imposing an evidential burden of proof on the defendant which would enable it to be compatible with Article 6(2).

(c) In *R v Offen and Others* [2001] 1 WLR 253, the Court of Appeal held that in s 2 of the Crime (Sentences) Act 1997 consolidated as s 109 of the Powers of Criminal Courts (Sentencing) Act 2000, the phrase 'exceptional circumstances' for not imposing an automatic life sentence for a second serious offence could be interpreted in accordance with the obligation under s 3 so that it did not result in offenders being sentenced to life imprisonment when they did not constitute a significant risk to the public.

(d) In *R v Carass* [2002] 1 WLR 1714, the Court of Appeal held that the burden of proof imposed under s 206(4) of the Insolvency Act 1986 was evidential only and that the word 'prove' in relation to the statutory defence of proving no intent to defraud was to be read as 'adduce sufficient evidence'.

(e) In *Attorney-General's Reference (No 1 of 2004) sub nom R v Edwards and Others* [2004] EWCA Crim 1025, the Court of Appeal provided guidance on the interpretation of statutory provisions imposing a reverse burden of proof.

(f) In *Attorney-General's Reference (No 4 of 2002) Sheldrake v DPP* [2004] UKHL 43, the House of Lords held that s 5(2) of the Road Traffic Act 1988 imposed a legal burden on a defendant charged with being in charge of a motor vehicle, with alcohol concentration above the prescribed limit, contrary to s 5(1)(b) of the Act. It was also held that the statutory defence in s 11(2) of the Terrorism Act 2000 to a charge of membership of a proscribed organisation was to be interpreted as imposing an evidential burden only.

19.2.2.4   Section 4—declaration of incompatibility

This section provides that the higher courts (the High Court and above) may make a declaration of incompatibility, declaring that a provision is incompatible with a Convention right. Some examples of declarations of incompatibility from recent case law are as follows:

(a) In *R (Holding & Barnes plc and Others) v Secretary of State for the Environment* [2001] 2 WLR 1389, the House of Lords reversed a declaration of incompatibility made by the Divisional Court in connection with the decision-making process of planning appeals and inquiries, on the basis that judicial review provided sufficient judicial control within the terms of Article 6.

(b) In *R (on the application of H) v Mental Health Review Tribunal and Secretary of State for Health* [2001] 3 WLR 512, the Court of Appeal made a declaration of incompatibility with Article 5(1) and Article 5(4) in relation to ss 72 and 73 of the Mental Health Act 1983 regarding a decision of the Mental Health Tribunal to detain a patient, as the sections placed a burden on the patient to prove that the criteria for detention had not been satisfied.

(c) In *Wilson v First County Trust* [2001] 3 WLR 42 the Court of Appeal made a declaration that s 127(3) of the Consumer Credit Act 1974 was incompatible with Article 6(1) and Protocol 1, Article 1, as it imposed an absolute bar to enforcement through the courts of a regulated agreement which did not contain prescribed terms, and was a disproportionate restriction on the rights of a lender. This decision was, however, reversed by the House of Lords in *Wilson v Secretary of State for Trade and Industry, sub nom Wilson v First County Trust (No 2)* [2003] UKHL 40; [2003] 3 WLR 568, where it was held that the Court of Appeal had been wrong to declare s 127(3) of the Consumer Credit Act to be incompatible with the Convention where the cause of action arose and the parties' rights were determined in the County Court before the Human Rights Act 1998 had come into force.

(d) In *International Transport Roth GMBH and Others v Secretary of State for the Home Department* [2002] 3 WLR 344, the Court of Appeal made a declaration, by a majority, that the scheme adopted under part II of the Immigration and Asylum Act 1999, which imposed penalties on carriers of clandestine entrants to the UK, was incompatible with Article 6 and Protocol 1, Article 1. The scheme was not, however, held to be inconsistent with European Community law.

(e) In *R (Anderson) v Secretary of State for the Home Department* The Times, 26 November 2002, a panel of seven judges in the House of Lords held unanimously that the court would make a declaration of incompatibility of s 29 of the Crime (Sentences) Act 1997 with Article 6(1) as the section left to the Home Secretary alone the decision on how long a prisoner sentenced to mandatory life for murder should remain in prison for punitive purposes. The tariff or minimum term should be fixed by an independent and impartial tribunal and the Home Secretary was not such a tribunal.

(f) In *Bellinger v Bellinger* [2003] UKHL 21; [2003] 2 AC 467, the House of Lords held that s 11(c) of the Matrimonial Causes Act 1973 was incompatible with Articles 8 and 12 as a post-operative transsexual was unable to have her marriage legally recognised.

(g) In *R (M) v Secretary of State for Health* [2003] EWHC 1094 (Admin) it was held that the automatic appointment of the nearest relative for persons detained under the

Mental Health Act 1983 and the inability of detainees to challenge that appointment rendered the provision incompatible with Article 8.

(h) In *R (Uttley) v Secretary of State for the Home Department* [2003] EWCA Civ 1130; [2003] 1 WLR 2590, a declaration of incompatibility with Article 7 was made in respect of s 33 of the Criminal Justice Act 1991 as the terms of the licence of a sentenced appellant imposed a heavier penalty than the one provided by the law at the time of the commission of the offences for which he was sentenced.

(i) In *R (Morris) v Westminster City Council & First Secretary of State* [2004] EWHC 2191 (Admin) it was held that s 185(4) of the Housing Act 1996 was incompatible with Article 14 in that it required the court to disregard a dependent child of a UK citizen, in a case where the child was subject to immigration control.

(j) In *R (Hammond) v Secretary of State for the Home Department* [2005] UKHL 69, the House of Lords held that para 11(1) of Sch 22 to the Criminal Justice Act 2003, which did not allow for an oral hearing to determine the minimum term of an existing prisoner, was incompatible with Article 6.

(k) In *R (Clift) v Secretary of State for the Home Department; Secretary of State for the Home Department v Hindawi and Headley* [2006] UKHL 54, the House of Lords made a declaration that the early release provisions contained in the Criminal Justice Act 1991 were incompatible with Articles 5 and 14, to the extent that they prevented foreign national prisoners liable for deportation from having their cases reviewed by the Parole Board in the same way as other long-term prisoners.

19.2.2.5   Section 5—right of Crown to intervene

This section provides that where a court is considering making a declaration of incompatibility, the Crown is entitled to notice. This enables the appropriate Minister to be involved in the proceedings at an early stage to prepare for any remedial action under s 10.

19.2.2.6   Section 6—acts of public authorities

This section introduced a new public law wrong by providing that it is unlawful for a public authority to act in a way which is incompatible with a Convention right. A 'public authority' includes a court or tribunal, but does not include either House of Parliament.

In *Aston Cantlow Parochial Church Council v Wallbank* [2003] UKHL 37; [2003] 3 WLR 283, the House of Lords held that a Parochial Church Council, enforcing a lay rector's liability for repairs to the chancel of a church, was not a public authority and in any event enforcing such a liability did not infringe the Convention rights of the rector.

19.2.2.7   Section 7—proceedings

This section provides that a victim of an unlawful act by a public authority may make a claim. A victim is a person who has been directly affected by the act or has been at risk of being so affected.

19.2.2.8   Section 8—judicial remedies

This section provides that the court may grant such relief or remedy, or make such order as it considers 'just and appropriate' including damages, provided that the court has power to make such orders. Section 8(3) provides that damages may only be awarded if necessary to afford 'just satisfaction', and s 8(4) provides that in determining whether to award damages, or the amount to award, the court must take account of the principles applied by the European Court of Human Rights in relation to the award of compensation under Article 41 of the Convention. In *R (Bernard and Another) v Enfield Borough Council* The Times, 8 November 2002, Sullivan J awarded £10,000 damages under s 8(1) of the Act against London Borough of Enfield for a breach of Article 8 due to the local authority's failure to provide suitable accommodation for a severely disabled wheelchair-dependent woman over a period of 20 months. In *R (Greenfield) v Secretary of State for the Home Department* [2005] UKHL 14, it was held by the House of Lords that when assessing awards of damages under s 8 of the Act, the principles applied in the European Court of Human Rights to awards of compensation should be applied in the domestic courts.

19.2.2.9 Section 9—judicial acts

This section provides that proceedings in respect of judicial acts may be brought on appeal or by judicial review.

19.2.2.10 Section 10—power to take remedial action

This section confirms the power of a Minister of the Crown to take remedial action to amend legislation in order to remove an incompatibility where legislation has been declared incompatible under s 4.

19.2.2.11 Section 11—safeguard for existing human rights

This section provides that reliance on the Convention rights referred to in the Act does not restrict any other rights or freedoms.

19.2.2.12 Section 12—freedom of expression

This section provides that courts must have particular regard to the importance of freedom of expression, and is of benefit to the media.

19.2.2.13 Section 13—freedom of thought, conscience and religion

This section provides that courts must have regard to the importance of freedom of thought, conscience and religion, and is of benefit to certain religious organisations.

19.3 Rights and freedoms under the Convention

19.3.1 Purpose of the Convention

Article 1 of the Convention states the obligation of contracting States to secure to everyone within those States' jurisdiction, the rights and freedoms defined in the Convention.

19.3.2 Restrictions on the rights and freedoms

Many of the rights and freedoms set out in the Convention contain restrictions. They are classified as absolute, qualified or limited rights.

19.3.2.1 Limitations on rights

Articles 2, 3, 4(1) and 7 are absolute rights and they may never be the subject of derogation, even in times of national emergency.

All rights which are not absolute are, in principle, derogable. This is a formal procedure requiring the lodging of an instrument of derogation with the Secretary General of the Council of Europe.

The rights contained in Articles 8 to 11 are qualified. The conditions under which the State may lawfully interfere with or restrict the exercise of each right is set out in the second paragraph to each Article. Article 14 and Protocol 1, Article 1 are also said to be qualified rights.

Articles 4(2), 4(3), 5, 6, 9(1) (freedom of thought), 12, Protocol 1 Article 2, Protocol 1 Article 3 and Protocol 6 Article 1 are regarded as limited rights.

Generally, any such limitations must satisfy the following criteria:

(a) It must be according to the rule of law (see *Sunday Times v UK* (1979–80) EHRR 245).

(b) It must be in pursuit of a 'legitimate aim', eg national security, public safety, the economic well-being of the country, the prevention of disorder or crime, the protection of health or morals, or the protection of the rights and freedoms of others.

(c) It must be proportionate. 'Necessary in a democratic society' has been defined as 'proportionate to the legitimate aim pursued' (*Handyside v UK* (1976) 1 EHRR 737). In *Silver v UK* (1983) 5 EHRR 344 it was stated that 'the interference must, inter alia, correspond to a pressing social need and be proportionate to the legitimate aim pursued'. In *Soering v UK* (1989) 11 EHRR 439 at para 89 it was stated that 'inherent in the whole of the Convention is a search for a fair balance between the demands of the general interests of the community and the requirement of the protection of the individual's fundamental rights'.

19.3.3 Human rights in the Convention

Schedule 1 of the Act sets out the Convention rights which are directly enforceable in domestic courts. They are as follows:

Part 1   *Article 2*   Right to life.

Article 3   Prohibition of torture and inhuman or degrading treatment or punishment.

Article 4   Prohibition of slavery and forced labour.

Article 5   Right to liberty and security.

Article 6   Right to a fair trial:

(a) In civil and criminal matters, the right to a fair and public hearing within a reasonable time by an independent and impartial tribunal established by law. In some circumstances the press and public may be excluded.

(b) Presumption of innocence on a criminal charge

(c) Minimum rights on a criminal charge:

(i) to be informed promptly in an understandable language and in detail of the nature and cause of the accusation;

(ii) to have adequate time and facilities for the preparation of one's defence;

(iii) to defend oneself in person or through legal assistance of one's own choosing, or to be given free assistance where no means to pay and interests of justice so require;

(iv) to examine or have examined witnesses and obtain the attendance of witnesses on one's behalf under the same conditions as witnesses against oneself;

(v) to have the free assistance of an interpreter if one cannot understand/speak the language in court.

	Article 7	Freedom from retrospective criminal law, and the principle of legal certainty and restrictive interpretation in criminal matters.
	Article 8	Right to respect for private and family life, home and correspondence.
	Article 9	Freedom of thought, conscience and religion.
	Article 10	Freedom of expression.
	Article 11	Freedom of peaceful assembly and association.
	Article 12	Right to marry and found a family.
	Article 14	Prohibition of discrimination in the enjoyment of Convention rights.
	Article 16	Restrictions on political activity of aliens.
	Article 17	Prohibition of abuse of rights.
	Article 18	Limitation on use of restrictions on rights.
Part 2	*The First Protocol*	
	Article 1	Protection of property.
	Article 2	Right to education.
	Article 3	Right to free elections.
Part 3	*The Sixth Protocol*	
	Article 1	Abolition of the death penalty.
	Article 2	Death penalty in time of war.

19.3.3.1   Article 2—right to life

Article 2 states:

> 1. *Everyone's right to life shall be protected by law. No one shall be deprived of his life intentionally save in the execution of a sentence of a court following his conviction of a crime for which this penalty is provided by law.*
>
> 2. *Deprivation of life shall not be regarded as inflicted in contravention of this article when it results from the use of force which is no more than absolutely necessary:*
>
> (a) *in defence of any person from unlawful violence;*
>
> (b) *in order to effect a lawful arrest or to prevent the escape of a person lawfully detained;*
>
> (c) *in action lawfully taken for the purpose of quelling a riot or insurrection.*

This is a fundamental right which places a corresponding positive duty on public authorities to protect life and a negative obligation to refrain from the unlawful taking of life. In *Venables & Thompson v News Group* [2001] 2 WLR 1038, it was held in the Family Division that the Convention and the law of confidence could be extended, in exceptional cases, to enable the court to grant injunctions to protect individuals who were seriously at risk of injury or death, if their identity or whereabouts became public knowledge. In *R (Pretty) v DPP* [2001] 3 WLR 1598 (House of Lords), *Pretty v UK* (2002) 35 EHRR 1 (European Court of Human Rights), the DPP had refused to undertake not to prosecute where the applicant, a sufferer of motor neurone disease, wished her husband to assist in her suicide. It was held by the House of Lords (a decision which was approved of by the European Court of Human Rights) that Articles 2 and 3 were aimed at the protection and preservation of life and the dignity of life, and were not aimed at protecting a person's right to procure his or her own death. There were no violations of Articles 2, 3, 8, 9 or 14. In *Edwards v UK* (2002) 35 EHRR 487, the applicants' son was stamped on and kicked to death by his cellmate in Chelmsford prison. The deceased was suffering from mental illness and the assailant was suffering from paranoid schizophrenia, yet they were placed in a cell together. It was held that there were violations of Articles 2 and 13. In *McShane v UK* (2002) 35 EHRR 593, the applicants' husband was killed when an armoured personnel carrier ran over him during a major disturbance in Londonderry,

Northern Ireland. The European Court of Human Rights held that there had been a violation of Article 2 in respect of failings in the investigative procedures concerning the death and that there was a further breach of the State's obligations under Article 34. In *R (Amin) v Secretary of State for the Home Department* [2003] UKHL 51; [2003] 3 WLR 1169, the deceased was beaten to death in a racist attack by a cellmate in Feltham Young Offender Institution. An internal inquiry was held by the Prison Service in addition to a police investigation and an investigation by the Commission for Racial Equality into racial discrimination in the Prison Service. It was held that an independent public investigation had to be conducted by the Secretary of State in order to fulfil the UK's obligations under Article 2. In *Finucane v United Kingdom* (2003) 37 EHRR 656, the Court held that there was a violation of Article 2 where a lawyer had been shot dead, as there had been no effective investigation into the circumstances leading to the death.

19.3.3.2 Article 3—prohibition of torture and freedom from inhuman or degrading treatment

Article 3 states:

> *No one shall be subjected to torture or to inhuman or degrading treatment or punishment.*

There is an absolute prohibition on torture and inhuman or degrading treatment or punishment. In *East African Asians v United Kingdom* (1981) 3 EHRR 76, the Commission decided that the denial of entry to the UK of British nationals, classified as 'overseas citizens', who were of Asian origin, amounted to degrading treatment. In *Selmouni v France* (2000) 29 EHRR 403, treatment was held by the European Court of Human Rights to amount to torture where the applicant was subjected to prolonged assaults in police custody, including beating, dragging by his hair, being urinated over, and threatened with blowlamps and a syringe. He was awarded 500,000 French francs in just satisfaction under Article 41. In *Hilal v United Kingdom* (2001) 33 EHRR 31, the Court held that there was a violation where a decision was made to deport an overstayer to Tanzania as his life would have been endangered by his return. In *Keenan v UK* (2001) 33 EHRR 38, the European Court of Human Rights held that there was a violation due to the treatment of a mentally disordered prisoner who committed suicide in the segregation unit of the prison the day after an adjudication in which he was ordered to serve an additional period of 28 days in custody. In *Price v UK* (2002) 34 EHRR 1285, the European Court of Human Rights held that there had been lack of care of a woman, severely disabled from thalidomide, who had been committed to custody in civil proceedings for a judgment debt and was held in a police cell not specially adapted. There were inadequate facilities in the police station and in prison with the result that male officers in the prison were required to assist in lifting her on and off the toilet. This was held to amount to degrading treatment. In *McGlinchey v United Kingdom* (2003) 37 EHRR 821, the Court held that there had been a violation of Article 3 on account of the failure of prison authorities to provide requisite medical care to a heroin addict who died in custody. In *Secretary of State for the Home Department v Wainwright and Another* [2003] UKHL 53; [2003] 3 WLR 1137, the House of Lords held that a strip search of visitors to an inmate in a prison did not give rise to a new common law tort of invasion of privacy.

In *R (Adam) & Others v Secretary of State for the Home Department* [2005] UKHL 66, the House of Lords held that refusal of asylum support had resulted in severe conditions suffered by asylum seekers, and amounted to a breach of Article 3. In *A and Others v Secretary of State for the Home Department* [2005] UKHL 71, the House of Lords held that the Special Immigration Appeals Commission should refuse to admit evidence if it concluded on a balance of probabilities that such evidence had been obtained by torture. If in doubt, however, the evidence should be admitted, subject to considerations of weight to be given to such evidence.

In *R (on the application of Graham) v Secretary of State for Justice; R (on the application of Allen) v Secretary of State for Justice* [2007] EWHC 2940 (Admin), it was held that the handcuffing of a prisoner while he was receiving chemotherapy treatment had breached his rights under Article 3, as he did not represent a risk to the public, there having been no risk of escape.

19.3.3.3 Article 4—prohibition of slavery and forced labour

Article 4 states:

1. *No one shall be held in slavery or servitude.*
2. *No one shall be required to perform forced or compulsory labour.*
3. *For the purpose of this article the term 'forced or compulsory labour' shall not include:*

    (a) any work required to be done in the ordinary course of detention imposed according to the provisions of Article 5 of this Convention or during conditional release from such detention;

    (b) any service of a military character or, in case of conscientious objectors in countries where they are recognised, service exacted instead of compulsory military service;

    (c) any service exacted in case of an emergency or calamity threatening the life or well-being of the community;

    (d) any work or service which forms part of normal civic obligations.

Article 4(1) contains an absolute prohibition on slavery or servitude.

19.3.3.4 Article 5—right to liberty and security

Article 5 states:

1. *Everyone has the right to liberty and security of person. No one shall be deprived of his liberty save in the following cases and in accordance with a procedure prescribed by law:*

    (a) the lawful detention of a person after conviction by a competent court;

    (b) the lawful arrest or detention of a person for non-compliance with the lawful order of a court or in order to secure the fulfilment of any obligation prescribed by law;

    (c) the lawful arrest or detention of a person effected for the purpose of bringing him before the competent legal authority on reasonable suspicion of having committed an offence or when it is reasonably considered necessary to prevent his committing an offence or fleeing after having done so;

    (d) the detention of a minor by lawful order for the purpose of educational supervision or his lawful detention for the purpose of bringing him before the competent legal authority;

    (e) the lawful detention of persons for the prevention of the spreading of infectious diseases, of persons of unsound mind, alcoholics or drug addicts or vagrants;

    (f) the lawful arrest or detention of a person to prevent his effecting an unauthorised entry into the country or of a person against whom action is being taken with a view to deportation or extradition.

2. *Everyone who is arrested shall be informed promptly, in a language which he understands, of the reasons for his arrest and of any charge against him.*

3. *Everyone arrested or detained in accordance with the provisions of paragraph 1 (c) of this article shall be brought promptly before a judge or other officer authorised by law to exercise judicial power and shall be entitled to trial within a reasonable time or to release pending trial. Release may be conditioned by guarantees to appear for trial.*

4. *Everyone who is deprived of his liberty by arrest or detention shall be entitled to take proceedings by which the lawfulness of his detention shall be decided speedily by a court and his release ordered if the detention is not lawful.*

5. *Everyone who has been the victim of arrest or detention in contravention of the provisions of this article shall have an enforceable right to compensation.*

The right under Article 5 is limited by the circumstances set out in the article.

Once a sentence of long-term detention is imposed, Article 5(4) requires periodic review by a judicial body of the sentence to ensure that it remains justified. The reviewing body must be independent of the executive, eg the Mental Health Review Tribunal; the Discretionary Lifer Panel of the Parole Board. *In Tv UK* (2000) 30 EHRR 121, there was held to have been a violation of Article 5(4) where there had been no review of the offenders' tariff once the Home Secretary's decision to set it had been quashed by the House of Lords in judicial review proceedings. Similarly, in *Curley v UK* (2000) 31 EHRR 401, a violation of Article 5(4) was found in the case of an offender detained during Her Majesty's pleasure whose release was always subject to the approval of the Secretary of State. In addition, Article 5(5) was breached because the offender had no enforceable claim for compensation under domestic law.

In *O'Hara v UK* (2002) 34 EHRR 812, the European Court of Human Rights held that there was a violation of Article 5(3) as the applicant, a prominent member of Sinn Fein, had been held in police detention for 6 days 13 hours before release and had not been 'brought promptly before a judge'. In *S.B.C. v UK* (2002) 34 EHRR 619 there were held to be violations of Article 5(3) and Article 5(5) on automatic denial of bail under s 25 of the Criminal Justice and Public Order Act 1994 (see also *Caballero v UK* (2000) 30 EHRR 643). In *Stafford v UK* (2002) 35 EHRR 1121, the European Court of Human Rights held that there were violations of Article 5(1) and Article 5(4) where the applicant had served 12 years for murder and had been released, but had been detained after completion of a further term for fraud. There was no justification for his continued detention by order of the Home Secretary as he presented no significant risk of committing further violent offences. In *Benjamin & Wilson v UK* (2003) 36 EHRR 1, the European Court of Human Rights held that there was a violation of Article 5(4) as there was no procedure for a speedy decision by a court of the lawfulness of detention of mentally ill prisoners sentenced to life but detained in hospital. The Secretary of State had the power to order the release of the applicants. In *R (Noorkoiv) v Secretary of State for the Home Department* The Times, 31 May 2002, the Court of Appeal held that delays in the Parole Board's current arrangements for determining the status of discretionary and automatic life prisoners infringed Article 5(4). In *R (Saadi and Others) v Secretary of State for the Home Department* The Times, 1 November 2002, the House of Lords held that detention of asylum seekers for approximately seven days at Oakington Reception Centre pending a fast-track decision on their applications was lawful and did not infringe Article 5(1)(f).

In *R (Clift) v Secretary of State for the Home Department; Secretary of State for the Home Department v Hindawi and Headley* [2006] UKHL 54, the House of Lords held that the early release provisions contained in the Criminal Justice Act 1991 were incompatible with Articles 5 and 14, to the extent that they provided for differential treatment of foreign national prisoners (see **19.2.2.4**).

In *Secretary of State for Justice v David Walker; Secretary of State for Justice v Brett James* [2008] EWCA Civ 30, the Court of Appeal held that the Secretary of State for Justice was in breach of his duty by failing to provide offending behaviour courses to enable prisoners, serving indeterminate sentences for public protection (IPP), to satisfy the Parole Board by the end of the minimum term of their sentences that their detention was no longer necessary for public protection.

19.3.3.5 Article 6—right to a fair trial

Article 6 states:

> 1.   *In the determination of his civil rights and obligations or of any criminal charge against him, everyone is entitled to a fair and public hearing within a reasonable time by an independent and impartial tribunal established by law. Judgment shall be pronounced publicly but the press and public may be excluded from all or part of the trial in the interest of morals, public order or national security in a democratic society, where the interests of juveniles or the protection of the private life of the parties so require, or to the extent strictly necessary in the opinion of the court in special circumstances where publicity would prejudice the interests of justice.*

2.   Everyone charged with a criminal offence shall be presumed innocent until proved guilty according to law.

3.   Everyone charged with a criminal offence has the following minimum rights:

(a) to be informed promptly, in a language which he understands and in detail, of the nature and cause of the accusation against him;

(b) to have adequate time and facilities for the preparation of his defence;

(c) to defend himself in person or through legal assistance of his own choosing or, if he has not sufficient means to pay for legal assistance, to be given it free when the interests of justice so require;

(d) to examine or have examined witnesses against him and to obtain the attendance and examination of witnesses on his behalf under the same conditions as witnesses against him;

(e) to have the free assistance of an interpreter if he cannot understand or speak the language used in court.

This article has given rise to extensive litigation.

The right to consult with a solicitor in a police station is fundamental to the preparation of a defence and is protected under Article 6(3). It has been held that, where adverse inferences can arise from an accused's silence when being questioned in the police station, access to a solicitor is of 'paramount importance' (*Murray v UK* (1996) 22 EHRR 29). See also *Magee v UK* (2001) 31 EHRR 822 and *Averill v UK* (2001) 31 EHRR 839, where the European Court of Human Rights held that violations of Article 6(1) and Article 6(3)(c) had occurred due to the lack of access to a lawyer for 48 hours and 24 hours respectively, during interrogation. In *Brennan v UK* (2002) 34 EHRR 507 the Court held that there was a violation of Article 6(1) and Article 6(3)(c) where a police officer remained within sight and earshot of a legal consultation.

The right to silence is an important right. In *Condron v UK* (2001) 31 EHRR 1 there was held to have been a violation due to failure of the trial judge to adequately direct the jury on an inference to be drawn from the suspects' silence whilst in custody. The European Court made the following points:

(a) The right to silence is at the heart of the notion of fair procedure under Article 6 and particular caution is required before a domestic court can invoke an accused's silence against him.

(b) The power to draw adverse inferences from the silence of the accused cannot of itself be considered incompatible with Article 6, but is a matter to be determined in light of all the circumstances of the case.

(c) It is incompatible with the right to silence to base a conviction solely or mainly on the accused's silence or refusal to answer questions, or give evidence.

(d) However, where a situation clearly called for an explanation from an accused, then his silence can be taken into account in assessing the persuasiveness of the evidence against him.

(e) In the instant case, it was more than merely desirable that the jury should have been directed that if they were satisfied that the applicants' silence at the police interview could not sensibly be attributed to their having no answer, or none that would stand up to cross-examination, then they should not draw the adverse inference.

In *Beckles v UK* (2003) 36 EHRR 162, the European Court of Human Rights held that there was a violation due to the failure of the trial judge to adequately direct the jury on the inference from silence.

It is essential that adequate disclosure is given to the defence in criminal trials. In *Edwards v UK* (1992) 15 EHRR 417, the Court held that 'it is a requirement of fairness under Article 6, indeed one which is recognised under English law, that the prosecution must disclose to the defence all material evidence for or against the accused'. The decision of the European Court of Human Rights in the case of *Rowe and Davis v United Kingdom* (2000) 30 EHRR 1, although avoiding a comprehensive critique of the domestic system for dealing with the disclosure of 'sensitive' material, established the following principles:

(a) The right to a fair trial means that the prosecution authorities should disclose to the defence all material evidence in their possession for and against the accused.

(b) That duty of disclosure is not absolute, and 'in any criminal proceedings there may be competing interests, such as national security or the need to protect witnesses at risk of reprisals or keep secret police methods of investigation which must be weighed against the rights of the accused'.

(c) Only such measures restricting the rights of the defence to disclosure as are strictly necessary are permissible under Article 6(1).

(d) Any difficulties caused to the defence by a limitation on its rights must be sufficiently counter-balanced by the procedure followed by the court.

The Court held that there was a violation of Article 6(1) due to failure of the prosecution to leave decisions on disclosure to the judge. Following that decision the Court of Appeal held that the convictions should be quashed (*R v Davis, Johnson & Rowe* [2000] Crim LR 1012). In *Atlan v UK* (2002) 34 EHRR 833 the European Court of Human Rights held that there was a violation of Article 6(1) for failure to lay relevant evidence before the trial judge to rule on disclosure.

Trials of very young defendants should not be subjected to the full publicity of criminal trials as in the case of adults. Measures ought to be taken to ensure that they receive a fair trial. In *T v UK; V v UK* (2000) 30 EHRR 121, it was held that the child killers of James Bulger had been denied a fair hearing in breach of their rights under Article 6. One of the reasons for this was that the trial took place in the glare of unprecedented media attention which, combined with other factors such as the layout of the court room, in the opinion of the Court, increased the defendants' sense of discomfort. Following the decision of the European Court of Human Rights in that case, the Court of Appeal laid down a *Practice Note (Crown Court: Trial of Children and Young Persons)* [2000] 1 WLR 659, to address the limitations of practice and procedure in relation to trials of young defendants in the Crown Court (see the **Criminal Litigation and Sentencing** manual).

In *Ezeh and Connors v UK* The Times, 30 July 2002, the applicants were prisoners charged with offences against prison discipline and were found guilty after an adjudication held by the Prison Governor and ordered to serve additional days in custody. They had been allowed to seek legal advice but denied legal representation. The European Court of Human Rights held that the proceedings were criminal in nature and there was a violation of Article 6(3)(c). Prison rules have since been changed—District Judges now hear cases and prisoners are offered legal representation.

In *Davies v UK* (2002) 35 EHRR 720, a delay of over five years in proceedings by the Secretary of State for Trade and Industry was held to be in violation of Article 6(1). In *Mellors v UK* (2004) 38 EHRR 189, the Court held that there had been a violation of Article 6.1 due to the unreasonable length of criminal proceedings. In *Cuscani v UK* (2003) 36 EHRR 11, the European Court of Human Rights held that there was a violation of Article 6(1) and Article 6(3)(e) due to the absence of an interpreter at the trial of the defendant, an Italian, manager of 'The Godfather Restaurant' in Newcastle, on VAT charges, for which he was sentenced to four years' imprisonment, as he had a very poor command of English. In *R v Looseley, Attorney-General's Reference (No 3 of 2000)* [2001] 1 WLR 2060,

L had supplied heroin to an undercover police officer who had telephoned him to place an order for the drugs. The House of Lords held that the police had done no more than provide L with an unexceptional opportunity to commit the offence and his appeal was dismissed. The acquitted defendant in the Attorney-General's Reference was charged with supplying heroin to undercover police officers who were offering contraband cigarettes for sale. It was held that the trial judge had been entitled to stay the proceedings as the officers had instigated the offence by offering inducements to a person who had not previously dealt in heroin. In *Texeira de Castro v Portugal* (1998) 28 EHRR 101, it was held that the right to a fair trial will be violated where police officers or participant informers have stepped beyond an 'essentially passive' investigation of a suspect's criminal activities, and have 'exercised an influence such as to incite the commission of an offence'. Such influence would amount to entrapment.

In *R v Saunders, Parnes, Ronson & Lyons* The Times, 15 November 2002, the House of Lords considered appeals against convictions where the European Court of Human Rights had previously held that there were violations of Article 6(1) in the Guinness serious fraud trial following the use at trial of evidence obtained under compulsion in an earlier Department of Trade and Industry investigation. The House of Lords held that the convictions were not unsafe as the law was applied as at the date of trial. The Human Rights Act 1998 did not have retrospective effect, even though the European Court of Human Rights had found that the trials were unfair (*Saunders v UK* (1996) 23 EHRR 313 and *IJL, GMR&AKP v UK* (2001) 33 EHRR 225).

In *Matthews v Ministry of Defence* [2003] UKHL 4; [2003] 1 AC 1163, it was held that the provision in s 10(1)(b) of the Crown Proceedings Act 1947 which prevented an ex-serviceman from bringing a personal injury claim against the Ministry of Defence was a substantive bar and was not incompatible with Article 6.1, which applied to procedural limitations, and was not engaged.

In *Edwards & Lewis v UK* [2003] Crim LR 891 the European Court of Human Rights held that there was a violation of Article 6.1 as the applicants had been convicted and sentenced to prison terms on the basis of evidence of undercover police officers who were stated to have entrapped the applicants into committing offences of possession, intent to supply heroin and possession of counterfeit notes.

In *R v H; R v C* [2003] EWCA Crim 2847; [2003] 1 WLR 3006, the Court of Appeal held that where there was a public interest immunity application, it was only in exceptional cases that the judge should invite the Attorney-General to appoint special independent counsel.

19.3.3.6   Article 7—no punishment without law

Article 7 states:

> 1. *No one shall be held guilty of any criminal offence on account of any act or omission which did not constitute a criminal offence under national or international law at the time when it was committed. Nor shall a heavier penalty be imposed than the one that was applicable at the time the criminal offence was committed.*
>
> 2. *This article shall not prejudice the trial and punishment of any person for any act or omission which, at the time when it was committed, was criminal according to the general principles of law recognised by civilised nations.*

This article prohibits the retrospective application of the criminal law.

19.3.3.7   Article 8—right to respect for a private and family life, home and correspondence

Article 8 states:

> 1. *Everyone has the right to respect for his private and family life, his home and his correspondence.*

2. There shall be no interference by a public authority with the exercise of this right except such as is in accordance with the law and is necessary in a democratic society in the interests of national security, public safety or the economic well-being of the country, for the prevention of disorder or crime, for the protection of health or morals, or for the protection of the rights and freedoms of others.

This article has enabled advocates to advance arguments in favour of a law of privacy in cases involving celebrities, based on the principle of the law of confidentiality. In *Douglas v Hello!* [2001] 2 WLR 992, an injunction restraining *Hello!* against publishing pictures of the wedding of the celebrities Michael Douglas and Catherine Zeta-Jones was discharged by the Court of Appeal, which held:

(a) that there was clearly a serious triable issue as to whether the photographs had been taken at a private function;

(b) English law recognised the right to privacy in Article 8, but there were different degrees of privacy which materially affected the interaction between the right to privacy and the right to freedom of expression conferred by Article 10;

(c) the wedding was far from being a private one, for the major part of the couple's privacy rights had been sold as part of a commercial transaction; and

(d) the balance of convenience militated against the grant of an injunction.

In *Beckham & Beckham v MGN Ltd* (2001) Lawtel 30.07.01 an injunction was continued against the publishers to prevent publication of pictures in the *Sunday People* of David and Victoria Beckham's new house as they argued that their security could have been breached. In *A v B plc and Another, Garry Flitcroft v Mirror Group Newspapers Ltd* [2002] 3 WLR 542, an injunction had been granted restraining newspaper publishers from disclosing or publishing information concerning sexual relationships between the claimant, a professional footballer, a married man with children, the second defendant and another woman. The injunction was set aside as the law of confidentiality would not grant the same protection in relation to transient relationships as it would to those concerning relationships in marriage.

Evidence obtained as a result of unregulated intrusive surveillance potentially infringes a suspect's rights under Article 8 (see *Khan v UK* (2001) 31 EHRR 1016). In *Allan v UK* (2003) 36 EHRR 143 the Court held that there were violations of Articles 6, 8 and 13 where there was use of a coached informer and covert recordings, but there was no statutory system of regulation in place.

In *Faulkner v UK* (2002) 35 EHRR 686 the Court held that there was a violation of Article 8 due to failure of the prison service to post a letter sent by a prisoner to a government Minister. In *Goodwin v UK* (2002) 35 EHRR 447 the Court held that there were violations of Articles 8 and 12 in the case of a male to female transsexual's rights to legal recognition of her new gender, and in *Peck v UK* (2003) 36 EHRR 719 the Court held that there were violations of Articles 8 and 13 in respect of the publication of CCTV footage and photographs of the applicant taken while he was making a suicide attempt.

In *Dennis v Ministry of Defence* [2003] EWHC 793, it was held that common law nuisance was sufficient to dispose of a claim by the owners of a Grade 1 listed mansion for damages in relation to noise disturbance emanating from RAF Harrier jets based at a nearby air force base. If necessary, the court would have held that rights under Article 8 and Protocol 1, Article 1 had been infringed.

In *Hatton and Others v United Kingdom* (2003) 37 EHRR 28, the Grand Chamber held by a majority of 11–6 that the UK had acted within its margin of appreciation when introducing night flight controls and that there had been no violation of Article 8. There was, however, a violation of Article 13 as there was no domestic remedy whereby the applicants could effectively challenge the interference with their private lives. Judicial review did not satisfy the requirements of Article 13.

In *AB (Jamaica) v Secretary of State for the Home Department* [2007] EWCA Civ 1302, the Court of Appeal held that the breach of immigration control by an overstayer who had married a British citizen was not so significant that it warranted disruption of the family's life by her and her daughters' removal to Jamaica. It was also unreasonable to expect her British husband to leave the UK to settle in Jamaica.

19.3.3.8   Article 9—freedom of thought, conscience and religion

Article 9 states:

> 1. *Everyone has the right to freedom of thought, conscience and religion; this right includes freedom to change his religion or belief and freedom, either alone or in community with others and in public or private, to manifest his religion or belief, in worship, teaching, practice and observance.*
>
> 2. *Freedom to manifest one's religion or beliefs shall be subject only to such limitations as are prescribed by law and are necessary in a democratic society in the interests of public safety, for the protection of public order, health or morals, or for the protection of the rights and freedoms of others.*

This article was argued unsuccessfully in the Court of Appeal on behalf of a Rastafarian who claimed a defence of religious use to a charge of possession of cannabis with intent to supply (*R v Taylor* [2002] Crim LR 314).

19.3.3.9   Article 10—freedom of expression

Article 10 states:

> 1. *Everyone has the right to freedom of expression. This right shall include freedom to hold opinions and to receive and impart information and ideas without interference by public authority and regardless of frontiers. This article shall not prevent States from requiring the licensing of broadcasting, television or cinema enterprises.*
>
> 2. *The exercise of these freedoms, since it carries with it duties and responsibilities, may be subject to such formalities, conditions, restrictions or penalties as are prescribed by law and are necessary in a democratic society, in the interests of national security, territorial integrity or public safety, for the prevention of disorder or crime, for the protection of health or morals, for the protection of the reputation or rights of others, for preventing the disclosure of information received in confidence, or for maintaining the authority and impartiality of the judiciary.*

This article has been relied on, together with s 12 of the Act, by the media, to counter arguments founded on Article 8.

In *R (ProLife Alliance) v BBC* [2003] UKHL 23; [2003] 2 WLR 1403, it was held that the BBC and other broadcasters were entitled to refuse to broadcast a party election broadcast which contained graphic images of abortion on the ground that it was offensive to public feeling. Article 10.1 was qualified by Article 10.2.

19.3.3.10   Article 11—freedom of assembly and association

Article 11 states:

> 1. *Everyone has the right to freedom of peaceful assembly and to freedom of association with others, including the right to form and to join trade unions for the protection of his interests.*
>
> 2. *No restrictions shall be placed on the exercise of these rights other than such as are prescribed by law and are necessary in a democratic society in the interests of national security or public safety, for the prevention of disorder or crime, for the protection of health or morals or for the protection of the rights and freedoms of others. This article shall not prevent the imposition of lawful restrictions on the exercise of these rights by members of the armed forces, of the police or of the administration of the State.*

This article relates to a right considered to be one of the foundations of a democratic society and is not restrictively interpreted. In *Wilson and Others v UK* (2002) 35 EHRR 523 the Court held that there was a violation of Article 11 where domestic law allowed for employers to cease to recognise trade unions in the work place and to abandon previous collective bargaining agreements.

In *R (Laporte) v Chief Constable of Gloucestershire* [2006] UKHL 55, the House of Lords held that the police had acted unlawfully in preventing coach passengers from reaching the site of an anti-war demonstration because it was unreasonable to have concluded that a breach of the peace was imminent at the point where the coaches had been stopped and escorted away. The interference with the demonstrators' rights was disproportionate and in violation of Articles 10 and 11.

19.3.3.11   Article 12—right to marry and found a family

Article 12 states:

> *Men and women of marriageable age have the right to marry and to found a family, according to the national laws governing the exercise of this right.*

In *R v Registrar General for Births, Deaths & Marriages, ex p CPS* The Times, 14 November 2002, the Court of Appeal held that there was no power to prevent a prisoner on remand from marrying a woman who was a prospective witness at his forthcoming trial and who would cease to be compellable by reason of s 80 of the Police and Criminal Evidence Act 1984.

19.3.3.12   Article 13—right to an effective remedy

Article 13 states:

> *Everyone whose rights and freedoms as set forth in this Convention are violated shall have an effective remedy before a national authority notwithstanding that the violation has been committed by persons acting in an official capacity.*

This right was omitted from the Convention rights referred to in the Human Rights Act 1998.

19.3.3.13   Article 14—prohibition of discrimination

Article 14 states:

> *The enjoyment of the rights and freedoms set forth in this Convention shall be secured without discrimination on any ground such as sex, race, colour, language, religion, political or other opinion, national or social origin, association with a national minority, property, birth or other status.*

This is not an independent prohibition, but lends support to other Convention rights, eg in *Abdulaziz, Cabales and Balkandali v UK* (1985) 7 EHRR 471 immigration rules were held to be discriminatory against women seeking permission for their husbands to enter the UK, ie discriminatory of their enjoyment of their right to a family life under Article 8. In *Willis v UK* (2002) 35 EHRR 547 the Court held that there was a violation of Article 14 and Protocol 1, Article 1 where the applicant had been refused social security benefits to which he would have been entitled had he been a woman in a similar position, namely the widowed mother's allowance and a widow's payment. Further, in *Mendoza v Ghaidan* [2004] UKHL 30, the House of Lords held that sexual orientation was an impermissible ground for discrimination and that a gay partner was entitled to be a survivor to a protected tenancy.

19.3.3.14   Article 15—derogation from the Convention

Article 15 states:

> *1. In time of war or other public emergency threatening the life of the nation any High Contracting Party may take measures derogating from its obligations under this Convention to the extent strictly required by*

the exigencies of the situation, provided that such measures are not inconsistent with its other obligations under international law.

2. No derogation from Article 2, except in respect of deaths resulting from lawful acts of war, or from Articles 3, 4 (paragraph 1) and 7 shall be made under this provision.

3. Any High Contracting Party availing itself of this right of derogation shall keep the Secretary General of the Council of Europe fully informed of the measures which it has taken and the reasons therefor. It shall also inform the Secretary General of the Council of Europe when such measures have ceased to operate and the provisions of the Convention are again being fully executed.

The derogation from Article 5(3) (no detention without prompt trial) was held by the Court in *Brannigan v UK* (1993) 17 EHRR 539 to have satisfied Article 15 as there was an emergency in Northern Ireland threatening the life of the nation, and detention for seven days without access to a court was necessary. A wide margin of appreciation was allowed to the UK.

The Government derogated from some of its obligations under the Convention when it enacted the Anti-terrorism, Crime and Security Act 2001 following the September 11th terrorist incidents and the military action in Afghanistan. In *A and Others v Secretary of State for the Home Department* [2004] UKHL 56, the House of Lords held, however, that detention of several non-national suspected terrorists was incompatible with the Convention and was disproportionate.

19.3.3.15   Articles 16, 17 and 18—additional restrictions and rights

Articles 16 to 18 state:

Article 16: Restrictions on political activity of aliens
Nothing in Articles 10, 11 and 14 shall be regarded as preventing the High Contracting Parties from imposing restrictions on the political activity of aliens.

Article 17: Prohibition of abuse of rights
Nothing in this Convention may be interpreted as implying for any State, group or person any right to engage in any activity or perform any act aimed at the destruction of any of the rights and freedoms set forth herein or at their limitation to a greater extent than is provided for in the Convention.

Article 18: Limitation on use of restrictions on rights
The restrictions permitted under this Convention to the said rights and freedoms shall not be applied for any purpose other than those for which they have been prescribed.

19.3.3.16   Articles 1 to 3 of the First Protocol

Articles 1 to 3 of Protocol 1 state:

Article 1: Protection of property
Every natural or legal person is entitled to the peaceful enjoyment of his possessions. No one shall be deprived of his possessions except in the public interest and subject to the conditions provided for by law and by the general principles of international law.

The preceding provisions shall not, however, in any way impair the right of a State to enforce such laws as it deems necessary to control the use of property in accordance with the general interest or to secure the payment of taxes or other contributions or penalties.

Article 2: Right to education
No person shall be denied the right to education. In the exercise of any functions which it assumes in relation to education and to teaching, the State shall respect the right of parents to ensure such education and teaching in conformity with their own religious and philosophical convictions.

Article 3: Right to free elections
The High Contracting Parties undertake to hold free elections at reasonable intervals by secret ballot, under conditions which will ensure the free expression of the opinion of the people in the choice of the legislature.

In *A v The Head Teacher and The Governors of A School* [2004] EWCA Civ 382, the Court of Appeal held that the claimant was entitled to damages where his right to education had been affected by his exclusion from school.

19.3.3.17   Articles 1 and 2 of the Sixth Protocol
Articles 1 and 2 of Protocol 6 state:

> *Article 1: Abolition of the death penalty*
> *The death penalty shall be abolished. No one shall be condemned to such penalty or executed.*

> *Article 2: Death penalty in time of war*
> *A State may make provision in its law for the death penalty in respect of acts committed in time of war or of imminent threat of war; such penalty shall be applied only in the instances laid down in the law and in accordance with its provisions. The State shall communicate to the Secretary General of the Council of Europe the relevant provisions of that law.*

19.4   Reports and further reading

19.4.1   Court reports

Butterworths Human Rights Direct <http://www.butterworths.com> <http://www.lexisnexis.co.uk>
Criminal Law Review (Human Rights Case Reports).
European Court of Human Rights (Judgments) <http://www.echr.coe.int>
European Human Rights Reports (EHRR).
Lawtel <http://www.lawtel.com>
The Times Law Reports.

19.4.2   Textbooks and periodicals

Clayton & Tomlinson, *The Law of Human Rights,* 3rd edn, Oxford University Press, 2003.
European Human Rights Law Review.
Leach, *Taking a Case to the European Court of Human Rights,* 2nd edn, Oxford University Press, 2005.
Legal Action.
Nash & Furse (eds), *Essential Human Rights Cases,* 2nd edn, Jordans, 2002.
New Law Journal.
Ovey, Jacobs & White, *The European Convention on Human Rights,* 4th edn, Oxford University Press, 2006.
Simor & Emmerson, *Human Rights Practice,* Sweet & Maxwell, 2006.
Solicitors Journal.
Starmer, *European Human Rights Law: The Human Rights Act 1998 and the European Convention on Human Rights,* Legal Action Group, 2006.
Wadham, Mountfield & Edmundson, *Blackstone's Guide to the Human Rights Act 1998,* 4th edn, Oxford University Press, 2006.

Class problems in contract and tort

In each of the following problems you are given a brief set of facts. In each case you should advise the client on appropriate remedies, taking as practical an approach as possible.

20.1 Martin Pender

Your Instructing Solicitors act for Martin Pender, whose business is that of car leasing. By a leasing agreement dated 3 January 2006 Mr Pender ('the owner') leased, and Jest Videos Company plc ('the hirer') took, for a term of three years from 1 February 2006, five cars at a rental of £18,000 p.a., payable yearly in advance on 1 February 2006 and the two subsequent anniversaries of that date. Clause 7 of the agreement provided that in the event of default being made in any yearly payment for 14 days or more after the due date, the owner might take possession of the goods.

During December 2005 the owner, in the expectation that the hirer would sign a leasing agreement, bought five new Ford Focus motor cars for £12,000 each which he had painted in accordance with the company's wishes, in company colours. The cost of the modifications was £6,000.

On 1 February 2006 he hirer took possession of the cars and paid the first year's rent. The hirer failed to pay the rent due on 1 February 2007 and on 16 February the owner repossessed the cars.

Between 16 February and 1 April 2007 the owner carried out at a cost of £3,000 repairs necessary to put the cars in a state fit for re-leasing, and on the latter date re-leased the cars to Dodgems Incorporated for two years at a rent of £9,000 p.a. Counsel may assume that no terms which would have been more favourable to the owner could have been found, and that it is unlikely that the cars can be leased again at the end of the two-year period, when they will probably be worth about £6,000 each.

As a result of the hirer's default in paying the amount due on 1 February 2007, the owner did not have in hand sufficient funds to fulfil an agreement which he had made to purchase a Renault van from the manufacturers with delivery and payment set for 1 March 2007. The owner managed to complete this purchase by borrowing £10,000 for six months at 20% p.a. from Grasping Finance Limited. Interest on this loan amounted to £1,000 and Grasping Finance Limited charged an 'arrangement' fee of £300.

Liability is unlikely to be an issue.

Counsel will please advise as to quantum.

20.2 Mr and Mrs Roberts

Mr and Mrs Roberts are the owners of farmland in Northumberland. In 1996 they granted a licence for three years to the Northern Gravel Company ('the Company') to extract gravel from one of their fields. The Company extracted a large amount of gravel, leaving a pit measuring 100 metres by 150 metres with a depth of 15 metres.

On 4 August 2001 Mr and Mrs Roberts entered into a second licence with the Company granting it the right to tip certain types of rubbish in the pit.

Clause 3 of the licence provided:

(a) The Company shall tip rubbish up to a level one metre below the natural surface of the pit.

(b) Upon completion of the tipping the Company shall place one metre of top soil evenly over the whole of the pit and such top soil shall be free from all impediments and materials which may turn a plough.

The Company completed tipping at the pit in September 2004. It then set about complying with Clause 3(b) of the licence. The Company claimed to have discharged its obligation by August 2005. However, in October 2005, when the field was being ploughed, the mechanical plough was fouled by an underground obstruction and badly damaged. Mr and Mrs Roberts immediately gave instructions for boring tests to be carried out, which revealed that there is only 70 cm of top soil and that there is a great deal of rubbish in it, including large concrete blocks.

Unfortunately Mr and Mrs Roberts have only just come to Instructing Solicitors concerning the matter, having relied on their land agent previously to obtain rectification of the position.

If possible Mr and Mrs Roberts would wish to force the Company to place another 30 cm of top soil on the site after the rubbish has been removed from the existing soil. Counsel is asked to advise:

(a) Whether it will be possible to obtain an order for specific performance against the Company.

(b) What will be the measure of damages if specific performance is not ordered and at what date damages will be assessed. The value of the field is now £40,000 but it would have been £60,000 if it were ploughable. The value of the whole farm is £500,000; with the field restored the farm would be worth £510,000. The cost of doing the necessary work to restore the field was £20,000 in 2005 but is now £30,000.

(c) What further damages may be recoverable in any event. As a result of the damage to the plough (which cost £1,000 to repair), Mr and Mrs Roberts were unable to plough another of their fields in time to sow a winter crop and so lost profit of £6,000. Further they have not been able to use the field in which the Company tipped rubbish for the planting of crops for the last three years, but only less profitably for the grazing of cattle, a loss of £4,000 per annum.

20.3 Newtown Theatre Company

Instructing Solicitors act for Newtown Theatre Company Ltd ('NTC'), a new company set up to run a theatre in Newtown and to tour the surrounding districts.

Counsel is instructed in relation to the employment of two actors, Mr Murray Clive, the well-known film and TV star, and Mr Siegfried Blackstone.

Mr Clive was engaged by NTC on the terms of a letter on NTC notepaper dated 15 September 2008, which reads as follows:

Dear Mr Clive,

This is to confirm the terms of the agreement made yesterday at your meeting with our Mr Selsdon.

1. You will be employed to act for our company from 18 September 2008 to 17 September 2009 at a salary of £3,000 per week.
2. You will act in such roles, and carry out such other duties incidental to the business of the company, as the company's management may direct.
3. You will be entitled to four weeks' paid holiday to be taken in accordance with the direction of the company's management.
4. You will not during the period of the agreement act in any other stage production in the United Kingdom.

Yours sincerely,
Newtown Theatre Co Ltd.

On 3 October NTC decided that its Christmas production would be *Aladdin* and cast Mr Clive in the role of Widow Twankey. Yesterday Mr Clive did not turn up to rehearsal, but sent a note saying that he was leaving the company and would be starting new employment with the Grabham Theatre Company in ten days' time.

Mr Blackstone was employed specifically for the production of *Aladdin,* in which he plays the Genie. His contract runs from 18 September to 31 December 2008. He is paid £1,000 per week. He has no written agreement, but was engaged orally by Mr Selsdon on behalf of NTC.

NTC has no specific information, but Mr Selsdon has heard a rumour that Mr Blackstone may have accepted an offer from a film company, and will leave their employment shortly before the opening on 1 November. In such an event, the company would be forced to abandon the production as it would be impossible to find a replacement, and there would be about £200,000 wasted expenditure on the publicity and settings, as well as the loss of box office profits.

The Company wishes to take proceedings against Mr Clive and wishes to be advised as to its position in relation to both Mr Clive and Mr Blackstone. In particular, it wishes to know whether there is any possibility of preventing Mr Clive or Mr Blackstone from leaving NTC, or, if not, on what basis damages would be awarded.

Counsel is requested to advise NTC what, if anything, can be done to protect its legitimate business interest.

20.4 Gordon Priestly

Mr Priestly previously lived in London with his wife Mary and two children aged eight and six. In 2007 the family decided to move into the country, where they would be able to afford a larger house. They wanted a larger house for two reasons: so that they could provide a home for Mr Priestly's mother, who is getting on in years and not well able to look after herself; and so that they could have a music studio in which to place a grand piano and in which Mary Priestly could supplement the family income by giving music lessons.

They were unable to find just the house they were looking for, but in September 2007 purchased a Victorian house called Mon Repos, Hobbs Green, Sussex, which stood in large grounds and could easily have an extension added.

Mr Priestly engaged Mr James Foyle, an architect, to design a two-storey extension which provided a large living area on the ground floor and a studio and bedroom on the floor above. Mr Foyle delivered the plans and specification in December 2007, and Mr Priestly engaged a local builder, Premier Builders Ltd, to construct the extension, commencing January 2008. He did not employ Mr Foyle or anyone else to supervise the building works, preferring to rely on his own experience as an interior designer.

After the usual delays Premier Builders Ltd completed the extension in June 2008 at a final agreed cost of £60,000. Mr Priestly then employed a local firm of decorators, R. B. Ricketts & Son, to decorate the extension to his design. The decorations included some ornamental plastering on the ceiling of the ground floor of the extension. Before R. B. Ricketts started work, Mrs Priestly's piano was moved into the upstairs studio (suitably protected with dust sheets and plastic wrapping), in order to save storage costs.

On the day they started work, Mr Ricketts senior pointed out to Mr Priestly that the floor of the upper storey seemed very springy and expressed some concern about this, but neither he nor Mr Priestly discussed the matter further. The ornamental plastering was completed, and on 29 June 2008 Mr Ricketts junior, a large man who must weigh about 14 stone, was standing on a ladder while painting in the studio, when suddenly the ladder fell through the floor. He was scarcely able to run out of the way before the piano also fell through the hole, taking most of the floor (and ceiling of the room downstairs) with it.

Mr Priestly called in another architect, Mr Basil Soole, to investigate the damage and supervise the repairs. Mr Soole found no fault with Mr Foyle's design, but reported that Premier Builders Ltd had constructed the floor in breach of the specification, good practice and the building regulations, in four main respects:

(a) The joists to the timber first-floor construction should have been at not more than 600 mm centres in order to comply with Building Regulation B19(3)(i). The joists fitted by Premier Builders were at varying centres, never less than 800 mm and at five places as much as 950 mm centres. There was therefore insufficient support for the floor.

(b) The floorboards should have been of a thickness of not less than 22 mm in order to comply with Building Regulation B21(2)(ii). They were in fact 15 mm throughout the extension.

(c) The specification called for softwood to be Douglas fir, western hemlock, European redwood or Canadian spruce. Premier Builders had used deal, a far inferior softwood to those specified.

(d) Contrary to good practice, Premier Builders had not properly secured the joists to the retaining walls.

The repairs took 10 weeks to complete and were carried out by Crabbe & Co at a cost of £25,000. In addition Mr Soole's fee was £2,500 and R. B. Ricketts charged £1,250 to redo the ornamental plastering. The piano was beyond repair. It was worth £3,000, but Mrs Priestly had to buy another at a cost of £5,000. She has lost £2,000 income from piano lessons because of the collapse of the floor. Finally, Mr Priestly's mother was not able to move in until three months after she had planned and Mr Priestly had to pay her rent over that period, a total of £1,200.

Counsel is asked to advise Mr Priestly as to liability and quantum.

20.5 Polly Partridge

Your Instructing Solicitors act for Polly Partridge, who is 45 years old and well known in the art world. After taking a degree in History of Art at Oxford University, Ms Partridge worked for ten years in various art galleries in France: she then returned to England, where she deals in paintings both on her own account and as agent for various collectors.

In December 2002 Ms Partridge saw advertised in the current catalogue of Quentin Quick Fine Art Limited a drawing described as 'Drawing in pen and ink by J A Dessain, 1921'. Dessain was an artist with whose work Ms Partridge was familiar. After inspecting the drawing, she was satisfied as to its authenticity, and purchased it from Quick for £18,750 on 19 December 2002.

On 1 February 2008 Ms Partridge sent the drawing for valuation to Dr Robert Rawthorne of Rawthorne and Son (Fine Art Valuations) Limited. On 3 February Dr Rawthorne advised Ms Partridge that the drawing was not by Dessain and that it was virtually worthless. He also stated that, if the drawing had been a genuine Dessain, it would have fetched at least £45,000 at auction. Counsel may assume that Dr Rawthorne's advice is correct. At the time it was given, Ms Partridge believed that the only remedies she could have against Quick would be in case of fraud; and Quick's conduct at the time of the sale was in fact entirely innocent.

On 1 May 2008 Ms Partridge offered the drawing for sale by advertisement in art magazines as 'Drawing in pen and ink in the style of Dessain. Artist unknown. About 1920', but received no offer above £250.

On 1 June 2008 Ms Partridge consulted your Instructing Solicitors and was for the first time advised that the remedy of rescission might be available. Your Instructing Solicitors wrote to Quick stating that Ms Partridge was entitled, upon return of the drawing, to the return of the price with interest. Solicitors acting for Quick have responded by saying that it is now too late for Ms Partridge to make any claim and that, in any event, her action in advertising the drawing for sale constituted an affirmation of the contract with Quick so as to deprive her of any right to equitable relief.

Will Counsel please advise Ms Partridge as to her remedies.

20.6 Dreamy Travel Ltd

Instructing Solicitors act for Dreamy Travel Ltd ('the Company'). The managing director and principal shareholder is Mr Basil Dream. The Company's business consists primarily of package holidays arranged by the Company, and sold to its customers from a brochure. The Company prides itself on providing a good service to its customers. Every year a brochure is prepared, which is sent out to all previous customers and to anybody who has expressed interest in the Company's holidays.

For several years, the Company has traded with Greed Hotels Ltd, whose managing director and principal shareholder is Mr Gregory Greed, and which operates several seaside hotels. Each year, the Company takes an allocation of rooms in several of Greed's hotels, and pays a fixed weekly rate for these rooms, on a full board basis, whether or not such rooms are occupied. Of course, in this way, the Company is able to have the advantage of a much cheaper rate than would otherwise be the case. The Company then endeavours to fill these rooms with its customers.

In 2005 Mr Greed informed Mr Dream that he had acquired a valuable site at Brighton, and was building a luxury hotel. On 17 December 2007 Mr Greed told Mr Dream over a lunch at the Greed Hotel, Bournemouth, that the hotel at Brighton was finished and would be available for the 2008 season, from the beginning of April 2008. He said that the hotel was in the 4-star luxury category, with an Olympic-size swimming pool, two saunas, three tennis courts, two large lounges, a bar, discotheque, games room, and smaller writing and television rooms. He said that the hotel was within a five-minute walk from the sea. He supplied Mr Dream with photographs, including a photograph of the swimming pool, which looked magnificent. Mr Dream was about to go on a cruise with his wife, and did not go to see the hotel, as he otherwise would have done.

On Mr Dream's instructions the Company wrote the following letter to Greed Hotels Ltd on 7 January 2008.

Dear Sirs,
This is to confirm that we wish to book the following allocation from 1 April to 30 September 2008.
Greed Hotel, Brighton
36 double rooms at £400 per week
12 single rooms at £300 per week
The above prices include room, full board (two persons per double room) all usual hotel services, and to include VAT.
Yours faithfully
Dreamy Travel Ltd

Greed confirmed the booking by letter dated 14 January 2008 signed by Gregory Greed to the Company. Payment of the full price (£468,000) was duly made on 22 March, before the beginning of the season.

The Company incorporated in its brochure package holidays based on the Greed Hotel, Brighton, describing it in glowing terms in accordance with Mr Greed's description to Mr Dream, and featuring a reproduction of the photograph of the swimming pool. All the rooms were booked for the whole season and paid for in advance. The Company charged its customers £600 p.w. for a double room and £450 p.w. for a single room.

From the start of the season, the Company received a stream of complaints about the Greed Hotel, Brighton. Mr Dream went down to see for himself on 9 May. The hotel was only partly finished. The builders were still on the premises, and there was considerable noise. The swimming pool was not complete, and it was clear that the photograph supplied to Mr Dream must have been of another swimming pool. One of the saunas was not complete. There was only one lounge. The second lounge was being used as a make-shift dining room, as the dining room was not complete. However, it was not suitable as a dining room, and there was considerable congestion. The games room was not operational as there were builders' tools in it. There was no television lounge. By no stretch of the imagination could the hotel be described as in the 4-star luxury class. Virtually every customer complained.

The Company was obliged to write to all its customers on 10 May. To those who had already stayed at the hotel, or were there at the time and completed their stay, it offered a 50% refund of their money plus compensation for distress and inconvenience and expenses. To those who had cut short their stay it offered a 100% refund plus the same compensation. A 100% refund was automatically sent to those who had heard of the difficulties and cancelled before arriving, even if this was at the last moment. Those customers who had yet to start their holidays were offered three choices: (i) a 50% refund if they took the holiday up; (ii) a 100% refund plus £20 for expenses if they cancelled; (iii) an equivalent holiday at no extra cost at another hotel, if possible in Brighton, otherwise elsewhere on the south coast.

The Company felt obliged to offer these generous terms in view of the volume of complaints from customers indicating that they would never book a holiday with Dreamy Travel again, and in view of some very bad press publicity which must reflect on the future goodwill of the Company.

Mr Dream was able to negotiate with Mr Greed a total cancellation of the booking from 22 July and a full refund of the money paid in respect of the remaining period (£180,000).

A total of £350,000 was paid back to customers by way of refunds, plus a further £46,000 in compensation. The rest of the money received from customers was retained, but the cost of alternative holidays for those customers was £320,000.

In order to make all the rearrangements and offers, the Company incurred postal and telephone costs of £976 and had to employ two extra temporary staff from an agency for two months, at a cost of £10,336.

Counsel is asked to advise the Company as to quantum.

20.7 Peter Boggis

Instructing Solicitors act for Mr Peter Boggis, who is a partner in a firm of architects, Goodhart Boggis & Co. Mr Boggis's car, a Volvo Estate reg. no. YP03 BOG, belongs to the firm, but is exclusively used by Mr Boggis. On about 13 July 2008 he telephoned Rural Motors Ltd and booked it in for service on 20 July 2008. He spoke to the service manager, a Mr Wort.

A few days later, Mr Boggis discovered that he was going to have to go abroad on business on 20 July. Therefore when he took the car in for service on 20 July he asked Mr Wort at the reception desk if Rural Motors could store the car for a few days until he was able to return and collect it. Mr Wort replied, 'OK, I'll store it for you, but if it's for too long we may have to charge you something extra.' Mr Boggis agreed to this.

Mr Boggis then drove his car into the service area, and was just about to leave when Mr Wort pointed out to him that there was a portable laptop computer on the back seat. This was Mr Boggis's personal property. Mr Boggis did not want to take it with him on his business trip, and had no time to return to the office before setting off, so he asked Mr Wort if it would be all right to leave the computer in the car. Mr Wort replied that it 'should be OK'. Mr Boggis accepted this remark without a second thought and left the car with the computer inside it.

As it turned out, Mr Boggis's trip lasted longer than expected and he did not return to collect his car until 3 August. He paid for the service using a cheque drawn on the partnership account. He was not charged for the storage. He then went to drive his car away and noticed that the computer was not inside it. He therefore returned to the reception desk and asked Mr Wort where it was. Mr Wort apologised, and went off to have a look for it. After about 10 minutes he returned empty-handed and said that the only explanation he could give was that 'it must have been nicked'. Mr Boggis told Mr Wort that he held Rural Motors Ltd responsible for the loss, but Mr Wort replied that they were not responsible and pointed out a notice over the reception desk which said:

Whilst Rural Motors Ltd will endeavour to take every reasonable precaution, it is regretted that no responsibility can be accepted for loss or damage to any property left inside vehicles.

Mr Wort went on to say that the computer might still be kicking around somewhere and that he would keep his eye open for it, but Mr Boggis was obliged to leave without it.

Instructing Solicitors have written to Rural Motors Ltd making a formal demand for the return of the computer, but received a reply from their Solicitors to the effect that (a) the loss of the computer was Mr Boggis's own responsibility since he chose to leave it in the car; (b) that the storage was free of charge and so the garage could not be held liable in any event; (c) that the garage was protected by the notice; and (d) that even if the garage was prima facie liable, Mr Boggis was contributorily negligent.

Counsel is asked to advise Mr Boggis whether he can recover the value of the computer (£3,199) from Rural Motors Ltd.

20.8 Roger Lucas

Roger Lucas was injured on 30 June 2005, on his last day of work for Don Godfrey & Co Ltd, before starting work as a long-distance lorry driver. His date of birth was 1 March 1977. Counsel is asked to advise on quantum.

Roger Lucas will say:

I was very severely injured in the accident, sustaining a paraplegia from which I have been told there is no hope of recovery and my life expectancy has been reduced by about 10 years. I am confined to a wheelchair. Jenny, my wife, has been a wonderful source of support. Before my accident she had two part-time jobs working as a nursing assistant at the nearby cottage hospital for five mornings a week, and as a receptionist/nurse for our local family general practitioner each weekday afternoon. She has given up the receptionist job to look after me and persuaded me to take a positive attitude to my misfortune. From June 2006 to May 2007 at the suggestion of the District Rehabilitation Officer I attended a course at the York Rehabilitation Centre training to become a pharmacy assistant. I passed the end of course exam with flying colours, but unfortunately have been quite unable to get a suitable job. Our local cottage hospital has no vacancy for a pharmacy assistant. Only one assistant is employed and she is still ten years' from retiring age. Whether the hospital will still be open in ten years time is a rather uncertain matter. The course organisers have told me that I could almost certainly get a job earning £300 per week net if I were to apply to a big city hospital. But this would entail moving to live in or close to a city which I do not want to do. Neither does my wife, though she too would have no difficulty obtaining employment as she is a trained nurse. We are both country folk born and bred. I have been quite unable to obtain work locally and can see little prospect of ever finding a job which I can conveniently reach from home. I can drive my specially adapted car, but not for distances of more than a few miles.

The losses which I would like to claim arising from my accident are as follows:

(a) Loss of earnings. At Don Godfrey & Co Ltd I received a net weekly wage of £300. As a long-distance lorry driver I would have netted at least £400 per week with a weekend working bonus of £100 net every fortnight. I had never worked weekends while in Don Godfrey & Co Ltd's employment. He had regular weekend drivers. Before I began my rehabilitation course I received £75 per week incapacity benefit. While on the course I was given a grant of £80 per week. I am now in receipt of £60 per week income support.

(b) The cost of building a ground floor extension to 14 Peel Road which is a threestorey cottage. My architect advises that it is quite impossible to fit disabled person's escalators to this old stone cottage so I am confined to the ground floor. The proposal is to build an extension into the garden which will give me as much accommodation on ground floor level as the cottage has on all three floors. Unfortunately access for contractors is very difficult to the rear of our cottage and the cost of the extension, including professional fees, will be in the region of £50,000. My solicitor points out that I could buy a three-bedroomed bungalow on a new estate about seven miles away for £65,995, but frankly I cannot face living on a new estate. My cottage is presently worth about £70,000.

(c) £200 per week net to my wife for looking after me each afternoon and at week-ends. This is what she has lost by giving up her job as a receptionist/nurse on 1 September 2005.

(d) £100 per week to my sister-in-law for looking after me in the mornings. She also comes in most weekends to give my wife a break. She has been doing this since 1 September 2005. I have not been paying anything to my sister-in-law, who is simply a housewife, but would like to do so. Professional nursing attendance for four hours a day, seven days a week, would cost £300 per week. Eight hours a day would cost £450 per week. It would cost another £150 a week to have a nurse on call at night.

(e) The cost of converting my car to enable me to drive it without feet controls. This was £1,000, and this expense will be repeated every, say, five years.

(f) The cost of a special battery-operated wheelchair which I find much more comfortable and versatile than the chair supplied free on the NHS, £3,500. The life of these chairs is about ten years.

(g) The cost of my lost fortnight's holiday in Portugal planned to start on 18 July 2005. The cost was £725 each for my wife and myself, covering flights and accommodation. The flight portion of the holiday was insured and I received £800 from the insurance company when I had to cancel. I had unfortunately decided against insuring the whole holiday which I could have done for an extra £10 premium.

(h) The cost of employing a professional decorator to decorate my lounge, labour charge £500 plus VAT.

20.9 James Davies

James Davies worked as a motorcycle courier until he was injured on 1 November 2004. His date of birth was 2 October 1979. Counsel is asked to advise on quantum.

James Davies will say:

I had pains in my right leg and shoulder so I went to the Accident Department of the hospital. A doctor carried out an X-ray and said that there was nothing wrong except rather severe bruising which would heal in a few weeks if I took things easy.

I stayed off work and rested but both my knee and ankle joints remained painful. I went to my GP in February 2005 and he referred me to a Consultant whom I saw on 1 and 15 March 2005. On the second occasion she told me that the results of my test were not certain, but that I had potentially serious injuries to both knee and ankle joints. My leg was put in plaster for three months. In June 2005 I was then told I should exercise the joints as I had some form of rare necrosis and might have to have an arthrodesis operation to pin the joints into a fixed position. My exercises and physiotherapy treatment were not successful, however, and in January 2006 an arthrodesis was performed to both joints. As a result, I cannot now bend my right knee, nor move my right ankle.

I have had to give up motorcycling and cannot undertake any physical work. I was earning £300 per week net when I stopped work. For a year after my accident I received £100 per week unemployment benefit and thereafter received £60 per week income support until I ceased to be eligible in May 2005. I had to sell my bike and my gear. I received £2,000 for the bike and £500 for the gear, which were good prices, but I had paid £4,000 and £750 respectively for these items originally.

Before I was injured I used to play the saxophone with local bands for fun and to earn extra money, almost £75 per week. I was unable to earn anything from saxophone playing between the date of my accident and 1 May 2006 when I resumed playing. Between 1 May 2006 and November 2007. I earned on average £150 per week. While off work I practised a great deal and improved considerably. In November 2007 I became a professional. I now earn about £600 net per week. I travel considerably for my work now and have to use public transport, which I estimate costs me at least £1,500 per year more than the cost of going by motorcycle.

There is however no job security in being a professional musician. If times get hard the work may dry up and nobody wants to employ an ex-musician. I am worried that I will find it very hard to gain alternative employment.

EXTRACT FROM MEDICAL REPORT of MR KENNETH BRAND, FRCS, of 100 Harley Street, London W1:

Opinion: . . . in conclusion the trauma of the relatively minor injury to both knee and ankle joints sustained by Mr Davies on 1 November 2004 was responsible for the necrosis which so affected the joints that there was no alternative to Mr Davies's medical advisors but to carry out an arthrodesis of both these joints.

20.10 John Simms

John Simms was injured in an explosion on 1 February 2007. His date of birth was 5 March 1952. Counsel is asked to advise on quantum.

John Simms will say:

I was in St George's Hospital, Tooting for a month. My head and neck were extremely painful and, despite physiotherapy treatment, I continue to suffer serious headaches and a lack of mobility in the neck. I have been declared unfit to drive fork lift trucks. My employers took me back on 1 August 2008 as a warehouse clerk which is a job I can manage, provided I do not have a serious headache. I get these about once a fortnight, and lesser headaches about three times a week. For about six months after the accident my sleep was regularly disturbed by headaches. I have been advised that I have a 10 per cent chance of suffering from post-traumatic epilepsy. From about six months after my accident I began to feel seriously depressed. I also found that I became very easily irritable and inconsiderate, whereas before the accident I had an easy-going affable personality. Although I have had treatment for this condition, I feel quite frankly that it has been of little use. My temper has been a problem at work and I have got into trouble with the warehouse foreman. I am presently on a final warning and I am worried that I may soon lose my job.

As a fork lift driver I took home £280 per week (p.w.). My net earnings as a warehouse clerk are £200 p.w. For 12 months after the accident I received DSS benefits of £80 p.w. and until I resumed work I then had income support of £60 p.w. My other losses are as follows. I am unable to do the home decorating and gardening which I did before the accident. I estimate that this will cost me on average £1,000 per annum. During the first 12 months after my accident my sister-in-law, Mrs Watkins, came every week-day to look after me as my wife, who works as a canteen assistant, could not take time off without losing her job. I paid her £30 p.w. but, considering the amount of work she did, I would like to have paid her £100 p.w. and would wish to make a claim for the higher sum.

I am also told that my pension when I retire will be affected. At the age of 65 I would have received a pension (based on my employers' contributions) of £160 per week, but in view of my reduced earnings this is now likely to be only £125 per week, assuming I do not lose my job.

EXTRACT FROM MEDICAL REPORT of MR KENNETH BRAND, FRCS, of 100 Harley Street, London W1:

Mr Simms' injuries may therefore be summarised as comprising:

(a) Three inch laceration of scalp over vertex, which has healed well with no noticeable scar.

(b) Head injury with concussion. There have been some complaints of nausea and dizziness. There is an increased risk of post-traumatic epilepsy in the order of 10 per cent. If Mr Simms is to suffer epilepsy it could be anything up to 10 years before this becomes apparent.

(c) Crush fracture of first cervical vertebra. Mr Simms has made a fair recovery from this injury but will suffer permanently from occasional pain and aching in the neck, and from his present 20 per cent limitation in movement.

(d) Depression, irritability. Mr Simms has been seen by Dr Bard, the eminent psychiatrist, but has not responded to treatment. Unfortunately Dr Bard arranged for him to be admitted to the Clapham Hospital for the Mentally Ill for tests and observation, but Mr Simms was so distressed to see his fellow patients that he left immediately. The prognosis is uncertain, but there are reasonable grounds for expecting this aspect of his condition to improve over the next two to three years.

(e) There is no reduction in life expectancy, which remains about 20 years.

20.11 Richard Reshirn

Richard Reshirn was a quantity surveyor who suffered an accident on 1 November 2005. His date of birth was 20 October 1975. Counsel is asked to advise on quantum.

Richard Reshirn will say:

I lost consciousness and came to in the Clifton Royal Infirmary. I was wearing a hard hat and this probably saved my life. My spine was severely injured, however, and I am now a paraplegic, having paralysis of the lower limbs, bladder and sexual function. I am confined to a wheelchair with no hope of recovery. My life expectancy is reduced to about 15 years. I am prone to bladder infections, respiratory infections and pressure sores.

After 10 weeks in hospital I went to the Westport Rehabilitation Centre where I was trained to cope as best I can with my physical difficulties, but I will always need some nursing assistance. This is at present provided by my wife Laura, who gave up her job on 1 March 2006 in order to be able to look after me. Her salary was £15,000 p.a. net. However, she is feeling the strain and wants to resume her career. I will need about 35 hours of nursing care per week at a current cost of £ 10.00 per hour plus a home help at £50 per week.

Before my accident I was earning £50,000 gross, £35,000 net, and had excellent prospects of promotion in 2007. If I had been promoted my salary would have been £45,000 p.a. net. I had a secure job and was likely to have become a partner by the age of 40, when I could have expected substantially higher earnings, typically £80,000 p.a. net. I am now unable to work except at home, because of the amount of care I need. I have been able to develop my artistic talents as an illustrator of children's books and have been earning about £15,000 p.a. net from this work since November 2006.

We have no children. We had planned to have children very shortly after my accident, but this is now uncertain. It might be possible through artificial insemination, but I could not cope with looking after children, so we would either need a full-time nanny, or Laura would have to give up work. We would like to have children, but only if we can afford it. I am however very distressed by the thought that I will not live to see them grown up.

As a result of my accident we had to sell our three-bedroomed flat, which was on the second floor of a block, for £100,000 and buy a house so that I could live on the ground floor. This is at present a small terraced house which we bought as a temporary measure for £80,000, but it is unsuitable in the long term, especially if we have a family. We will need to buy a three-bedroomed house with downstairs accommodation for me. This is likely to cost £150,000, and a further £30,000 in special adaptation for my needs.

20.12 Albert Corey, deceased

Albert Corey died on 17 October 2005, leaving a widow, Barbara, and two children. Albert was a fitter earning £205.34 per week net at the date of his death with additional regular overtime. Albert consistently kept 25 per cent of his take-home pay and 65 per cent of his overtime for himself; the rest he gave to Barbara, who spent it on running the household, keeping the family and paying rent and rates. Nothing was saved. Of the money Albert gave Barbara, 12 per cent was consistently spent by Barbara on Albert's upkeep, the rest on herself and the children and on expenditure for the family as a whole which has not diminished since Albert's death. Of the money Albert kept for himself, 5 per cent was consistently spent on gifts and entertainments for Barbara and the children.

Before Albert's death Barbara worked full-time earning £174.30 per week net, but since his death she has had to give up full-time work so as to look after the children. She quit her job on 1 November 2005 and took up part-time work from that date initially earning £90.98 per week net, rising to £93.32 per week net on 1 September 2006, and £98.85 on 1 September 2007. Her salary in full-time work would have risen to £180.06 per week net on 1 January 2006, £187.20 per week net on 1 January 2007 and £191.62 per week net on 1 January 2008. Had Albert not died, his earnings would have risen to £217.61 per week net on 1 March 2006, £225.38 per week net on 1 March 2007 and £239.70 per week net on 1 March 2008. Overtime opportunities at Albert's place of work are spread evenly and fitters of Albert's seniority earned an average of £128.40 per month net in 2005, £129.15 per month net in 2006, £136.80 per month net in 2007 and so far in 2008, £119.20 per month net.

Albert used to do D-I-Y work and repair work around the home. Barbara has so far spent £637.20 on workmen's bills for work Albert would have done and has done no redecoration or home improvement, some of which is now urgent and will cost £775. Barbara has spent more on baby-sitting since Albert's death: an extra £15.00 per week.

What is the total financial loss suffered by Barbara and the children in consequence of Albert's death as at 1 September 2008?

20.13 David Morgan, deceased

Counsel is instructed by Bruce & Bruce of 14a High Street, Tisborough, Northampton-shire. Your Instructing Solicitors are instructed by Mrs Annette Morgan, who is looking after her two grandchildren following the deaths of Mr and Mrs David Morgan. Mrs Annette Morgan has taken out letters of administration of the estates of both her son and daughter-in-law and wishes to pursue a claim on behalf of her grandchildren. Your Instructing Solicitors have been negotiating with the insurers of Manorborn Builders Limited, who have indicated that they might be prepared to pay £120,000, if this is acceptable.

Would counsel please advise on quantum, and in the light of that advice state whether an offer of £120,000 should be accepted.

Arnold Manor will say:

I am the managing director of Manorborn Builders Limited.

Mr Morgan was a good workman who had been with the company for many years. He had a basic pay which after deductions amounted to £16,200 p.a., and in addition he would earn overtime money during the summer months when we were busy. On average I would expect him to work overtime on about 20 weeks of the year. He would then be given approximately £120 in cash for a week's overtime.

Annette Morgan will say:

I am the mother of David Morgan. His father died in 2004. David was born on 14 September 1980, and followed his father into the building trade. Although he did so well at school I always thought he could have done better. In June 2001 he married Daisy Johnson and they had two children, Maxine who was born on 2 May 2002 and Marcus, born on 5 September 2004. They lived in 'The Willows', which David was buying on an endowment mortgage costing £420 a month. When he died the insurance company paid off the mortgage. David was killed at work on 5 September 2007. The funeral was on 12 September 2007 and cost £1,100, paid for by Daisy.

Unfortunately, only three weeks after David's death Daisy had a fatal car accident. It was entirely her fault. I then moved into 'The Willows' to look after the children. I was born in 1960 and am very fit so I expect that I shall be able to look after them through school and, if appropriate, college. I have been asked about the family's living expenses before David's death. Fortunately Daisy was a very methodical person. She kept an account of all the family's expenditure. Her books show that over the year before David died the family spent on average £62 p.w. on food and drink, £45 p.w. on council tax, gas, electricity and general household items, £30 p.w. on clothing, and £53 p.w. on the car (which was written off in Daisy's fatal crash), travel and entertainment. In addition, each week David put aside £10 for each of the children into an endowment policy which would be payable when they reached the age of 18. My impression was that David spent very little on himself, not more than £50 p. w. in addition to the above. And if any job needed doing in the house he would do it.

Daisy did not work after she married David, though I think she wanted to go back to her job as a solicitor's clerk when Marcus went to school in September. I enjoy looking after the children. They were very cheerful souls, but I find it difficult to manage financially. Since Daisy died I find that it costs me about £3,000 a year to pay all the outgoings on 'The Willows', including the gas, electricity, maintenance and so on, and the children cost at least £1,750 p.a. each to feed, clothe and take on holiday. The jobs around the home which David used to do are costing me about £750 a year. Also, as a special gift, I continue the £10 p.w. endowment policies which David started.

20.14   Susanna and Emma Williams, deceased

Counsel has herewith: Statement of Michael Morley.

Counsel is instructed by Gatwicks on behalf of Mr Michael Morley, the executor of the estate of his late cohabitee, Susanna Williams, who died in a tragic accident on 6 February 2008, together with their daughter, Emma. Probate of Miss Williams's estate was granted to Mr Morley out of the Brighton District Probate Registry on 28 July 2008.

Counsel is requested to advise whether it would be worthwhile bringing proceedings in respect of Emma Williams's death and on quantum.

Michael Morley of 18 Carlton Terrace, London SW1 will say:

I was born on 21 November 1978 and have since 2002 been living with Susanna Williams at the above address. We considered ourselves to have a stable relationship, but we never married. We had two children, Mark, who was born on 3 March 2001, and Emma, who was born on 12 October 2007. I am presently unemployed, having been dismissed from my job as an investment analyst at the Biological Bank on 1 November 2007.

I had been earning £150,000 per annum. I was given a severance payment of £60,000 and since then I have been unable to find a job and have had no income.

Susanna Williams was born on 14 October 1978. Throughout our relationship she worked as a commodity broker for Bowyers, Pierce and Green. At the time of her death her remuneration package was a basic salary of £120,000 per annum plus annual bonus which, on 1 January 2008 had been £30,000. This financial year her net income would have been about £90,000 net of tax and National Insurance. She had a company car and her employers also paid her private medical insurance (BUPA) subscription of £1,000 per annum, permanent health insurance premium of £2,000 per annum, fitness club subscription of £1,000 per annum and car running expenses up to £1,000 per annum. Our children were looked after by a full-time, live-in nanny whom we paid £150 per week plus board and lodging.

Since the tragedy I have felt unable to continue looking for work and I now look after my son, Mark. Had Susanna lived I expect I would have found a job by now at a salary of about £40,000 net, but at present I am just not interested in working. The nanny has left and I have not replaced her. Susanna and I paid all our earnings when we were both working into a joint account out of which we paid all our expenses. The primary expense was our mortgages. We each had a mortgage with interest payments of £1,500 per month. Our other expenses included council tax of £1,500 each, electricity, gas and water at about £1,500 per annum and entertainment expenses of about £2,000 per month. Susanna dressed well and I would estimate that she spent about £7,500 per annum on clothes and accessories. Our holidays and out-of-town breaks cost about £7,500 each year.

I now go out very little, though I have bought a car to replace the car which Susanna had as part of her remuneration package. It cost me £10,000. Mark will start at St Michael's Preparatory School, Belgravia this term. The fees are £2,000 per term and would have been paid by Susanna had she lived. I receive £15,000 per quarter from an insurance policy which Susanna took out before her death, and will continue to receive this until October 2038, when Susanna would have been 60 years old. Susanna and Emma are buried in the graveyard of their home village near Brighton. The funerals cost me £2,500 and £1,000 respectively and I am erecting an ornamental marble tombstone suitable for a woman of Susanna's achievements at a cost of £6,275.

INDEX